BLACK TO NATURE

BLACK TO NATURE

Pastoral Return and African American Culture

Stefanie K. Dunning

University Press of Mississippi / Jackson

The University Press of Mississippi is the scholarly publishing agency of
the Mississippi Institutions of Higher Learning: Alcorn State University,
Delta State University, Jackson State University, Mississippi State University,
Mississippi University for Women, Mississippi Valley State University,
University of Mississippi, and University of Southern Mississippi.

www.upress.state.ms.us

The University Press of Mississippi is a member
of the Association of University Presses.

Copyright © 2021 by University Press of Mississippi
All rights reserved

Lucille Clifton, "the earth is a living thing" and "*won't you celebrate with me*"
from *The Book of Light*. Copyright © 1993 by Lucille Clifton. Reprinted with the
permission of The Permissions Company, LLC on behalf of Copper Canyon
Press, coppercanyonpress.org

First printing 2021

∞

Library of Congress Cataloging-in-Publication Data

Names: Dunning, Stefanie K., 1973– author.
Title: Black to nature : pastoral return and African American culture /
Stefanie K. Dunning.
Description: Jackson : University Press of Mississippi, 2021. | Includes
bibliographical references and index.
Identifiers: LCCN 2020054621 (print) | LCCN 2020054622 (ebook) | ISBN
9781496832948 (hardback) | ISBN 9781496832931 (trade paperback) | ISBN
9781496832955 (epub) | ISBN 9781496832962 (epub) | ISBN 9781496832979
(pdf) | ISBN 9781496832986 (pdf)
Subjects: LCSH: American literature—African American authors—History and
criticism. | Nature in literature.
Classification: LCC PS153.N5 D857 2021 (print) | LCC PS153.N5 (ebook) |
DDC 810.9/896073—dc23
LC record available at https://lccn.loc.gov/2020054621
LC ebook record available at https://lccn.loc.gov/2020054622

British Library Cataloging-in-Publication Data available

Dedicated to

Omi Jayasena-Dunning and Andrew Brath

For your love, endless support, and willingness to hike

CONTENTS

3   Introduction: "a black and living thing"

29   Chapter One: Natural Women

61   Chapter Two: Dead Wild

91   Chapter Three: Flesh of the Earth

125   Chapter Four: Plant Life (Notes on the End of the World)

155   Coda: Take Me Outside

159   Acknowledgments

161   Notes

179   Bibliography

189   Index

BLACK TO NATURE

INTRODUCTION

"a black and living thing"

the earth is a living thing

is a black shambling bear
ruffling its wild back and tossing
mountains into the sea

is a black hawk circling
the burying ground circling the bones
picked clean and discarded

is a fish black blind in the belly of water
is a diamond blind in the black belly of coal

is a black and living thing
is a favorite child
of the universe
feel her rolling her hand
in its kinky hair
feel her brushing it clean
—Lucille Clifton[1]

Ruptures

It is July 2016, and I'm riding in my cousin's big Suburban in rural North Georgia. She's invited me to a resort where a coworker has gifted her a big multiroom suite. There isn't much to do at this resort if you don't play golf, except go to the swimming pool. The first day we go to the swimming pool, we're relieved that our family isn't the only Black family there. Our sheer numbers seem to diffuse the discomfort of the white swimmers.

Almost. I try not to notice as white people slowly leave the pool when we enter. I manage to focus on my family, the sunshine, and the fresh crisp smell of the southern spring air. On the second day, my cousin tells me there are some beautiful waterfalls nearby. It's a short hike from the trailhead to the waterfall, and we all set off—me, my daughter, my cousin and her mother, her son, and two other cousins and their children. In all, we are five women with five children. We pull up directions on my phone's GPS app. It takes us deeper into the woods, into the country, until there is no longer a signal. We find ourselves creeping up a graveled road too narrow for two cars to pass side by side. There are few signs and no other travelers. My cousin gets nervous, and as we round a corner only to reveal more unending country gravel road, she stops the car and backs up.

"What are you doing?" I ask. I'm a hiker, a backpacker, a regular camper. I was looking forward to this family hike.

"It's too deserted. I can't do this. I can't take the chance."

"The chance of what?" I ask.

"Of bumping into the wrong white people out there."

My cousin had a point: the woods and white people are the stuff of Black nightmares. The incident caused me to contemplate the relationship Black people have (or don't) to nature, especially because for most of my life, I have nurtured a deep love for the natural world. Neither my love for nature nor my cousin's legitimate fear of it is at odds with what is a long and deep ecological Black history. Lucille Clifton, in her poem "the earth is a living thing," asserts that the earth is alive—a critical observation for the revelations of this volume—and she aligns the living earth with Blackness when she writes that the earth "is a black and living thing." Throughout the poem Clifton aligns animals, plants, and *being* with Blackness, thereby naturalizing Black life relative to the earth environment. Like Clifton's poem, *Black to Nature* is doubly invested in thinking about the earth as alive and about Black people's relationship to it. But public perception leans heavily toward the notion that Black people and nature don't mix. There is a well-known *Funny or Die* skit called the "Black Hiker."[2] In it the actor Blair Underwood is hiking in a pastoral setting. As he encounters whites on the trail, they act shocked to see him, and the skit gets funnier as the people he encounters become increasingly more open about their sense of surprise that a Black person is hiking, asking to take pictures with him and calling their friends over to witness the "Black hiker." The idea that Black people do not enjoy nature is prevalent throughout our culture, not just in this skit. The narrative of the nature-aversive Black person is echoed in headlines like "National Parks Reach out to Blacks Who Aren't Visiting"[3] and "Why People of Color Don't Visit National Parks."[4] A simple Google search returns hundreds of articles that attempt to explain the absence of Black people from recreational nature sites and activities. Operating in tandem with this perception of nature, in a recreational or even rural sense, as being white territory is the construction of Black people as "urban" subjects. It is not my intention to assert that it is "untrue" that many Black people live in cities and are averse to nature-centered activities. Rather, I propose that in the late twentieth and early twenty-first centuries, many Black texts (and some centered on, but not authored by, Black characters) revisit the site of the agrarian, the rural, or the natural world and that this "pastoral return" can be read as a symbolic deployment of the argument for the abolition of civil society. If it is true, as scholars such as Orlando Patterson, Jared Sexton, Frank B. Wilderson III, and Saidiya Hartman assert, that Black people "embody a *meta-aporia* for Humanist thought and action," which proceeds from slavery, then the abolition we have all been waiting for has yet to arrive.[5]

Explaining this perhaps startling insight, Frank B. Wilderson III writes, "Blackness is coterminous with Slaveness. Blackness is social death, which is to say that there was never a prior meta-moment of plentitude, never a moment of equilibrium, never a moment of social life. Blackness, as a paradigmatic position . . . cannot be disimbricated from slavery."[6] Abolition, by this account, is not simply mobilizing a "rights" discourse or changing a few laws; it is the complete dismantling and collapse of civilization as we know it. Calvin Warren speaks of this collapse as "the end of the world."[7] What is meant is not the end of the *earth*, but rather the end of civil society, which is the only way the Black person can ever be liberated from the "afterlife of slavery."[8] Importantly for this volume, the collapse of civilization in the texts I analyze here—or of any hierarchical social structure—is often imagined as a return to nature, since we have all been encouraged to view nature as anathema to forward progress and to believe that such progress equals freedom. The texts I analyze here contest the construction of nature as "other" and implicitly reject the notion that human evolution can be measured by the degree to which we are in control of the natural environment. In my focus on nature in the chapters that follow, I build on the Zen concept of "interbeing," first articulated by Thich Nhat Hanh, to describe what I see as a distinct way that Black texts engage nature.[9] And, as I show below, both nature and Blackness are defined as "outside" of society (both are "socially dead"), and the unchecked freedom of either represents a subversion of the law and order of Western civilization.

In this introduction I outline what I call "ruptures" from nature that explain and reveal what is at stake in Black claiming or disclaiming of nature. I discuss the following historical and epistemological factors: a) discourses of primitivism; b) forced agrarian labor, that is, chattel slavery; and c) pastoral violence, that is, lynching. These factors inform and structure Black nature discourses and reveal the at-once problematic and productive possibilities of explorations and representations of nature in Black texts. I should pause here to acknowledge the fraught and overdetermined use of the word "nature." Nature, wilderness, the rural, and the agrarian are all "racially and culturally particular constructions[s] with intellectual and aesthetic origins in Romantic sublimity and American transcendentalism," according to Paul Outka's analysis.[10] It will be evident enough as we proceed, if it isn't already, that the "natural world" as a construction, and all that this implies and entails, has been used as a symbol of both evil and goodness but has no inherent moral or immoral quality. Yet the historical and epistemological meanings that cohere in the term "nature" mean that to evoke it is to reference a complicated and violent history in relation to race. Outka goes on to note that American wilderness is "always already saturated with the authority of slavery and the possibility of violent punishment."[11] It is not my intention to either elide or gloss these connotations, but rather to show that because of, and despite, the violence that the "idea" of nature, and nature itself, has been made to do against the Black person, Black representations of nature in the twentieth and twenty-first centuries signal a "rescrambling [of] the dichotomy between objectified bodies" that "disrupts presumptive knowledges of black subjectivity," as Uri McMillan argues in another context.[12] I hope to show in this book that nature, in the Black texts I examine here, is deployed as a means of "rescrambling" the teleology of the Western progress narrative. In doing so, these texts both implicitly and explicitly acknowledge the need for abolition, referencing the natural world as a site of the antisocial.[13] Thus, nature is utilized in this volume in both literal and figurative ways, naming both extant things (landscape, animals, and plants) and protean notions about bodies relative to hair and skin color, as well as lighting and mise-en-scène. I do not use the term "nature" to suggest or imply support of the transphobic idea that there is "natural gender" or the essentialist notion that there is biological race; my discussions herein about nature refer to the environmental world and the ways in which it is signified upon and utilized by the artists I discuss in this volume. My motley use of nature relies upon an understanding of it as a shifting signifier that aligns with the manifold ways it is cited in the texts I examine. The capaciousness of nature in these Black texts defies an understanding of it—understood in Western society as a material object occupying a nonhuman elsewhere—as simply one thing. Instead, both "actual" nature (the outside world, as it were) and the concept of it are in constant flux in the representational universe of these various texts.

The theoretical and critical investments of this project are neither eco-critical nor posthumanist, even as those theoretical traditions are also concerned with "nature," writ large. The texts I examine are not about environmentalism, nor are they about seeing nature as an "active, relational agent that meets us halfway."[14] In the essay "Why Do We Care About Post-humanism? A Critical Note," Bo Allesøe Christensen argues that posthumanist discourses, despite their attempts to counter the problematic humanism of the Anthropocene, actually only reify the "human" as a "stable and coherent category": "Being in a post-human age, in distinction from a previous age with boundaries between human and non-human sustained, creates, dialectically, a problem. Distinguishing between a post-human and a human age requires of the post-human age that it defines itself up against the previous age. Posthumanism thereby reinstalls the necessity of what it questions the existence of, namely the human."[15] Christensen's point is that the "post" in posthumanist discourses relies upon the category of the human, as an intact social construction, to make its claims. So we might understand posthumanism as reliant upon, and following from, the flawed logic of humanism. And, as many critical race theory scholars of late have observed, "human" has always meant, and still means, "white." Writing in "The Free Black is Nothing," Calvin L. Warren asks in an analysis of the phrase "Black Lives Matter," "Can blacks have life? What would such life *mean* within an antiblack world?"[16] Post-humanism, despite its compelling attempt to decenter the human (read, white person), is hindered by its failure to recognize the ways in which the term "human" still drives the mechanisms of anti-Blackness that bars Black people from either a humanist or posthumanist existence. Writing about posthumanism in the work of N. Katherine Hayles, Alex Weheliye points out that despite Hayles's "desire to redraft this hegemonic Western version of personhood, her singular focus on this particular historical composite unnecessarily weighs down her project, since the posthuman frequently appears as little more than the white liberal subject in techno-informational disguise."[17] Hence, despite posthumanist attempts to flatten the old distinctions of human versus a natural other, given that it has yet to reckon with the ways in which some humans are not yet actually perceived to be such, its theoretical framework cannot contain or explain how Black artists represent and engage nature in their work. Likewise, as many critics have noted, eco-criticism, as it historically unfolded, did so without regard for the particular ways that nature and the environment figured in nonwhite contexts, and reproduced many of the most problematic ideas about race within the broader culture.[18]

How, then, can we theorize the representation of nature in Black texts, which is often celebratory, and yet somehow distinct from the ontological and geographical aims of transcendentalism, environmentalism, and posthumanism? I propose that we think about nature in Black texts through the sign of the "unsovereign." Writing about the unsovereign in his essay "The Vel of Slavery," Jared Sexton notes:

> Abolition, the political dream of Black Studies, its unconscious thinking, consists in the affirmation of the unsovereign slave—the affectable, the derelict, the monstrous, the wretched—figures of an order altogether different from (even when they coincide or cohabit with) the colonized native—the occupied, undocumented, the unprotected, the oppressed. Abolition is beyond the restoration of sovereignty. Beyond the restoration of a lost commons through radical redistribution (everything for everyone), there is the unimaginable loss of that all too imaginable loss itself (nothing for no one).[19]

"Nothing for no one" is the abolition of borders, of sovereignty, of rule, of police, of the state. Within abolition—nothing for no one—is the recognition that laying claim to any "location" is always after the fact of interbeing, something added to the irreducible, and ultimately indescribable, entity we call "nature."

Rupture 1.0: Discourses of Primitivism

> There is a very rigid etiquette as a compensation for the extreme looseness of the Negro. We found that ourselves; as soon as we were in the wilds, we became very particular that our boys should be clean . . . we were very strict about the cleanliness of the boys. They liked to be as dirty as possible but when serving at table, they had to wear white turbans and white shokas; we made it ceremonial. And you felt that if you did not shave for one day you would never shave again. You would get out of your own hands, you would practically lose yourself, and that is the beginning of the going black.
> —Carl Jung, 1925[20]

the earth is a living thing. Human beings bloomed from its womb, earthly consequence, not earthly cause. *is a black shambling bear.* Like an apple tree *apples* (verb), the earth *peoples* (verb).[21] Black people, earth's first people, are a burst of space, dark matter, bending a parabola of the branch, earth-fruit dropped upon rich soil, ripe with life and human origin. *is a black hawk circling.* Language cannot capture the inescapable truth of our belonging to this particular planet, to this earth. This overdetermined word, *nature*, bears the historical trace of divinity, some faint echo of a grand, organic spinning: Anansi[22] as God; the world as web. *is a black and living thing. is a favorite child of the universe.* The earth precedes humans in every cultural account, and there has never been any question that the earth is the womb from which we arose. As the philosopher Alan Watts argues, we did not come "into" this world, we came *out* of it.[23] Out of the primordial soup of the seas we came, breaking our mother's water, wiggling to land, looking for our feet. When Lucille Clifton asserts, and in fact feels the necessity of asserting, that *the earth is a living thing,* she is speaking against the pervasive notion that the earth is a dead and inanimate thing, an Enlightenment notion that inaugurates the anti-Blackness upon which the foundation of Western civilization rests.

In the epigraph above, Carl Jung reveals that his perception of the "dirtiness" of the Africans he's charged with serving him on his expedition makes him feel that he will "get out of his own hands." It is not enough for Jung and his men to maintain the obsessive-compulsive body cleaning that convinces them that they are civilized; they must also impose that order of action upon the Africans working for them, forcing them to bathe on their schedule and then swaddling them in white. Let us take note that for Jung, the "Negroes" and "dirt" occupy the same category of being, the white clothing a "buffer" between his own constructed whiteness, with shaving and grooming being the only ways he can maintain it. In other words, in his cosmology "dirt," the soil of the earth, inheres to Blackness such that both must be guarded against, controlled, and managed via various constructions of whiteness.

The earth was the European's first *other*. Nature was the European's first dead "thing," to be used, without recourse or consequence, as he saw fit. In an article titled "How the Enlightenment Separated Humanity from Nature," Alexander Blum explains, "Beginning with early scientific thinkers like Francis Bacon and René Descartes, the study of observable nature was divorced from the study of human beings, and ever since, our relationship to the natural world has been fraught with utopian error."[24] This "error," he goes on to argue, is founded in Cartesian dualism:

> In order to progress scientifically, a distinction had to be made between the intractable problems of self-consciousness and the objective, measurable world. Descartes proposed a solution: The entire world was to be reduced entirely to "measure and number," the founding reductionist principles of science, save for human minds, God, and angels. Through his Cartesian dualism, which enabled the flourishing of modern science by removing psyche from the world, Descartes inadvertently structured modern science to conceive of the human being as outside of nature.[25]

If human beings were "outside" of nature, separate from it, and if it could only be seen as inanimate in opposition to the animation that characterizes humans, it stood to reason that "man" could do whatever he wanted to nature. Francis Bacon went so far as to define nature as a slave or servant:

If humankind was distinct from the natural world, then we could in fact treat it as our servant, our slave. The sciences would be aimed toward the development of new technology, the contortions and enslavement of nature made to suit our alien human whims. Bacon wrote that the scientist must steal the secrets of nature in Promethean fashion, "as torture may compel an unwilling witness to reveal what he has been concealing." One could scarcely imagine a worse relationship between human beings and nature than that of torturer and victim sprawled across the rack.[26]

This view of nature as a recalcitrant resource that must be beaten into submission and made subordinate to "man" bears nascent relation to the place that the African comes to occupy in the imagination of the Enlightenment European. Hence, European notions about nature set the stage for the violations of the Middle Passage and chattel slavery in the Americas. It makes sense, then, that one of the earliest ways Europeans characterized Africans was as primitives, as those as of yet uncoupled from nature. For the Enlightenment European, anyone who lived in harmony with nature, or who did not live as they did, was always already a "thing," the same kind of "thing" that nature was seen to be. And "things," in this exploitative cosmology, were meant to be used, mined, and made to work for the (hu)*man*. A whole world of exploitation rotates on the axis of this insight, as the rupture from nature in European thinking is the primal ground upon which subsequent blood is shed. In other words, philosophical notions about nature provide scaffolding for a range of other areas of human/other interaction and activity, and the "otherizing" of nature enacted by Enlightenment thinkers enables the anti-Blackness of Western society.

A stunning parallelism characterizes the treatment of both the natural world and Black people. Writing about anti-Black brutality, Calvin Warren says that the world can be understood as one "in which black torture, dismemberment, fatality, and fracturing are routinized and ritualized."[27] Warren's characterization of Black torture aligns with Bacon's thinking about nature. If nature was a "body to be tortured," then tortured bodies in essence become nature, beastly "things," for whom no human compassion need be cultivated. In *Novum Organum* (1620), Bacon writes, "Let the human race recover that right over nature which belongs to it by divine bequest," dripping with the same rhetoric of dominance and rule that suggests that Bacon saw himself as "outside" of nature, and as a force that could act upon and against nature itself.[28] Bacon's statement also reveals a kind of anxiety about nature, a desire and need to subdue it, so as to "put right" that which was broken in the fall from grace. "As a consequence of his expulsion from the Garden of Eden, man was condemned to a life of hard work. Work became the only means he could count on to make nature subordinate to his needs," writes E. Montuschi in her essay on Bacon.[29] Hence, Bacon's emphasis on the domination of nature can be read as a deep insecurity related to the biblical notion of the fall from grace. Writing about Francis Bacon's discourses on nature, and on late Renaissance writings on nature in general, Richard Serjeantson notes that "there was an intimate connection in the Renaissance 'between the interpretation of Scripture and the interpretation of nature.'"[30] Though Bacon was not the only thinker of his day interpreting nature, he is widely recognized as the dominant Enlightenment thinker whose writing framed broad cultural approaches to nature.

We can trace the elision of nature with Africans along the interstice of scriptural and natural interpretation through European representations of Africans as primitive. Specifically, frequent depictions of Africans menaced by snakes in the Garden of Eden demonstrate the ways in which discourses about correcting the mistake of the fall from grace merged with the Black body. Iterations of primitivism are anchored in both time and space, marking the African, and eventually Black people, as geo-temporal anomalies, anathema to Western progress and civilization. This rendering of the African, and ultimately the Black person, as primitive, as nature *itself* in the same way that nonhuman animals *are* nature, propels a rupture between the Black person and nature by incentivizing Black disavowal of it. This rupture follows from an Enlightenment internalization of the biblical story about being cast out of the Garden of Eden. In other words, Black rupture from nature is preceded by, and follows from, a European one. This is so much the case that we could read the history of European conquest as almost always preceded by a natural rupture that echoes through every society and culture made to submit to the will of the slave master or the colonizer.

In Henri Rousseau's painting *The Snake Charmer* (1907), that rupture is reimagined in specifically racial terms. Instead of being harassed and threatened by the snake, here the Black Eve is in harmony with the snakes and nature itself. Rousseau at once evokes a primal story of natural rupture and suggests that the Black Eve is still at one with nature—which again represents her in Hegelian terms as outside of history, as belonging to the mythical and unreal past. In this way, the Black subject becomes the object upon which the European can project a relationship to nature not characterized by danger and expulsion. In doing so, however, he puts the African in another category of being from himself, and so like the flora and fauna, the Black person is fair game for environmental conquest, the Black person is hence "socially dead."[31] In Rousseau's painting, the snake charmer represents his fascination with what he saw as a primitive being; he himself is the snake, wrapped around the finger, if you will, of the sexualized and exotic primitive Eve, who by 1903 was "emancipated" from chattel slavery.

The Snake Charmer, Henri Rousseau, 1907.

Tree of Snakes, Edouard Riou, 1863.

If we look at a pre-emancipation image of a Black person with snakes, such as Edouard Riou's 1863 illustration *The Tree of Snakes*, we see that the African is menaced by snakes all around, in mortal danger. Here the African is at the mercy of nature rather than the master of it, precariously perched on the edge of a branch with nowhere to go. Even falling in this scenario would mean being bitten, and so he is left in limbo (literally on a limb). The imagined utopic harmony with nature evident in Rousseau's (later) painting is absent here, as the fantasy of the endangered and vulnerable African plays out as a rehearsal of the archetypal story of the fall from grace, as a projection of European anxiety about nature superimposed upon the African other. Eerily, the depictions of Black people in the Garden of Eden, menaced or not, resonates with a reading of the slave trade as the end of a Black Eden[32] and the inauguration of the natal alienation and placelessness[33] that characterize Black (social) life in the West today.

Rupture 2.0: Slave Work

> *Sun-up to sundown, picking that cotton!*
> *Sun-up to sundown, whipped by the master!*
> *Sun-up to sundown, chains and shackles!*
> *No more auction block for me!*
> —Negro spiritual as sung by Sounds of Blackness[34]

> *I am a reaper whose muscles set at sun-down. All my oats are cradled.*
> *But I am too chilled, and too fatigued to bind them. And I hunger.*
> —Jean Toomer, *Cane*[35]

If we can accept the premise that Enlightenment Europeans, following Bacon's philosophical musings on nature, saw their goal as taming wilderness so as to restore the divine order of Eden, then the land they would call America must have seemed quite a wicked place indeed. Despite contemporary celebrations of the "wild" in mainstream American letters and media, early colonial settlers (those very first slave masters) saw the American wilderness as dangerous and in need of transformation. Outka notes that "what might well seem to contemporary Americans, at least in their imagination, a breathtaking view back to an untouched, uncreated natural beauty, was something quite different to most of these early settlers. Rather than a carefully cultivated (by the Native people living there) landscape that emphasized ecological harmony, they saw an unredeemed in-between state, predated by a biblical origin story for the wilds before them."[36] The endless pine forests that flanked the East Coast of the United States were a formidable barrier to the establishment of a European-style "civilized" society in the "New" world, in the mind of the European settler. As Outka goes on to explain, the wilderness for Europeans was associated with savagery, with Native Americans, and represented a threat to their project of a New Jerusalem, a city on a hill. The slave, then, becomes a tool through which Europeans "beat back" the wilderness and, by extension and implication, also "beat back" Native Americans with the spread of monocrop agriculture, which radically damaged and altered the landscape in ecologically and culturally violent ways.

To be a slave was to be an unwilling party to multiple violations of the natural world; it was to participate in a system of extraction that was also extracting humanity out of you; it was a compulsory victimization that exploited both the land and yourself. In the twelfth chapter of *12 Years a Slave*, Solomon Northup describes the ordeal of working on a plantation picking cotton. For the novice picking cotton was painful because the cotton fluff contains within it a sharp barb that can easily cut one's hands. How much blood was washed from cotton yields; how much residue of Black blood was spun into fabric? Northup talks about the beauty of the cotton field but then juxtaposes that against the persistent fear and fatigue of the slave, echoing Toomer's insights from "Harvest Song" featured in the epigraph above: "The cotton grows from five to seven feet high, each stalk having a great many branches, shooting out in all directions, and lapping each other above the water furrow. There are few sights more pleasant to the eye, than a wide cotton field when it is in bloom. It presents an appearance of purity, like an immaculate expanse of light, new-fallen snow."[37] Yet despite the billowy beauty of the cotton fields, the slave lives in perpetual fear that his or her bag of cotton will be too heavy or too light; and, because they worked sunup to sundown, they were always tired:

> An hour before day light the horn is blown. Then the slaves arouse, prepare their breakfast, fill a gourd with water, in another deposit their dinner of cold bacon and corn cake, and hurry to the field again. It is an offence invariably followed by a flogging, to be found at the quarters after day-break. Then the fears and labors of another day begin; and until its close there is no such thing as rest. He fears he will be caught lagging through the day; he fears to approach the gin-house with his basket-load of cotton at night; he fears, when he lies down, that he will oversleep himself in the morning. Such is a true, faithful, unexaggerated picture and description of the slave's daily life, during the time of cotton-picking, on the shores of Bayou Boeuf.[38]

This fear, induced by forced labor, racializes the landscape such that feelings about one's own freedom, and one's own engagement with nature, with the land, become dependent upon one's bondage. "Slave agriculture and the systems of control it depended on put slaves in a conflicted relationship to the land," Kimberly Smith writes. She goes on to argue that freedom, then, becomes correlated with "certain ways of interacting with and controlling nature."[39] The slave was unlikely to "love" the land given that his bondage was intimately tied to it; thus, the experience of slavery not surprisingly structures the Black person's relationship to nature as oppressive. "Working the land" produces a kind of automatic oppositional relationship, especially for those working it against their will. Slave agrarian labor, then, functions as another site of Black rupture from nature. Smith notes, "Black theorists reasoned that race slavery and post-Emancipation racial oppression put black Americans into a conflicted relationship to the land—by coercing their labor, restricting their ability to own land, and impairing their ability to interpret the landscape."[40] If discourses of primitivism functioned to alienate the Black subject from nature ideologically, being forced to "work" the land put the Black person at odds with land itself, making of the American landscape a kind of material enemy. Being prevented from owning land, even after slavery fell, continues to hamper the Black person's engagement with land and with nature. This persistent alienation from the land echoes back to us when we find ourselves wanting to engage nature—as my cousin did that day—and yet facing paralyzing existential terror at the historical memory of vulnerability and violence pastoral spaces evoke for the Black person.

Reaching back into slave narratives, we get a glimpse of what Black relation to the land *could* have been if not interrupted by slavery and Jim Crow. The relationship that some West Africans had to the land, before slavery, is best captured in the *The Interesting Narrative of the Life of Olaudah Equiano or Gustavus Vassa, The African* (1789). He writes,

> Our land is uncommonly rich and fruitful, and produces all kinds of vegetables in great abundance. We have plenty of Indian corn, and vast quantities of cotton and tobacco. Pine-apples grow without culture; they are about the size of the largest sugar loaf, and finely flavoured. We have also spices of different kinds, particularly pepper; and a variety of delicious fruits which I have never seen in Europe; together with gums of various kinds, and honey in abundance. All of our industry is exerted to improve those blessings of nature. Agriculture is our chief employment; and everyone, even the children and women, is engaged in it. Thus we are habituated to labour from our earliest years. Every one contributes something to the common stock: and as we are unacquainted with idleness, we have no beggars. The benefits of such a mode of living are obvious.[41]

Agricultural work, farming, and land cultivation were not unknown (or unwelcome), according to Equiano, to West Africans. He describes above an almost idyllic relationship with the land in West Africa, emphasizing harmony between nature ("Our land is uncommonly rich and fruitful") and human labor ("All of our industry is exerted to improve those blessings of nature"). And though the land of eastern North America was, and is, also "rich and uncommonly fruitful," the lash transforms the "blessings of nature" into a curse. I emphasize Equiano's description of West African agriculture and affective relationship to the land in order to reveal alternative land-based modalities that existed among those Africans conscripted into bondage. It seems logical, then, to expect that once slavery is abolished, the relationship between the Black farmer and the land would harmonize, the adversarial perception of nature I describe herein would recede, and the conditions of joyful labor to "improve the blessings of nature" would arise once again. But even after slavery is over, the Black person's relationship to the land remains vexed, due to the way endemic racism disrupts both land ownership and enjoyment of nature.

The first postslavery precedent of this was the overturning of the Sherman's Field Order No. 15, which is the source of the famous phrase "40 acres and a mule."[42] While the mule was not originally promised to the formerly enslaved in the field order, the forty acres were. The field order allocated 400,000 acres of land for formerly enslaved people. Sherman took his order to President Lincoln, who met with Black leaders in Savannah, Georgia, and approved the reallocation of those lands for the freedmen. It seemed a stunning victory for the freedman! It was short-lived, though, because Lincoln was soon assassinated. Had the order not been overturned by Vice President Andrew Johnson, it would have given the formerly enslaved their own means of livelihood, their own communities, and power over their own affairs. They would have then worked land for themselves, not for another. We can imagine that the vexed relationship to the land of the slave may have radically shifted. The overturning of Sherman's field order meant that instead of getting land along with their freedom, most former slaves ended up working as sharecroppers, which some scholars argue was worse than slavery.[43] This was a pivotal moment in the history of the Black American's relationship to the land. Nature, like the Black folks forced to work it, was not "free." It had been chained into an ownership system, a property system, that whites were determined to keep "white." The revocation of Sherman's field order was a postslavery theft of land from Black people by the government and would set the pattern for the Black person's relationship to the land, to ownership, and to nature for generations to come. Yet history suggests that all the progress narratives which inhere in "the Negro problem" never manage to transform the Black slave into a human being. In other words, even if land had been procured, the existential crisis that characterizes Black existence in this society would still assert itself. Thus, the theft of the forty acres was not the cause, but simply the sign, of the intractable nature of Black social death in Western society.

Rupture 3.0: Lynching

> *Southern trees bear a strange fruit*
> *Blood on the leaves and blood at the root*
> *Black body swinging in the Southern breeze*
> *Strange fruit hanging from the poplar trees.*
> —Sung by Billie Holiday, "Strange Fruit," by Abel Meeropol

Richard Wright's poem "Between the World and Me" begins with the line "And one morning while in the woods I stumbled." The casual tone of the first line suggests that walking in the woods was a common, normal occurrence for the speaker—not an extraordinary or singular experience. But his woodland idyll is interrupted by a "thing":

> And one morning while in the woods I stumbled
>   suddenly upon the thing,
> Stumbled upon it in a grassy clearing guarded by scaly
>   oaks and elms.
> And the sooty details of the scene rose, thrusting
>   themselves between the world and me.[44]

This "thing" is a lynching scene, which the rest of Wright's poem describes in vivid detail. The speaker goes on to imagine himself as the lynched man as he observes the scene: "And then they had me, stripped me, battering my teeth/ into my throat till I swallowed my own blood."[45] Walking in the woods forces the speaker into a confrontation with the violence of lynching, literally separating him "from the world," that is, the natural world. Presumably intended to enjoy the beauty of nature, his walk is interrupted by the evidence of a murder. Wright's poem perfectly demonstrates that the Black person's relationship to nature has been interrupted by racist violence, and that it is this violence that stands between Black people and "the world," the natural world.

The exploration of this palpable rupture from nature can also be felt in Billie Holiday's famous recording of the song "Strange Fruit."[46] Through its emphasis on blood, bodies, and rot, the song marries nature to Black death. The lynched bodies of Black people become the "fruit" of southern trees, which suggests that what blooms in the South—what the southern earth produces—is violence against the Black body. It's important to think about the "space of lynching" in the context of the pastoral and what the pastoral setting suggests about the particular nature of lynching violence. That it takes place outside in nature with the forced collusion of trees animates nature with a sense of danger, a sense of threat. To be outside, isolated in nature, then, for the Black American can be a mnemonic reminder of lynching. It is undoubtedly these images that haunted the mind of my cousin when she turned her car around and abandoned our woodland hike.

If discourses of primitivism and forced agrarian labor weren't enough to put the Black person in a vexed relationship to the land, lynching certainly was. The importance of lynching as a factor motivating a break with the agrarian and pastoral lifestyle of the South, via migration to northern cities, cannot be overstated. Lynching was epidemic in the South after the end of Reconstruction, and the NAACP estimates that between 1882 and 1968, some 3,446 Black people were lynched. Over an eighty-six-year period, that comes to approximately forty people per year, which is roughly three people per month, every month, for eighty-six years.[47] Lynching terrorism was, according to Isabel Wilkerson, the single most important factor driving the Great Migration of Black folks out of the South into northern and western cities. In *The Warmth of Other Suns* (2010), she writes, "They did what human beings looking for freedom, throughout history, have often done. They left."[48] Discussing the damage done by the terror of lynching, Bryan Stevenson, director of the Equal Justice Initiative, states,

> There are very few people who have an awareness of how widespread this terrorism and violence was, and the way it now shapes the geography of the United States. We've got majority black cities in Detroit, Chicago, large black populations in Oakland and Cleveland and Los Angeles and Boston, and other cities in the Northeast. And the African Americans in these communities did not come as immigrants looking for economic opportunities, they came as refugees, exiles from lands in the South where they were being terrorized.[49]

As Stevenson notes here, the cities we now associate with Black America arose because of the terrorism of lynching. These cities facilitated a shift in seeing the Black American as an urban rather than an agrarian subject. This is evident in Alain Locke's volume *The New Negro* (1925), where in an essay by James Weldon Johnson, Harlem is declared the "culture capital" of Black America. Johnson writes, "I believe the Negro's advantages and opportunities are greater in Harlem than in any other place in the country."[50] This perception of the contemporary Black subject as a city-dweller, along with the terrors of slavery and lynching, drives a discursive and literal wedge between Black people and nature.

The association between nature, particularly the woods, and Black death is so strong that in Jordan Peele's 2017 film *Get Out*, the opening credits set the eerie tone for the rest of the film through a montage of a car rushing past endless forest.[51] The protagonist of the film, Chris, is warned by his best friend, Rod, not to go into the woods with white people. Chris doesn't listen and the result is tragic; Rod is ultimately correct in his read of the white people in the film, of the setting in which they live, and their intentions toward Chris and Black people in general. The film effectively builds upon the notion that a Black person isolated in the woods is a dangerous situation and hence reinforces the association between the pastoral and Black death. This association is responsible in large part for Black aversion to natural spaces. The fear of encountering a violent racist, or even just an annoying one, persists in relation to green space. This well-founded fear continues to shape and determine Black interaction with nature (or lack thereof) in the contemporary moment. But, as I hope to show in the next section and throughout this book, pervasive racist violence throughout and all over the United States, without regard for North/South or urban/rural dichotomies, has precipitated a shift in the representation of natural space in Black texts.

Sutures

I am fifteen and at a church youth camp, the only Black person at this Episcopal gathering. It is late spring in Georgia, and the air is simultaneously warm and cool, springy with the slight, intimate humidity that feels delicious in a way that only southerners understand. I can smell pine in the air as we walk to the meeting hall to do "ice breakers," and the sun is setting in the distance, cloaking the sky in orange and pink hues like rippling silk across the fading blue sky. During the "ice breakers," we complete a strange exercise where we must pick a celebrity spouse for each person in the group. When the group reveals who they have chosen for me, it is Arnold SchwarzaNIGGER, they say, laughing to themselves as if I didn't get their "joke." None of the camp counselors correct the other teenagers, and I'm left to ignore what they've said. I glance outside and see that it is dark now. The black velvet of the night sky, and the gentle chorus of crickets, invites me out. So when the groups break up for informal socializing, I make my escape.

I leave the meeting hall and go out into the dark night. The campsite where the retreat is being held is empty, so as I walk farther away from the meeting hall, I find myself quite alone. Their laughter and voices disappear beneath soft, gentle outside noises. I allow the coo of an owl and the rustling of leaves, and the slight murmur of wind, to suppress the memory of my peers. I find a stump and sit on it and idly glance up. The sky is cloudless, and now very Black, alight with more stars than I've ever seen in my life. I'm filled with awe and a sense of poignancy I cannot describe. So striking was the starry sky that for one second, I almost could not catch my breath.

Tended by moonlight, I survived through the manna of the wilderness. This powerful moment in nature did not in any way strike a blow against those white campers; but it did bolster and sustain me. So while my argument is not that nature is the "cure" for the social ills of racism, I do contend that natural space enables an affective experience of freedom that is not only a (temporary) relief from the persistence of oppression; its appearance in Black texts is a gesture toward another world and another space of being. In *Black to Nature* I intend to show that Black people have a stake in nature that has been suppressed and ignored, and that the growing awareness of the geographically universal nature of anti-Black violence has precipitated a revisitation of nature in contemporary Black texts. In her groundbreaking book *Black Faces, White Spaces: Reimagining the Relationship of African Americans to the Great Outdoors* (2014), Carolyn Finney argues that African Americans have a unique and suppressed history of nature loving that has been excluded from mainstream depictions of environmentalism: "From Wynton Marsalis to Toni Morrison to Will Allen and Majora Carter to a woman named Pearl, African Americans toiled, sang songs, wrote stories, and transformed the landscape with hard work, big dreams, and a belief that African Americans have and have always had an intimate, ever-changing and significant relationship with the natural environment" (xvi). As a geographer and social scientist, Finney is primarily interested in real people and their experiences with the natural world. She goes on to write, "By investigating the shifting 'cognitive maps' of the spaces we think of as the 'natural environment,' we have an opportunity to rethink how African Americans in the United States have engaged those spaces."[52] This volume is invested in a similar, textual project that examines the way nature is evoked in Black texts as a way to get at the idea of abolition, and ultimately of freedom. Though *Black to Nature* is concerned primarily with text and representation, it seems clear that the appearance of nature in Black texts tracks to renewed attention to it in real life. Finney's work, along with that of Lauret Savoy, whom I discuss in more detail below, represents an excavation of a lost history of Black nature discourses and practices. Additionally, groups like Outdoor Afro, which dubs itself with the subtitle "Where Black People and Nature Meet," and the less-well-known Melanin Base Camp, work to facilitate Black people's relationship with nature through nationwide chapters that plan outdoor activities and raise media attention and public consciousness of Black outdoorsmanship.[53] Additionally, a number of volumes devoted specifically to Blackness and nature have appeared recently.⁵⁴ Writing in a volume titled *The Colors of Nature* (2002), bell hooks argues, "Before the mass migrations to northern cities in the early nineteen hundreds, more than 90 percent of all black folks lived in the agrarian south. We were indeed a people of the earth."⁵⁵

I argue herein that this willingness to claim natural and pastoral space, which once defined Black existence, marks a representational shift in contemporary Black culture. *Black to Nature* is an attempt to pay attention to, and enjoy, the textual magic and beauty produced by this renewed attention to nature in Black texts. Though a kind of readerly joy around the texts I discuss herein motivated my writing of it, I am also struck by the ways in which the decline of Western society is entwined with an emphasis on the natural world. Hence, I take up the previously mentioned idea articulated by Jared Sexton in his essay "The Vel of Slavery: Tracking the Figure of the Unsovereign" that the ultimate goal of Black studies lies in "abolition," or "nothing for no one."⁵⁶ I argue throughout *Black to Nature* that nature discourses in Black texts are not romantic appeals to the restoration of any kind of Black power, nor pleas for the "restoration of a lost commons,"⁵⁷ but rather that these natural spaces in Black texts are adjacent to this notion of abolition, that they signal the end of civil society—which would be the end of anti-Blackness—as we know it.

Thus, I take up a variety of texts in this book that critique—directly or indirectly—the once-hoped-for promise that living in cities would protect Black people from racial violence and oppression. Many of these texts, I argue, "return" their characters to rural, often (though not always) southern, agrarian settings through the tropes of self-discovery, coming home, healing, and communalism. Like the Great Migration, which created the Black urbanity we associate with the contemporary Black person, the "return," if you will, to agrarian, natural, and pastoral settings and themes in Black texts parallels a movement of Black Americans from the North to the South. The recent phenomenon of Black people moving back to the South was chronicled in *USA Today* with the article "After Nearly 100 Years, Great Migration Begins Reversal."⁵⁸ The Great Migration was fueled largely by epidemic lynching and racial violence in the South and the optimistic notion that in the North one would be safer. If it was ever true that the North was safer than the South, it is certainly not true now. With the epidemic of police brutality and murder that plagues most cities with sizable Black populations, it is clear that the city has its own form of lynching, strange fruit hanging not from poplar trees but bleeding on the sidewalks of New York, Chicago, Baltimore, Los Angeles, New Orleans, and Ferguson. Reniqua Allen addresses this point in an article for the *New York Times* titled "Racism Is Everywhere, So Why Not Move South?"⁵⁹ In it, Allen doesn't make an argument for southern *rural* locales, but if northern cities aren't any safer than any other place in the United States for Black people, then the agrarian, natural settings left behind in the cosmopolitan progress narrative of the twentieth century might necessitate a second look at rural, pastoral locales.

In the same way that Black millennials are recognizing that racism is an American phenomenon and not a consequence of North or South, I am hoping to implicitly evoke a critique of the city as a "safe haven" against the violence of racism. In this sense, the "feeling" about nature is, I would like to argue, being reconfigured in the face of a growing recognition of the threat to Black life that pervades American culture, such that no change in locale actually affects one's survival outcomes in relation to racial violence. In other words, if nature was understood as dangerous because of lynching, the notion that the city would be free of Black suffering and death is now, in 2019, exposed as only the wish that it was. The seemingly unsophisticated "old Negro" of the South that the cosmopolitanism of the Harlem Renaissance presumably solved is now laid bare as a kind of respectability politics in disguise. It was never the case that becoming urbane, "worldly" subjects would inaugurate the Black person into Western humanity. In other words, becoming cosmopolitan subjects did nothing to undo the violent effects of white supremacy. Indeed, as critics like Saidiya Hartman, Jared Sexton, Calvin Warren, Christina Sharpe, and Frank B. Wilderson III have aptly demonstrated, such a transition—from thing to human—is impossible in the context of this civil society.[60]

Writing about longing for a return to her southern home, Sharon P. Holland beautifully captures the pastoral joy that has been neglected in the mainstream representation of almost exclusively urban Black life: "I wanted to go *back* home, to the place where I could still hear the faint echo of my grandmother's voice above the rhythmic creaking of the makeshift rope swing we erected one summer near the creek; to the place where I could smell the mix of cedar and pine needle in the side-yard on Otis Street."[61] But the joy and comfort captured in Holland's words doesn't mean that she is blind to the ongoing presence and history of violence and racism:

> Whether coming or going, our feelings about home are always ambivalent. This idea of home can perhaps be even more fraught in southern life because living "it" means both to repudiate and to cling to tradition. How do we love Jackson, Mississippi or Selma, Alabama or Chapel Hill in 1963? And for that matter, how do we embrace Durham in the fall of 2013 or Sanford, Florida in the winter of 2012?[62]

It isn't that one situation (either longing for and loving one's southern and/or rural home) operates against the other (knowing and remembering things that have happened down home), but rather that they exist simultaneously, with neither denied or repudiated. It is this complicated coterminous relationship between Blackness and nature that I examine in the texts in this volume.

Black to Nature is concerned with nature and the Black person in the context of American geography, and the way that racism shapes experiences of the natural world. Lauret Savoy, in her book *Trace: Memory, History, Race, and the American Landscape*, accurately illustrates this when she writes, "As I crossed the Continental Divide, the questions became so urgent they soon composed the journey. High in Colorado's Rocky Mountains, where the Arkansas River rises, I decided to try to trace family, and myself, from storied places and recorded history. But *where* to start?"[63] Savoy shows that her efforts to craft a family history and genealogy returns her to *places*, to the land—but to where and what land? Savoy's memoir tells the story of her life through descriptions of the various places she has been, alone and with her family, as a way for her to recover a family history that includes, and is not simply set against, the land itself. In a broader American cultural context, some of the relevance and impact of Savoy's work might be lost. But in the context of being Black in American society, Savoy's weaving of a certain kind of geographical claim into her Black American genealogy shifts the contextual field to reveal that Savoy's project is deeply invested in a radical act of reclamation of the natural world for Blackness. *Black to Nature* is a book that examines texts that, in various ways, similarly seek to reclaim the natural world for the Black person via the abolition of civil society.

The implications of the shift from "rural" to "urban" in the context of Blackness were profound in that the shift radically increased the Black person's sense of "placelessness," which—as Katherine McKittrick demonstrates in her work—is indelibly tied to racial alienation and oppression. What, then, does it mean for the Black urban person to return to the pastoral, the rural, and in many cases the South, when these places have historically been the sites of lynching, slavery, and Jim Crow?[64] And how do the authors and artists I discuss in this book reconcile their pastoral and natural imagery with the overburdened history of racist violence in natural spaces? The texts I study confront this historical dilemma by rejecting the framing logic of Eurocentric environmentalism and by reclaiming and recoding nature as contiguous with Blackness, as the site of a subversive antihuman ontology. By considering a largely discarded pastoral ethos, these texts productively question the contemporary boundaries of Black ontology and stake a claim for the contemporary Black person in both time and place. Writing in her essay "Earthbound," bell hooks notes:

> Backwoods folks tend to ignore the rules of society, the rules of law. In the backwoods one learned to trust only the spirit, to follow where the spirit moved.

> Ultimately, no matter what was said or done, the spirit called us from a place beyond words, from a place beyond man-made law. The wild spirit of unspoiled nature worked its way into the folk of the backwoods, an ancestral legacy, handed down from generation to generation. And its fundamental gift, the cherishing of that which is most precious, freedom. And to be fully free one had to embrace the organic rights of the earth.[65]

hooks's formulation here seems to me to speak to the kind of abolition Sexton writes about in the aforementioned essay. This vision of freedom is not related to civil rights or the language of equality; in fact, hooks's construction of freedom here is outside of society and beyond the law. Saidiya Hartman articulates the limits and problems of this historical civil rights progress narrative when she writes about how laws can "dissimulate the encroaching and invasive forms of social control" enacted against Black people.[66] *Black to Nature* embraces hooks's notion that to be "fully free," one must "embrace the organic rights of the earth." As such, I am interested in the way nature arises in works whose texture and tone is nihilistic and pessimistic as evidence of what happens when the rainbow is enuf.[67] At the same time, these texts carve out space—natural space—for their Black characters to feel at home on the earth in ways that are unimaginable under the regime of white supremacist society.

Though the theoretical frame for this book relies heavily upon Afro-pessimism and critical race theory, all of the texts I examine in *Black to Nature* either feature Black women and/or girls as their protagonists or are authored by Black women. Though there are no transgender women characters in any of the texts I examine in this volume, I want to emphasize that my broader claims about nature and Black womanhood rest upon a recognition that the category of "woman" describes both cisgender and transgender women. My emphasis on race, rather than a more detailed discussion of gender, in this introduction relates to the ways in which Black rupture from nature is tied to specifically racialized violence, which is somewhat different from the problematic ways in which women are constructed as Mother Nature. Susan McFarland notes that typically representations of women have been "historically negative," though nature has not been the site of the kind of gendered violence that lynching is.[68] Likewise, Black men and women were equally forced into "working the land" in ways that white women were not, so that disavowal of nature in a Black context is related in particular ways to racialized arrangements. So, while white feminists construct their exclusion from nature and wild spaces as a function of a patriarchal order that allows access to the pastoral to white men, Black rupture from nature equally distances Black men and women from the pastoral. Despite these critical differences, feminist articulations of nature are important for this volume, because contemporary Black women's work could be read as participating in a project of "powerfully resist[ing] the erasure of women from wilderness" and crafting from a historical negative a "positive experience."[69] Nature, in recent women's texts, has been "used as an agent of resistance," as women imagine an antipatriarchal world of gender liberation.[70] I hesitate to embrace the term "eco-feminism," because of the ways in which it has failed to reckon with women of color in its theorizations, which often results in the reproduction of racially oppressive structures from within. Throughout this volume I rely upon the work of Black feminist scholars—bell hooks, Sharon P. Holland, Saidiya Hartman, Hortense Spillers, and Christina Sharpe—and Black women's theorizations and work enable the readings I perform here. Feminist readings of beauty and of the idea of Mother Nature pervade this volume, since the authors of these texts point toward the same kind of radical abolition of oppressive structures that groups like the Combahee River Collective do.[71] Because of the ways that Black women—and throughout this volume when I refer to Black women I am speaking of both transgender and cisgender women—are multiply excluded in Western society, discourses of abolition and liberation articulated by Black women stand in for the whole race. Anna Julia Cooper expressed this when she wrote, "Only the Black Woman can say, 'when and where I enter ... then and there, the whole race enters with me.'"[72] Cooper's insight also applies to the entire (human) race, because if this society—which holds in its power at varying degrees many other oppressed people and which premises its hierarchy on anti-Blackness—no longer has this foundation to rest upon, then the whole oppressive house of cards comes tumbling down. This would liberate not only Black women but everyone else in civil society who is held in a subordinate position. These texts, then, speak for us all, because the liberation of the Black woman is the liberation of the world.

Chapter 1, "Natural Women," explores the idea of reverse migration in two contemporary Black women's texts. I argue that Beyoncé's *Lemonade* (2016), ostensibly about marital infidelity, functions as a critique of the Black progress narrative by representing the pastoral South as a site of Black love and wholeness. As *Lemonade* visually and thematically references Julie Dash's film *Daughters of the Dust* (1991), I argue that both texts contend for a version of Black life that is not urban, and that returns the Black woman (and family, by extension) to the land in order to contend for Black self-love via a rejection of Western values and ontology. In this chapter I show how nature is utilized to rebut claims about the unlovability of Black women so prevalent in Western society.

Chapter 2, "Dead Wild," discusses Hurricane Katrina as a landmark moment in contemporary discourses about nature and Blackness through Jesmyn Ward's novel *Salvage the Bones* (2011), and Benh Zeitlin's 2012 film *Beasts of the Southern*

Wild. Both texts are concerned with natural disaster, climate change, Black girlhood, and animals. Zeitlin's text is not a Black woman's text, though it features a Black girl protagonist. The film, I argue, takes up the same issues as Ward's novel but manages to recirculate images and ideas of anti-Black precarity. Esch, Ward's protagonist, I argue demonstrates through her view of the world Black interbeing with nature, which radically subverts notions of Black existence under the regime of civil society. My discussion in this chapter focuses on the intersection between natural disasters and Black death, specifically in relation to Hurricane Katrina, as well as examining the ways in which theories of the animal highlight the non-mattering of Black life in American society.

Chapter 3, "Flesh of the Earth," is an analysis of the television show *Queen Sugar* (2016) and Kaitlyn Greenidge's novel *We Love You, Charlie Freeman* (2014) through Jared Sexton's articulation of abolition as "no(where) for no(body)." I consider in this chapter the idea of homelessness (nowhere) and selflessness (nobody), by revealing the ways that land ownership and "the self" are social constructions upon which civil society, and hence oppression, rely for structural coherence. My discussion leads me to a consideration of Zen discourses, which suggest a framework for thinking through Sexton's notion of abolition. In *Queen Sugar* I consider the way that land ownership, and material acquisition, vex the possibility of Black liberation. In *We Love You, Charlie Freeman*, I analyze how the self, or the ontology of the human as a Western construction, is undermined by Greenidge's exploration of the human/animal divide through the character of a chimpanzee named Charlie. Both texts reveal the untenable, violent nature of land ownership and self-making, which in the West always excludes Blackness and also relies upon those exclusions to structure the social hierarchies that govern our lives.

In the fourth chapter, "Plant Life (Notes on the End of the World)," I turn to Octavia Butler's *Parable of the Sower* (1993) and Colm McCarthy's film *The Girl with All the Gifts* (2016) as a kind of representational end point to the arc of epistemological nature texts explored in the book. Butler's novel anticipates the collapse of Western civilization and suggests that returning to nature is more than simply a notion, but rather a necessity. Referencing Black survivalists like Harriet Tubman and Malidoma Somé, I argue that nature—in all these texts, but most notably in Butler's—represents an alternative space of mediation, where a "taste" of freedom can be experienced. Both of these texts show that the collapse of the system is synonymous with the liberation of the Black person. Hence, the ultimate implication of Black nature discourses is one of liberating anarchy. Though it is outside of the canon of African American texts, my discussion of the British film *The Girl with All the Gifts* (2017) productively addresses many of the same issues of social collapse and abolition present in

Butler's text. Both texts turn, I argue, to "plant life" as a rebuttal of Western ontology and the articulation of a way of being that sutures the Black person into the natural world.

I conceive of *Black to Nature* as a double homage to nature and to the artists who feature it in their texts. It is a love song to the sky and to the earth, to these stories and images. My intention is to place work that features pastoral, agrarian, and rural imagery and themes at the center, rather than the margin, of our consideration of contemporary Blackness. Underlying all the chapters in this book, though each chapter considers and constructs nature in a different way than the one before, is an implication that by evoking nature, in all its symbolic and literal diversity, these authors suggest something generative about the deconstruction of the leviathan of Western society. I am interested throughout *Black to Nature* in the ways that nature signals a reimagining of categories of experience—from beauty to love to place to existence to alternate ontologies—in ways that point toward liberation. I invite the reader to consider the possibilities of the abolition of civil society, of the death of anti-Blackness, and what the achievement of both might mean about our place in the natural world.

CHAPTER ONE

Natural Women

You make me feel,
You make me feel like
A natural woman.
—Sung by Aretha Franklin, "A Natural Woman," by Gerry Goffin, Carole King, and Jerry Wexler[1]

I am the first and the last. I am the honored one and the scorned one. I am the whore and the holy one. I am the wife and the virgin. I am the barren one and many are my daughters. I am the silence that you cannot understand. I am the utterance of my name.
—Nana Peazant, *Daughters of the Dust*

On May 29, 1851, Sojourner Truth delivered an oft-cited speech to the mostly white audience at the Women's Rights Convention in Akron, Ohio. In her address, Truth brilliantly turned the ontological and theological basis for women's subordination on its head. First, Truth connects women's liberation to Black liberation by arguing that if both women and Black people get rights, white men might find themselves "in a fix." She then goes on to rebut the notion that women are not as physically strong as men:

> That man over there says that women need to be helped into carriages, and lifted over ditches, and to have the best place everywhere. Nobody ever helps me into carriages, or over mud-puddles, or gives me any best place! And ain't I a woman? Look at me! Look at my arm! I have ploughed and planted, and gathered into barns, and no man could head me! And ain't I a woman? I could work as much and eat as much as a man—when I could get it—and bear the lash as well! And

ain't I a woman? I have borne thirteen children, and seen most all sold off to slavery, and when I cried out with my mother's grief, none but Jesus heard me! And ain't I a woman?[2]

Truth uses the ways in which she was treated as "less than" a woman to deconstruct claims about inherent female fragility. In doing so, she also subtly refuses the primal ground of racial thinking, which conceptualizes the Black woman's body and the white woman's body as inherently different. Later in her speech, Truth subverts the theological claim that women are inferior to men because Jesus was a man by pointing out that Jesus, in all his divinity, came from a woman. And, instead of allowing Eve to be seen as the "bad" woman who caused the human fall from grace, Truth argues that if Eve had enough power to get us out of the garden, then surely she is powerful enough to be seen as a man's equal in this imperfect world. Truth's short speech is a generative intersectional analysis of race and gender that succinctly undermines the theo-ontological basis of both American racism and sexism, and stands today as a landmark moment that captures both the dilemma and the solution to the seeming conundrum of Black womanhood.

Though she gave her speech in 1851, more than 150 years ago, these questions about Black womanhood persist. Two contemporary texts, Julie Dash's *Daughters of the Dust* (1991) and Beyoncé's *Lemonade* (2016), are concerned with the same issues of misogynoir in ways that build upon the foundational insights articulated by Truth and that extend her argument for the recognition of a powerful, natural, and spiritually grounded Black womanhood. What would it mean for Black women, both cisgender and transgender, to feel like "natural" women, women who are not defined by a politics of indecency, but rather felt their place as a *desired given* in this world? And how does feeling like a "natural woman" support the Black woman's existence in the face of a world that, as Aretha conveys so convincingly, makes one feel so tired?

Say Her Name: Black Interbeing with Nature

I discuss *Daughters of the Dust* and *Lemonade* in this chapter with special emphasis on nature, arguing that the visual evocation of nature in both of these texts stages the Black woman's belonging in the world as a rebuttal to the corrosive idea that there is no place for Black women and girls, and that Black women always already represent a kind of excess that "civilized" society cannot countenance. In the epigraph above, from Julie Dash's *Daughters of the Dust*, words from the Gnostic text *The Nag Hammadi*[3] are adapted to speak specifically to what Hortense Spillers calls a "locus of confounded identities,"[4] which describes the situation of Black women in America. Dash, with the same deft rhetorical spellcasting conjured by Truth, does not argue against the suggestion that "black woman can be seen as a particular figuration of the split subject,"[5] but rather she makes the split subject an expression of the divine: "I am the silence you cannot understand; I am the utterance of my name."[6] Black women, in Dash's film and Beyoncé's visual album, come to signify the magnificent totality, the alpha and the omega of being. These visual texts transmit another set of implications through their striking and poignant mise-en-scène that enmesh Black women in nature, elevating our understanding of Black womanhood to one of spiritual significance.

I first saw *Daughters of the Dust* as a student at Spelman College. It was 1993 and a screening had been arranged. The room filled to capacity as we, all young Black women, sat and watched ourselves unfold on the screen. I remember the stillness of the room as we took in the lush, refreshing images. I remember the quiet walk back to a friend's dorm room, words too feeble to capture the poignancy of the experience. What moved inside of me? It was something deep and ancient, motivated by recognition and longing. Viewing *Lemonade* was a similar experience of witnessing the affective life of Black womanhood turned into art. I stayed up late to watch it the night it came out. I texted my best friend—we met at Spelman—and I shared with her my immediate sense that *Lemonade* was Beyoncé's magnum opus. The significance of viewing Dash's film and Beyoncé's *Lemonade* might make more sense if I mention the violence and hostility that characterizes the lives of Black women and girls. Though we didn't have cell phone cameras to capture it all back then, the unfolding scenes of violence directed at Black women and girls today is historical and recurring. A police officer sitting on a Black girl's back in Texas is burned into my memory.[7] The image of a police officer beating a Black girl at her school desk intrudes upon my consciousness.[8] Names of Black women who died for being so come to mind: Sandra Bland, Rekia Boyd, Shukri Ali Said, and Breonna Taylor. In their efforts to bring attention to the violence Black girls and women face, Brittany Cooper and others have coined the phrase "Say Her Name" to remind us of the importance of remembering the suffering and death of Black women in the wake of state-sanctioned brutality.[9]

The "Say Her Name" movement asks that we think about the weight of violence, disdain, and repudiation Black women bear under the white gaze and about how Black women and girls are always made to feel that we do not belong, that we are best hidden or even disappeared, that there is no place for us, that our presence is always wrong and unnatural and that we must progress, improve, and "get with it." The word "natural" here not only implies something about "the natural world" but also suggests something about expectation. When something seems logical and in place, we say "naturally": "I was so tired that naturally I fell asleep as soon as I got home." So the use of "natural" here signifies on what belongs and what doesn't, what we expect to occur and what we don't. When Aretha sings that being loved makes her feel like a natural woman, this is a profound statement in the context of Black womanhood about how love can ameliorate the existential crisis white supremacy presents for Black women.

W. E. B. Du Bois famously asked, "How does it feel to be a problem?"[10] I'd like to use Du Bois's schematic of "the problem" to think through several aspects of Black womanhood that have been "problematized" under white supremacy. Both *Daughters* and *Lemonade* address three important problematized sites, all raised via embodiment, that inhere to the ontology of the Black woman: skin, hair, and sex. Dash and Beyoncé implicitly and explicitly critique the idea that the Black woman's body—via her skin, hair, and sex—is a problem. I argue here that the figuration of the "natural" undoes the logic of the "problem," as the metaphor of nature in relation to Black women suggests both the inevitability and the "rightness" of Black womanhood. What moved in me when I saw *Daughters of the Dust* was the mitigation of this feeling of being a problem. The film does revolutionary damage to the hatred of Black women in this society and so powerfully clears space for another way of being and thinking about oneself. The weight of being seen as the world's problem is backbreaking; but at Spelman, amongst ourselves, we were no one's problem. And in a theater-darkened room viewing *Daughters of the Dust*, we could feel Paul D's words to Sethe in *Beloved* (1987): "You your own best thing."[11] I see the ethos of both *Daughters of the Dust* and *Lemonade* as related to this recognition that we ourselves are the ones we have been waiting for. Nature is at the center of how both of these texts reject a history of misogynoir. As I show here, in Beyoncé's *Lemonade* and Dash's *Daughters of the Dust*, nature functions as a visual metaphor that subverts mainstream representations of Black women. At first glance, *Lemonade* is about marital infidelity. Likewise, at the most superficial level, the film *Daughters of the Dust* is about a family's migration from the Sea Islands of the South to the mainland and eventually to the North. I hope to show here, though, that in both texts references to "real" and "historical" events encourage a deeper exploration of belonging, nature, and Black womanhood. In both texts, natural mise-en-scène frames profound narratives about Black women's bodies and self-discovery.

Daughters of the Dust tells the story of the Peazant family, in 1905, who live in Igbo Landing, on the Sea Islands off coastal Georgia. Some members of the family are migrating to the North and/or to the mainland, and the film unfolds over their last day on the island. Through flashbacks and voiceovers, we learn about the family matriarch's life under slavery, as well as the recent history of various members of the family. Of particular note is the story of Eula and Eli, a young married couple expecting a child. Eula has been raped and refuses to tell Eli who raped her for fear that he might seek revenge. The implication is that she was raped by a white man and telling Eli would put him in danger of being lynched. Throughout the film, Eli and Eula's unborn child appears as a spirit to narrate her family's history and spiritual growth. Several cousins arrive at Igbo Landing, where the Peazants live, to see their family members make the historical crossing from island to mainland. Among them is a character called Yellow Mary, a woman who is an outcast among her relatives because she was a sex worker and a wet nurse. *Daughters of the Dust* builds narrative tension around Eli's insecurity about the paternity of Eula's baby, around Yellow Mary's journey to self-acceptance, around the retention (or purposeful forgetting) of West African spiritual beliefs, and around the question of racial progress. Significantly, Dash's film not only narratively rewrote the book on Black women and filmic representation but also reclaimed the Black woman's body from the dehumanizing gaze of white supremacy by filming characters in ways that highlight their humanity and wisdom.

Writing about Dash's film, Toni Cade Bambara referred to it as a "historical marker," and Ruth Elizabeth Burks argued that the film "deliberately resisted dominant discursive patterns."[12] Critics of the film agree that it represents "radical textual practice" precisely because it disrupts a long history of representing Black women as undesirable, excessive, and anathema to a "pure" womanhood.[13] Dash's film articulates a pessimism about the civil rights progress narrative, while also simultaneously highlighting the ways in which Black culture in the US is distinct from white culture. Likewise, it visually and ideologically foregrounds nature in a way that locates its characters in an African-inflected spirituality that radically renounces every aspect of Western society's contextualization of Blackness. Though the film's plot concerns members of the Peazant family migrating to the mainland/to the North, the film itself stands as a kind of meta-textual reverse migration, since it implicitly discredits the idea that migration North somehow successfully addresses the problem of the color line. The film stands as a kind of ideological return to the old folkways of Black people, to the pre-Christian identity of the formerly enslaved, and to a rejection of technology, cosmopolitanism, and Western cultural values. Black women are at the narrative and visual center of Dash's text, and central to its radical turn is how it films them.

Students of popular culture and critical race theory[14] know that one of the major problems plaguing Western cinema has been how it lights scenes specifically and exclusively for white people. The traditional three-point lighting system used in classical film has often left Black actors either over- or underexposed, producing images that distort the Black person's appearance. This is such a big issue in mainstream TV and film that when the cinematographer for HBO's show *Insecure* (2016) did such a good job lighting its (almost entirely) Black cast, it made headlines. With titles like "It's Lit! How Film Finally Learned to Light Black Skin!,"[15] "A Look at How HBO's *Insecure* Lights Black Actors So Well,"[16] and "The Art of Lighting Dark Skin for Film and HD,"[17] it's clear that dark skin has long been framed as a "problem" for filmmakers, as if somehow dark skin itself was inherently unfilmable. However, in Dash's film, which is praised as much for its visual beauty as its groundbreaking narrative, little to no artificial light was used. Writing about Dash and cinematographer Arthur Jafa's visual style in the film, Diana Pozo notes,

> While Technicolor's aesthetics required painstakingly designed artificial lighting to achieve naturalist effects, *Daughters of the Dust* uses primarily natural lighting to produce a surreal colorscape.... This radical aesthetics of color disrupts classical notions about color and cinema in several ways: it supports Dash's radical feminist narrative style, challenges the purity of whiteness and the notion that dark skin tones are difficult to film, and historicizes the power relations of color pigment production.[18]

The supposed difficulty of filming dark skin is revealed, through Dash's film, as yet another way mainstream American culture represents Blackness as visually reprehensible, hence structuring our view of the Black body through disgust and repudiation. Dash's film doesn't "get lighting right"; it simply films Black people in *natural* light, and in doing so, reveals that Black skin tones do not present a "problem" for the art of filmmaking. Arthur Jafa's organic cinematography underscores Dash's critique of the assertion that Black people are "hard to film" and simultaneously emphasizes a connection between people and nature that negates the Cartesian dualism that constructs these as opposites. Nature, then, via natural light at all times of day, became Dash's ally in her mission to reveal the richness of Black life, and specifically to rescue the Black woman's body from the technologies of an otherizing white gaze.

Dash purposely relied upon tableau vivant in this film in order to push back against a media that obscures, erases, and elides Black women's significance. "Tableau vivant" literally means "living picture" in French, and Dash's film accomplishes a texture of proximal "aliveness" in each multiply layered shot. Speaking about the film, Dash said that she wanted to create "frescoes" in the viewer's mind for strong visual impact.[19] These "frescoes" are created through the striking cinematography of the Sea Islands, all of which were shot with

Beach scene, *Daughters of the Dust* (1991), directed by Julie Dash.

natural light. The set for *Daughters of the Dust* is nature itself, as almost none of the narrative takes place "inside." Each shot and scene in the film provokes a deep sense of natural connectedness and wonder, which invites us to rethink the cultural dismissal of Black women. In this way nature functions cooperatively with Dash as a filmic interlocutor to stage questions of comfort, love, and place in relation to Black womanhood. The image from the film here is an example of the way Dash sets Black women *within* (as opposed to against) a natural landscape, bathed in natural light, to suggest an alternative schematic for looking at Black women. The yellow tones of the umbrella pick up the same colors in their skin and clothing, as does the blue-white overexposure of the sand and ocean behind them. Thus, through a monochromatic palette, Dash's film highlights the enmeshment of the women and nature.

One way Black women are maligned in white supremacist culture is by being made to feel "ugly." In 2011 an economics scholar from London published an article in *Psychology Today* that asserted that Black women were uglier than women of other races.[20] After backlash to the article, *Psychology Today* removed it; but the very fact that it took hundreds of articles and comments to point out the misogynoir of the piece shows that the editors of that publication had already internalized the belief that Black women are ugly. Given that in mainstream American society beauty is the highest achievement a woman can attain,[21] the fact that Black women are categorically defined as inherently unattractive is tied to discourses of both racism and sexism. Writing about the ways in which Black women—no matter what they look like—can (n)ever be perceived as beautiful under white supremacy, Tressie McMillan Cottom reveals how racism turns upon the idea that only whiteness is beautiful. She narrates how she learned, as a school-aged girl, that "nothing was more beautiful than blonde."[22] She goes on to write, "That is because beauty isn't actually what you look like; beauty is the preferences that reproduce the existing social order."[23] Following Cottom's logic, since Black women are always already a threat to the social order, they can never be seen as beautiful under white supremacy.[24] Cottom goes on to define beauty as a reprehensible constraint, a thing to strive *against* and not for:

> Black women have worked hard to write a counter-narrative of our worth in a global system where beauty is the only legitimate capital allowed women without legal, political, and economic challenge. That last bit is important. Beauty is not good capital. It compounds the oppression of gender. It constrains those who identify as women against their will. It costs money and demands money. It colonizes. It hurts. It is painful. It can never be fully satisfied. It is not useful for human flourishing.[25]

Cottom spurns beauty as the ground upon which she anchors her worth. She ends her essay by explicitly repudiating beauty because to want it is to become an "economic subject," where "desire becomes a market."[26] Furthermore, if Black women get caught up in attaining beauty, they do so at the risk of reinforcing whiteness. "White women need me to believe I can earn beauty, because when I want what I cannot have, what they have becomes all the more valuable. I refuse them."[27] One way that these discourses of beauty work in society in relation to Black women is to make clear that Black women's *natural*, actual bodies are unacceptable. Black women's natural hair, body size, and shape are often maligned, ridiculed, and held up as an example of what "ugly" is.

There are volumes of academic and mainstream writing by Black women on the topic of "natural" hair, which is essentially hair that has not been chemically straightened (typically) and then styled in ways associated with white women's hairstyles.[28] The importance of hair in both *Daughters of the Dust* and *Lemonade* reveals the extent to which society acts against Black women at the site of their hair, using it to define them as other. The link between the word "natural" and Black women's hair in the construction above is important, since nature is associated here with rejecting a practice (chemically straightening one's hair) that has been understood—at least since the Black Power Movement of the 1960s—to be aligned with racial self-hatred. I do not intend to rehearse the debate around hair straightening (perms) versus natural hair, because ultimately each Black woman has the right to decide what to do with her own hair and that right is central to the practice of (personal) freedom. But

I do want to think about how natural hair can be read as a trope that addresses the ideological rupture of Black people from nature, and how both nature and natural hair suggest that, contrary to racist discourse, Black women belong to and in this world *as we were born*.

The relationship between nature and Black women's hair is visualized beautifully in the work of artist Pierre Jean-Louis. In his series titled "Black Girl Magic," Jean-Louis merges images of nature with Black women's natural hair to stunning effect.[29] In doing so he radically and instantly transforms our view of Black women's natural hair.[30] The locks that may have previously been perceived as "unruly," "wild," and "unkempt" are now revealed to be as majestic and transcendent as the earth, and the universe, itself. Black women's bodies, hair, and "looks" are contested ground, because Black women are often constructed as excessive and out of place. It is from within this discourse that these radical representations emerge to startle the dismissal with which Black women are so often greeted. The importance of Dash's decision to emphasize Black women's natural, non-Western hairstyles was not lost on Black women viewers. Writing in another context about Black women's hair, Kristen Denise Rowe explains, "These hair reveals hold great meaning for Black women, due to their complex, often politicized, and historically rooted relationship with hegemonic standards of beauty."[31] Hence, Dash's focus on natural Black hair in *Daughters of the Dust* is not incidental and represents a broader reframing of Black women and their bodies. Many of the hairstyles in the film could not be worn by anyone with thin, silky, or even slightly curly hair. Natural hair in the film, then, signifies a renunciation of Eurocentric standards of beauty. Writing about hair politics, Cheryl Thompson argues that for Black women, hair is a "matter of being," and she ties a reading of natural or "unnatural" hairstyles to an ontology of Black womanhood. She argues that "the Eurocentric beauty standard of straight, long and flowing hair" profoundly impacts "black women's notions of physical attractiveness, but also . . . courtship, self-esteem, and identity."[32] Dash's rejection, via hair, of white standards of beauty is not just skin deep, because discourses of feminine beauty are oppressively tied to patriarchal and global capital in ways that are devastating for both Black and white women. Hence, in Dash's emphasis on natural Black hairstyles, she also fundamentally critiques the hegemon of Western capitalism, which arose out of the degradation of slavery. Nature, then, is multiply iterated in Dash's text at the locus of the Black woman's body to argue for the right to exist as one's natural Black self.

Skin color is also a site of analysis in Dash's film, and the link between problematized skin color, hair texture, and sex is made explicit through the characters of Yellow Mary and Eula. In the case of Yellow Mary, who Cousin

"Black Girl Magic Series," Pierre Jean-Louis.

Viola points out is "not so yellow as some," her "lighter" skin is connected to the sex work she was forced to take up for survival. Hence, a Black woman's lighter skin—typically an advantage in white supremacist society—only increases the degree to which Yellow Mary is sexually othered and exploited as both a prostitute and wet nurse. Dash highlights the fact that light-skinned privilege did not save Yellow Mary from the ravages of anti-Black sexism and exposes the ways in which a woman's appearance—whether it is the repudiated looks of Black women or the valorized looks of white women—is co-opted by patriarchy as a means to keep women subordinate to men. Hence, Black women's phenotype (via skin color and hair texture) is intimately connected to the exploitation of their sex, which is another site of "the problem" in the discourses around Black womanhood. The same complicated set of problems is evident in Eula's character, who has been raped. Eli, her husband, is tortured by his wife's violation, in part because he fears the unborn child may not be his own. Further, it is implied that the rapist is white. When Eli asks Eula, "Who done this to us?" She replies, "No good can come from knowing," which means that justice is not even a glimmering possibility; this likely means that the rapist is white. Along with the emotional and physical violation Eula's rape is, there is also the fear that Eula will give birth to a white man's child—a child that may have lighter skin and straighter hair. The internalization of white beauty standards has led to the rise of colorism in the Black community, which has meant that lighter skin and silky hair textures were (and still are) sometimes preferred among some Black people. Writing about the history of colorism, Margaret Hunter notes, "The maintenance of white supremacy (aesthetic, ideological, and material) is predicated on the notion that dark skin represents savagery, irrationality, ugliness, and inferiority. White skin, and, thus, whiteness itself, is defined by the opposite: civility, rationality, beauty, and superiority. These contrasting definitions are the foundation for colorism."[33] Given the social advantages of lighter skin and straighter hair in American society, colorism can be read as consequence of the hierarchies of phenotype that are the result of racism. And though the relationship between colorism and white supremacy may seem obvious, this connection has not stopped mainstream culture from embracing the politics of colorism, specifically in relation to Black women. Yet Dash subverts the signifiers around light skin and straighter hair by making the possibility of a mixed-race child the site of crisis. Narratively, the film prompts us to long for the unborn child's African features, because the absence of white physical features in the child facilitates the healing of Eli and Eula's family.

The love of dark skin and natural hair is imbricated in Dash's film with a critique of the racial progress narrative, where racial uplift is represented by cultural assimilation. For many Black people in the early twentieth century, migration to the North seemed the only hope for bettering their social and economic position in American society. Dash's film critiques the idea that leaving the South, and all the traditional ways of Black life, represents "progress." Dash also reveals the ways in which some of the women of the Peazant family believe that migrating north, and embracing Christianity and the "cult of true womanhood," will ameliorate their position as sexual and racial victims of violence. Eula's rape, which occurs on the island, and Yellow Mary's sexual exploitation, which occurs "in the world outside Igbo Landing," function as bookends of sexual assault that frame the Black woman's existence in the United States. On the one end is the historical record of rape under slavery and Jim Crow, represented by Eula's experience of sexual assault; on the other is Yellow Mary's dislocation from her people and herself, which causes her to literally maim her own breasts in order to be released from her duties as wet nurse to a white family. When Yellow Mary shows up at Igbo Landing, she hands Haagar—her biggest critic—a tin of store-bought biscuits. It is precisely because of such "modern" pleasures that the mainland is associated with wealth, abundance, and progress. But Yellow Mary's brokenness, shattered as she was by misogynoir, reveals the truth of Nana Peazant's words to Eli about migration to the North: "You ain't gonna find no land of milk and honey up North, Eli Peazant." The migration to the North is an attempt to shake off the yoke of history, but in doing so Dash suggests that the ones who leave also lose their vital link to nature, to the ancestors, and ultimately to themselves. Part of what they are running from is precisely the sexual violence and the lynching violence that are central to Eula and Eli's conflict.

Hence, the third "problem" of Black womanhood relates to sexual violence, and the ways Black women have been made to bear the burden of deviant sexuality in Western society. Writing about captivity and sex, Hortense Spillers notes that "the captive body becomes the source of an irresistible, destructive sensuality."[34] Dash's film upends the "problem" of Black women's sexual exploitation by revealing that white supremacy always already constructs Black women as sexually "other," regardless of the Black woman's behavior. In essence, like Cottom, Dash *refuses* the terms of respectability and progress as they have been defined by the broader culture. This is most clear in a scene where Eula intervenes in the attacks being directed at Yellow Mary by Haagar and some other women. Eula, in a monologue on the beach, rebukes her family members for their exclusion of Yellow Mary as well as their belief that the progress narrative represented by migration to the North can somehow erase or undo a history of racial and sexual violence. She tells her kinfolk that the city (represented as the North and/or the mainland) will not save them from what they are running from:

Eula speaks, *Daughters of the Dust* (1991), directed by Julie Dash.

If you're so ashamed of Yellow Mary because you say she got ruined . . . what you say about me? As far as this place is concerned, we never was a pure woman. Deep inside we believed they ruined our mothers. And their mothers what come before them. And we live our lives always expecting worse because we believe we don't deserve no better. Deep inside, we believe that even God can't heal the wound of our past, or protect us from the world that put shackles on our feet. Even though you're going up North, you all think about being ruined too. Y'all think you can cross over to the mainland and run away from it? If you love yourself . . . love Yellow Mary. She a part of you . . . just like we a part of our mothers.³⁵

Eula reveals the implicitly anti-Black nature of the aspersions cast at Yellow Mary by historicizing sexual violence against Black women along a timeline from Yellow Mary, to herself, to all of the named and unnamed Black women who were sexually exploited during and after slavery. This scene is shot on the beach, subtly reminding of us of the ocean voyages that brought Africans to the shores of America. Anissa J. Wardi explains that Black texts "construe bodies of water as haunted by the bodies of those who lost their lives in their currents. Water, then, the course of travel, marks severed paths to home, family, landscape and even life."³⁶ Hence, in this scene the beachy landscape situates the Peazant family historically in relation to the Middle Passage and to slavery.

Yet the film's cinematography imbues another layer of meaning to the nature-function of this scene. By graphically matching the clothing of the Peazant women in the washed-out white-sand beach and the sunlit overexposure of the ocean behind them, we are invited to see the resilience and wisdom of Eula, and her kinfolk, despite the violations of slavery. As we can see in the image above, their white clothing mirrors the beach itself, drawing our attention to the contiguity between them and the earth, between people and place.

Daughters of the Dust not only uses mise-en-scène to connect Black women to nature but, through its representation of an African-inflected spirituality, rejects the axiological whiteness and sexism of Western Christianity. Spirituality in *Daughters of the Dust* critiques the progress narrative represented by crossing over to the mainland, as well as rejects the patriarchal arrangements of Christianity. Viola, who has already migrated to the mainland and comes back to Igbo Landing a fully committed Christian, defines progress and Christianity as the same thing. Sitting on the beach with a group of children, one of them asks her what is "over there on the mainland." She replies, "The Son of God, child, the Son of God." Later, Nana Peazant—in an attempt to blend her neo-African spiritual beliefs with the Christianity that those emigrating are embracing—wraps some roots and a bit of her hair, and her mother's hair, around a Bible. Haagar, who spends most of her time maligning Yellow Mary, yells "Hoodoo! Hoodoo!" and shoos her daughter away from kissing the Africanized Bible held by Nana Peazant.[37] The fear around non-Christian spirituality relates to the ways in which African culture was defined as primitive and other; so Haagar and Viola's disavowal of Nana's spiritual instruction is not necessarily related to a theological aversion so much as it is aligned in their minds with "backwardness," and hence an abomination to the notions of Western progress they have so eagerly embraced. Christianity, then, is seen as the means by which the Black person can successfully assimilate into American society.[38] But in Dash's film, Nana's spirituality is an important signifier of an African-inflected, woman-centered existence.

The negative associations of "Hoodoo" or "Voodoo" police traditional Black beliefs and subsequently act as a check on Black freedom. Writing about Voodoo, Ishmael Reed explains,

> The enemies of Voodoo have exploited rumors associating the Secte Rouge, a Petro sect, with human sacrifice in order to defame Voodoo, less a religion than the common language of slaves from different African tribes, thrown together in the Americas for commercial reasons. This common language was feared because it not only united the Africans but also made it easier for them to forge alliances with those Native Americans whose customs were similar. Voodoo has been the

inspiration for the major slave revolts in this hemisphere, including the one that ousted the French from Haiti, but just as Christianity has been used by tyrants as a means for persecuting their opponents, Voodoo has been similarly abused.[39]

Nana's melding of her Neo-African (Voodoo) beliefs with Christianity demonstrates how Black people in the Diaspora have made Christianity their own.[40] What's important about Voodoo for my discussion here is the way in which Voodoo's cosmology is shaped by an understanding of the power and totality of the natural world as a divine force. Gods and goddesses in Voodoo (Loas) are often associated with elements, directions, animals, rocks, and plants. Voodoo cosmology is based less on a monarchical model (as we see in Western Christian liturgy, where God is a kind of ruler or king) and more on a holistic engagement with nature and the universe. Hence, the sign of neo-African spirituality in *Daughters of the Dust* connects to nature and Blackness because it provides the epistemological and spiritual framework for Black (self) love.

Writing about Voodoo in Jamaica, Zora Neale Hurston notes, "The black people of Jamaica are beginning to respect themselves. They are beginning to love their own things like their songs, their Anansi stories and proverbs and dances."[41] Hurston explicitly links the practice of African spirituality with self-love, and both *Lemonade* and *Daughters* evoke this connection between self-love and spirituality. Neo-African spirituality in *Daughters of the Dust*, much like natural hair, represents self-respect and self-love. When Nana ties the charm she's made to the Bible, this is significant not only because it shows the flexibility of her worldview but also because she includes a piece of her hair and her mother's hair in it. Thus, the actual hair of the ancestors can be kept as a historical trace that connects her descendants to their Blackness, which they can use as a tool to navigate the dangers of a white supremacist society on the mainland.[42] Spirituality in *Daughters of the Dust* is inextricably tied to nature, as the Voodoo cosmology is one where nature is central —not peripheral—to the human experience. Voodoo and/or neo-African religion in *Daughters of the Dust* not only informs people's interaction with nature but also undoes the ideological basis for patriarchy and racism. It's a totally "Voodoo" move when Sojourner Truth reframes the maligned figure of Eve through a discourse of power and ability rather than as the cause of all the world's problems. Likewise, Nana's spiritual instruction to her descendants is grounded in the same liberating ideology evinced by Truth.

The impact of an African-inflected spiritual practice on how one negotiates the complicated effects of white supremacy and patriarchy is evident in the scene at the graveyard between Eli and Nana, where Nana's spiritual framework intervenes at the problematic site of sex and Black womanhood.

Eli articulates his angst about his wife's rape through the language of ownership. "I don't feel like she's mine anymore," he shouts to Nana. Nana quickly corrects him, "Eula never belonged to you; she married you." So for Eli, Eula's rape is primarily a violation of his masculine "right" over his wife's body and sex. This idea, that the rape impugns his rights as a man, aligns with white supremacist ideas about women as objects in need of protection. Just as the fantasy of the Black male rapist menacing white women prevalent in American society is not actually about the safety of white women but is instead about policing Black masculinity, Eli's reaction to Eula's rape is not at all about Eula but is instead about his negotiation of his place as a man in American society vis-à-vis white men. It is quite literally a matter "between men," to reference Eve Sedgwick,[43] and thereby decenters women in the rape narrative. Nana not only knows that Eli is wrong to construct Eula as his purloined and violated property but emphasizes to him that realizing this is not just a matter of him feeling better but is a matter of his spiritual growth and development. For Nana, Eli's struggle to overcome his feelings about Eula's rape is a crisis related to remaining connected to ancestral knowledge rather than capitulate to the gendered epistemology of the West. We can connect Nana's critique of Eli's patriarchal outrage all the way back to Sojourner Truth's speech, where she rebuts the argument that women are incapable of protecting themselves or, implicitly for this reading, of healing themselves.

This scene connects to the one I talk about above, where Eula explains that in the context of white supremacy, all Black women are "ruined." Refusing to embrace the belief that women can be whole only if they are free from both sexual desire and violation is a central part of overcoming the internalized inferiority that white supremacy bequeaths to Black people. For Eli to see Eula as "ruined" because she was raped is to view her through the same lens the larger society does, and—perhaps even more importantly—it is also to see all the Black women who came before as "ruined," unworthy, and degraded, for rape is as ubiquitous to the Black experience in America as is racism.

This wisdom articulated by Nana Peazant, in her emphasis on place, family, and the ancestors, resonates with the idea of "interbeing," a concept coined by the Zen teacher Thich Nhat Hanh. The Zen concept of "oneness" also characterizes Voodoo cosmology, where separation is de-emphasized and interconnectedness is highlighted. But the term also perfectly describes the way nature is represented in *Daughters*. Hanh defines interbeing as "the essential interconnectedness of the universe. It challenges us to look beyond the world of concepts and opposites. If we look deeply into the nature of our universe, we can see all things as profoundly interdependent."[44] Hanh explicitly tied his conception of interbeing to nature, articulating a view of nature that ceases to see it as "other." The use of nature simply as "landscape," and as a backdrop for human activity, is not how nature functions in *Daughters of the Dust*. The characters do not *look at* nature but rather are enmeshed in nature as a "given" part of existence. The distinction between *enjoying nature* and *interbeing* with nature is a critical one. In the former construction, nature is an "other" to be consumed through the senses or otherwise; in the latter, nature is not separate from oneself, but rather exists as a continuation of one's own being, different only in texture and viscosity. Hence, Dash's film corrects the delusional premise that between nature and people lies a boundary, and instead flattens the visual and epistemological field between person and place. This interbeing with nature characterizes Blackhood, a term coined by Mali Collins-White in her analysis of respectability politics. Writing about Blackhood, she notes, "I envision Blackhood to be a radical subjectivity overflowing with the known and unknown of the Diaspora: an amalgamation of what one would have been without the Diaspora, who one is with it, and what one desires or does not desire to be, utterly and forcefully for their Black selves."[45] This idea of Blackhood, as way of thinking about the intersection of Blackness, interbeing, and nature, speaks to the way that emphasis on the natural undoes the presumption of Black womanhood as a problem.

Forward: Interbeing as Black Praxis

A politics of Blackhood characterizes *Daughters of the Dust* and definitely describes all of Beyoncé's work since her self-titled album released three years before *Lemonade*. That album, which included the well-known hit "Drunk in Love," marked a swift turn toward Blackhood for Beyoncé. Many people describe the album's aesthetics (visually and musically) as "ratchet," which was different from the pop diva aesthetic Beyoncé previously cultivated. As a term, "ratchet" describes an aspect of Black life that is decidedly "disrespectful" of the norms of polite, white society. "Ratchet," as correctly defined by the online *Urban Dictionary*, means "ghetto" and/or "trashy."[46] Hence, ratchet performances are literally a middle finger to respectability politics. With its emphasis on sexuality and relationships, the album *Beyoncé* positioned its artist firmly within the realm of a kind of Blackhood that was and is often repudiated in mainstream society. At first glance, such moves within the realm of sex, marriage, and desire might seem like petty pandering to a culture of "low art." Yet when we consider that the respectability politics that held Beyoncé's image in check previously function as "a historical instrument of control"[47]—not just for her but for all Black women—we can see embedded in this turn toward the Blackhood of ratchetness a deeper political implication. The Blackness of the 2013 album *Beyoncé* primed a pop audience for the release of an even more subversively Black text three years later in *Lemonade*.

When *Lemonade* was released, many people recognized its intertextual link to Dash's film; and partly because of Beyoncé's album, *Daughters of the Dust*—over twenty years after being released—was trending. In fact, Dash's film is now (as of this writing) available on Netflix. When Dash was asked what she thought about *Lemonade*, she described it as a "masterpiece."[48] In *Lemonade*, Beyoncé returns to her southern and agrarian roots, drawing upon pastoral imagery reminiscent of Dash's film. While doing so she takes up the ways in which Black women are "unwanted" in a society that values whiteness—both phenotypically and culturally—over the antirespectability of Blackhood "rooted in African-centered ways of knowing and a simultaneous release of Western constructions of time, space, gender, sexuality, and being."[49] The same locus of problems—skin, hair, and sex—which I argue informs the radical Black feminist praxis of *Daughters of the Dust*, also inflects *Lemonade*'s structure and ethos. And like Dash's film, *Lemonade* emphasizes pastoral return and southern roots as an antidote to the fraught project of the traditional racial progress narrative. Both *Lemonade* and *Daughters*, I argue, are invested in a co-inscription of nature and Black womanhood in order to refuse the terms of white supremacy. As such, *Lemonade* is a tour-de-force that draws from the same contextual frame as Dash's film and much for the same reason—to address the experience of gendered and racial violence through a Black woman's lens. As I indicate above, *Lemonade* is about infidelity and love—which, as in the 2013 album, might seem predictably heteronormative. Writing about Angela Davis's reading of freedom and love, Lindsey Stewart notes, "Davis' insight is that . . . sexual love acts as a metonym for freedom." She goes on to show that in *Blues Legacies and Black Feminism* (2011), Davis argues that sexual love is a "tangible expression of freedom" for Black people post-slavery.[50] *Lemonade* takes seriously the claim that love, especially love between Black people, is another modality of freedom. Hence, love's failure in *Lemonade* is narratively tied to the ways in which the Black woman's body is constructed as a problem in Western society. And, like *Daughters of the Dust*, *Lemonade* refuses the idea of a problematized Black womanhood through an evocation of the "natural" that is then visually aligned with Black women.

Lemonade begins with two alternating scenes, one of Beyoncé onstage, in a black hoodie, against a red curtain, and the other of her in the same hoodie in a field of tall grass blowing gently in the wind. Beyoncé is alone, on the stage, and in the field, and this aloneness captures the ontological crisis of Black womanhood in American society, as well as Beyoncé's personal sense of abandonment. Walking, in the fields, Beyoncé reminds us of our American origins, that our first "place" here was on the land, in the fields, as slaves. Her presence in the field, along with her hooded jacket, implies that she is alone, that she is hiding, that perhaps she is looking for something she lost. The hoodie, now a ubiquitous visual cue to Black death since the brutal killing of Trayvon Martin, also marks the phenomenon of Black bondage. Thus, the hoodie and her presence in the field point to a Black American starting point and proceeds to a literal "deep dive" into the liberating "elsewhere" of love, as Beyoncé jumps from the top of a building. In this opening scene, she is returning to the site of a uniquely American crime—a crime against Black people that began on slave ships and continued in the fields of slavery, where people were transformed into "things," and human beings became captive bodies.

Writing about this, Spillers argues,

> The captive body, then, brings into focus a gathering of social realities as well as a metaphor for value so thoroughly interwoven in their literal and figurative emphases that distinctions between them are virtually useless. Even though the captive flesh/body has been "liberated," and no one need pretend that even the quotation marks do not matter, the dominant symbolic activity, the ruling episteme that releases the dynamics of naming and valuation, remains grounded in the originating metaphors of captivity and mutilation so that it is as if neither time nor history, nor historiography and its topics, shows movement, as the human subject is "murdered" over and over again by the passions of a bloodless and anonymous archaism, showing itself in endless disguise.[51]

Following Spiller's conclusion that in relation to the captive body, "distinctions between them are virtually useless," I argue that Beyoncé's opening scene in the bottle grass reminds us of the fields that distorted relations between Black people, such that Black women continue to be dismissed and read as undesirable partners as a result, even from "within" the race. *Lemonade*, at once beautiful to watch and painful to contemplate, reveals how Black women's bodies have been made to bear the representational burdens of the captive body, a body from which everyone—including some Black men—is fleeing. Thus, Beyoncé contextualizes Jay-Z's infidelity through discourses of Black pain and suffering, metaphorizing the breakdown of the Black family through tropes of slavery and labor. Healing, then, from infidelity and from the ways in which white supremacy intervenes in Black (self) love, occurs at the natural site, where we are visually reminded that Black women are as necessary and fundamental to existence as are water, air, fire, and earth.

Lemonade visually reminds us of Dash's film as it uses the same tableau technique to create images that disrupt the forward momentum of the nar-

Beyoncé in the field, *Lemonade* (2016), directed by Kahlil Joseph.

Women in white, *Lemonade* (2016), directed by Kahlil Joseph.

rative; and it uses nature as a trope to reject stereotypes about Black women's undesirability, while simultaneously negotiating the intersection of intimacy and racial violence. *Lemonade* also references *Daughters of the Dust* through its mise-en-scène, which adorns the Black women in Beyoncé's film in styles similar to those in Dash's film. Most of the women in Dash's film wear white, which contributes to the poignant and lush visual field of the film. Many scenes in *Lemonade* also feature women dressed in white, located in pastoral settings. Though it is common at Black funerals for people to wear white instead of Black, and hence we could read the white clothing in both texts as symbolic of the end of something, it is also the case that for those practicing a Yoruba-inflected spiritual tradition, white clothing represents a shield of protection.[52] Aesthetically, white also draws our attention to the darkness of the skin of the women, emphasizing, rather than hiding, their Blackness.

Lemonade is tied to *Daughters of the Dust* not only via its citational imagery and use of tableaux, but also through the set of concerns that structure Beyoncé's narrative. Like Dash's film, Beyoncé's visual album is concerned with Black women, racial violence, and love, and contests the American progress narrative. Beyoncé schematizes these profound epistemological issues via the body and through an explicit identification of the ways in which white supremacist rhetoric about the body disrupts Black (self) love. While *Daughters of the Dust* only tangentially refers to white people, Beyoncé's album suggests that her husband is cheating with a white woman or a woman who looks "less Black." This is clear from the now-famous line "Better call Becky with the good hair." "Becky" is a common slang term that means "white woman," and *Lemonade* aptly ties the infidelity in this particular case to a larger political failure to love Black women. In this one, critical line, Beyoncé identifies skin color (Becky = whiteness), hair texture ("good hair"), and sex (call, as in "call girl") as the site of a racialized and gendered trauma. This line is delivered at the end of the song "Sorry," where the refrain of the chorus is "Sorry . . . I ain't sorry." In the video for this song, Beyoncé is with Serena Williams, who dances sexily throughout. The inclusion of Serena is vital to unraveling the ways in which *Lemonade* is explicitly about misogynoir, and its impact on how Black women feel about themselves.

Serena Williams has experienced an onslaught of white supremacist and sexist attacks about her appearance. Much of that vitriol is directed at what mainstream society sees as Serena's "masculine" body type, which reinforces Spiller's contention that captive bodies are "ungendered" and "unprotected."[53] In an interview with *Harper's Bazaar UK*, Williams comments on how people have speculated that she was "born a guy," and how body shaming has been a persistent issue she has had to respond to over the course of her career.[54]

Serena bringing it, *Lemonade* (2016), directed by Kahlil Joseph.

"Body shaming," a newer coinage that characterizes Black women's experience in America since slavery, might stand in as a term that describes how Black women have always been defined as embodied "problems." The inclusion of Serena in the video for "Sorry" is an explicit critique of the ways in which Black women's bodies have been rejected. In this video, Serena is seen descending a staircase and walking down a hall toward Beyoncé, who sits in a chair. As the song proceeds, Serena begins to twerk and dance suggestively around Beyoncé, while she sings (to the implied male listener), "I ain't thinking 'bout you." Serena's presence also allows Beyoncé to critique both colorism and "good hair," because Beyoncé is often accused of an illegitimate and insincere pro-Black politics because of her lighter skin. Hence, we could read Serena as the recipient of Beyoncé's desire, not only in a (necessarily exclusively) sexual way, but also in a cathected way—where Serena's darker skin is celebrated and loved as if it were Beyoncé's own.

Throughout *Lemonade*, Beyoncé articulates her love for Blackness—visually and lyrically. On "Formation," she famously sings, "I like my baby's hair with baby hair and Afros; I like my Negro nose with Jackson Five nostrils." This complicated line—which requires the listener to know that "baby hair" and "baby's hair" here is not a repetitive aesthetic flourish but two very distinct though interrelated things—allows Beyoncé to avow her love of Black phenotype. *Lemonade* is a love song to everything about Blackness, especially to the very Black "look" that American society defines as repugnant through its demonization of Black women and their bodies. Writing about the radical nature of Black feminism and pleasure, Ruth Nicole Brown argues, "Desire can lead you to a life's work with people who make the language of just how good it feels felt, thereby giving everyone in the place, a politic to live up to. The analytic here is

Beyoncé admires Serena, *Lemonade* (2016), directed by Kahlil Joseph.

a Black feminist homegirl coupling of reproduction and pleasure."[55] Between Serena and Beyoncé on the pivotal song "Sorry," we witness a life's work of desire centered on Blackness and womanhood, where Black women love themselves in ways no one in the world of the album—not even one's Black husband in the context of *Lemonade*—has yet been healed enough to do.

Serena's dancing, and Beyoncé's homoerotic spectatorship of it, undermines respectability politics and thereby validates Serena's (and all Black women's) existence—not by suggesting she is a "worthy" sex object but by behaving in precisely the ways the white gaze views as disreputable. Furthermore, the video—with only women throughout—implies that this is a uniquely Black woman's space, and that this dancing is not for the male gaze, but rather for (self) pleasure. There is no capitulation to Western standards of beauty, sexiness, or appropriate behavior; instead, we see two Black women, alone, pleasuring each other with their song and dance. This scene is part of the radical praxis of *Lemonade*, as it centers an ethos of Blackhood that functions as an ideological wedge against white supremacy. Collins-White could have been writing about *Lemonade* when she wrote, "Blackhood imagines African bodies beyond these early projections that defined categories of Black womanhood and Black manhood as hypersexual and bestial, our intimacy as breeding, and pleasure central to a phenomenology only accessible to our captors."[56] The pleasures offered by this scene of Beyoncé and Serena together may not be accessible to either white or male viewers, and as such centers Black women and womanish desire in ways rarely seen in the texts we are most often given mainstream access to.

As *Lemonade* proceeds, Beyoncé broadens the film's critique to suggest that failure to love Black women weakens the Black community and participates in the same white supremacist discourses responsible for the extrajudicial murders of Black men and women by police and vigilantes. At stake in *Lemonade* is not just one marriage but a way of thinking about oneself, one's partner, and one's community that either strengthens Black people or colludes with structural racism. As in *Daughters of the Dust*, nature functions in *Lemonade* to reveal the complexity and wisdom of Black women, as well as to highlight the agrarian South as the spiritual home of Black Americans. Spirituality is also implicated in this conjunction of Black womanhood and nature. In much the same way that Nana's Black feminist politics are inflected by an African spiritual view of the world, so, too, does *Lemonade* reference an alternative spiritual tradition to reframe the Black woman's emplacement in the world, and—via the invocation of African goddesses—to reject Western patriarchy.

In her essay "Work the Root: Black Feminism, Hoodoo, Love Rituals, and Practices of Freedom," Lindsey Stewart writes, "I argue that we cannot understand . . . freedom without the cosmology the blues borrows from spirit work practices—for it is these practices that *imbued* sexual love with emancipatory possibilities."[57] Likewise, the spiritual references to West African cosmology in *Lemonade* ground Beyoncé's critique of white supremacy in a Blackhood that affirms an older Black tradition, where Black women were not only loved but worshipped, hence drawing our attention to the aspect of divinity articulated in the feminist dualism of the *Nag Hammadi*. The spiritual implications of *Lemonade* have been written about by many fans of the visual album. In the article "Our Goddess Beyoncé: Yoruba Goddesses in *Lemonade*," Annie Earnshaw explains the symbolic invocation of the Black and matriarchal divine in the album.[58] In addition to visually signaling Yoruba goddesses in her work, Beyoncé refers throughout *Lemonade* to the elders and to her ancestors; like Nana in *Daughters of the Dust*, the poetry she recites throughout—written by the Somali poet Warsan Shire—narrativizes Beyoncé's struggle with power and love across multiple generations. On the song "Redemption," Beyoncé recites, "Grandmother, the alchemist, you spun gold out of this hard life, conjured beauty from the things left behind. Found healing where it did not live. You passed these instructions down to your daughter who then passed it down to her daughter."

This is the same ethos that defines Nana's advice to Eli: "Call on the old souls. They will come to you when you least expect 'em." This reliance upon spiritual, ancestral, and oral knowledge turns away from Western epistemologies, grounding these characters in a singularly Black cosmology, decentering white supremacy and all that it projects onto Black women. The radical potential of *Lemonade*'s spiritual politics is nowhere more evident than in the ways that Beyoncé, in the subcultures of YouTube, 4chan, and Reddit, has been accused of being in the "Illuminati." A Google search with the words "Beyoncé" and

"Illuminati" returns thousands of hits; it is such a dangerous yet persistent issue that Beyoncé addresses it herself on "Formation" when she sings, "Y'all haters corny with that Illuminati mess." This conspiracy theory, which is too fringe for primetime but powerful nonetheless, argues that Beyoncé—and many other famous and influential people—are in a secret society and satanic cult whose goal is to control and subdue the masses.[59] The conspiracy theories about Beyoncé's purported satanism pathologize her in ways that are specifically raced and gendered; their effect is to "check" both the cultural and ideological influence of Beyoncé as a figure of liberation. The conspiracy theories about Beyoncé's spiritual beliefs confirm my argument here that Voodoo/neo-African spirituality supports an antipatriarchal and pro-Black spiritual ethos that empowers Black people, and especially Black women. Like Haagar, who yelled "Hoodoo!" at Nana Peazant when she witnessed the respect and veneration being given to her, these conspiracy theorists—in the face of Beyoncé's cultural influence and artistry—are yelling "Hoodoo" at her, and much for the same reason: to invalidate her Blackhood project. Yet the presence of neo-African spirituality in *Lemonade* points to an ephemeral and epistemological "elsewhere," where everything that was not previously available to Black women in society—love, comfort, acceptance—becomes imaginable and possible. Thus, tying together love, spirituality, and nature as it does, *Lemonade* reveals the path toward a Black feminist elsewhere, where "emancipatory possibilities" abound. This elsewhere is, I argue, symbolically referenced via the pastoral, where the supposed problematic of Black womanhood is undone and replaced by a sense of one's belonging in the world as one's "natural" self.

If the "problem" of Black womanhood is intimately tied to the ways in which our skin, hair, and sex are deemed "excessive" and "disreputable" by white supremacist discourses, then Dash and Beyoncé counter that narrative by filming *only* Black bodies, shifting the gravitational "center" of our racialized viewing. In both *Daughters of the Dust* and *Lemonade*, white people are visually absent. The only white people we see in *Lemonade* are a line of police officers in the "Formation" video (which runs as a postcredit cut scene) and a few shots of white people in couples during the song "All Night." Thus, while white supremacy is a kind of ghost that haunts Beyoncé throughout the album, whiteness is visually displaced off-screen. The absence of visual whiteness in both of these texts centers the Black gaze, making unnecessary the cultivation of what bell hooks has called the "oppositional gaze."[60] The most poignant moments in *Lemonade* when white supremacy is referenced are on the songs "Freedom" and "Forward." The song "Freedom" is preceded by the song "Forward," which includes a montage of real-life mothers whose sons have been killed by police. These mothers are dressed in African clothes and hold pictures of

Sybrina Fulton and her son Trayvon Martin, *Lemonade* (2016), directed by Kahlil Joseph.

Lesley McSpadden and her son Mike Brown, *Lemonade* (2016), directed by Kahlil Joseph.

Gwen Carr and her son Eric Garner, *Lemonade* (2016), directed by Kahlil Joseph.

their sons. Mike Brown's mother unsuccessfully fights back tears as the camera pans in, moving closer to her and the portrait of her son in graduation attire. This song occurs in the narrative after Beyoncé has forgiven Jay-Z for his infidelity. But it forces us to think about all the ways in which Black women lose Black men—not just as husbands and partners, but also as sons, brothers, and uncles. It relocates the rupture of the Black family in white supremacy and so the narrative invites us to consider and compare the ways in which whiteness, both through physical violence in the form of police brutality and through the epistemic violence that causes the internalization of values about "good hair" and white/light skin, undoes Black women literally and figuratively.

By dressing the mothers in African attire, *Lemonade* visually references Africa, and Black goddesses, while the deaths of the sons stand in for the ongoing anti-Blackness of American society. This accumulation of Black death is historicized in *Lemonade* from the Middle Passage, to slavery, to the extrajudicial murders of Black people. The faces of these mothers ask us to consider what we have been made to bear. The majesty of their African attire stands in painful opposition to the one-dimensionality of the photographs of their sons, all of whom were taken senselessly by racial violence. The photographs positioned against the living and royally attired women emphasizes the absence of these sons, who should be alive. These horrifically common racially motivated murders can be traced back to the vestibular predicament of the Middle Passage, with imagistic reference to West African culture bringing these women's pain into sharp relief.

Baptismal scene, *Lemonade* (2016), directed by Kahlil Joseph.

Baptismal scene, *Daughters of the Dust* (1991), directed by Julie Dash.

The specter of the Middle Passage haunts both *Daughters* and *Lemonade*, such that the presence of water in these texts co-evokes trauma and healing. Water is featured throughout *Lemonade* and often serves to mark a transition from one song to another. When Beyoncé jumps from a building at the beginning of *Lemonade*, she emerges in a watery space, which can be read as a womb. Water operates as a double signifier in these Black women's texts, and in Beyoncé's water represents both death and rebirth, as symbolized by her emergence from an aperture with water rushing from behind her. Water can be understood in this text as way of mediating "survival and trauma, diasporic and regional connections, and physical and psychological dislocations."[61] Water, then, is simultaneously a site of healing and trauma, a graveyard and a baptismal font. In the image above, the women are dressed in white, a reference to traditional rural baptism, signaling rebirth and renewal. This is not unlike a scene in *Daughters of the Dust*, when we see a group of Christians headed to the water for a baptism. These images, both in *Lemonade* and *Daughters of the Dust*, gesture toward earlier moments in Black history. The clothing in both instances conjures a sense of the past, reminding us of forgotten scenes in historical Black American life. The conjoining of water, Blackness, and the pastoral evinces Black American beginnings, implicitly undermining the sense of teleological movement "forward." In Beyoncé's song of the same name, the line "Best foot forward just in case," speaks to the instability of linear narratives of progress. "Just in case" implies something has been given up, as if the singer is hedging his bets concerning forward momentum. In other words, eliciting ancestral and historical memory through the signifier of Blackness undermines the progress narrative, by at once revealing the impossibility of Black liberation in a system that requires, in toto, anti-Blackness to operate and demonstrating that it was never the Black person who needed to change or to "evolve." Therefore, by returning to pastoral sites, both *Daughters* and *Lemonade* undermine the construction of Black women as a "problem."

Lemonade ends with forgiveness and reconciliation yet continues to center women, and a woman-centered community, throughout. As Beyoncé recites the words, "So we're going to heal," we see women in the garden, harvesting food, and then sitting together on a porch. These images foreground Black women and situate healing in the context of both nature and women's community. Such images seem textured by the past, allowing us to recall a tradition that was neglected in the rush toward cosmopolitan "progress." Like the protagonist in *Invisible Man* (1952), who after many painful experiences in the North can finally proclaim in celebration of his southern roots, "I yam what I yam," these texts demonstrate that not only was the North not, in the words of Nana

Harvesting vegetables, *Lemonade* (2016), directed by Kahlil Joseph.

Women gathered on the porch, *Lemonade* (2016), directed by Kahlil Joseph.

Peazant, a land of milk and honey but there is generative value in the places and practices of the Black agrarian past.

On Sapelo

The insights of Dash's and Beyoncé's texts are not simply intellectual for me; they are proximal. As a Black woman and as a southerner, I've experienced the feeling that perhaps up North there would be less racism and more opportunity. As a high school student, it was my dream to go to New York City. Even still, when it came time for me to go to college—despite being heavily recruited by well-known institutions far north of the Mason-Dixon Line—I could not bring myself to choose those institutions over Spelman. Because I grew up in predominantly white environments my whole life, I knew that the Black woman space of Spelman was something I needed. So I stayed in the South but spent two summers in a row in New York City. Once there, I quickly learned that it was not a land of milk and honey. Indeed, it was just as racist as the South, different only in its codes of racism. Furthermore, I discovered that I did not enjoy the city, and I longed to get back to the rich greenness of Atlanta and to the rural areas I visited often down home. When I finally knew that the city wasn't for me, a deep interest in the natural world blossomed in my consciousness, and I found myself curious about my grandparents' agrarian roots and background. Both of my grandparents, who were born in 1915, grew up in rural Georgia—in Taliaferro County. My grandmother's family worked as sharecroppers, and my grandfather's family, who were better off, owned their own farm. Through their stories, I began to suspect that my grandmother's grandparents may have come from the Sea Islands. When I asked my grandmother about this, she had little to say—either because she didn't know or because of the reputation of Gullah/GeeChee culture, specifically as it relates to neo-African religion.

Yet in so much of my grandmother's way of speaking, her way of seeing the world, and her spiritual commitment, I could see traces of a West African culture that seemed more present than distant. It was in the way she built community wherever she went and the way she accepted me that seemed to acknowledge that I too am the fruit of an ancient tree. In her there was a model of self-love that resonates in these Black women's texts. I feel her in these texts, as if they provide an entry into a secret but powerful coda that ties me to her and to all the Black women who came before me. In her and me, the past and the present meet, because through me the imprint of the ancestors echoes through time and space. In these texts bits of my actual life come back to me. It was my grandmother Elizabeth Frazier who asked me, when I told her I was going to graduate

Sign on Sapelo Island to Cabretta Beach. Photo by Stefanie K. Dunning.

school in California, how I could leave the place where my dead relatives were buried, much the same way Nana poses this question to her children who are migrating to the mainland. When she died, my grandfather insisted that her tombstone be engraved with a telephone, because she spent so much time calling people. It's an African-inflected practice to bury people with their beloved items, and this was a gesture to that tradition. After my grandmother died, she came to me in a dream one night. She was standing in a field of purple flowers, wearing purple herself, looking young and restored. Though my grandmother's body is no longer here, the earth(ly) body remains, which ties me to her via an unbreakable bond. In search of my grandmother, I find this unexpected and rich natural experience, my birthright, my right to exist as I am.

I go to Sapelo Island looking for the sound and smell of my grandmother. I took this photograph there. This sign, and others like it, highlight a resistance to mainland norms in favor of a whimsical, improvisational discursive relationship to place and to the natural world. The sign shown here, which is actually a "street sign," uses animals as symbols to point the way. The snake here is "pointing" toward the beach; so it's at once art and direction. For me this sign not only shows an appreciation for the natural but also represents how people can mediate their relationship to space when they are free. I hold these texts and spaces close, because they celebrate resistant modalities that concretize, rather than obscure, the Black woman's natural right to be, so that when I step outside, whether finding myself in the forest or on the beach, I know that I am home.

CHAPTER TWO

Dead Wild

The tears get close to my eyes ... and I have this feeling in the pit of my stomach that if I start crying, the sobs will kill me, ... I feel like if I started crying now, I'd never stop.
—Denise Moore, on "After the Flood," *This American Life*

What if some subjects never achieve, in the eyes of others, the status of the "living?" What if these subjects merely haunt the periphery of the encountering person's vision, remaining, like the past and the ancestors who inhabit it, at one with the dead—seldom recognized and, because of the circum-Atlantic traffic in human cargo or because of removal, often unnamed?
—Sharon P. Holland, *Raising the Dead*

In the video for the song "Formation" (2016), we hear a voiceover of a woman saying, "Look at all that water, boy!" as Beyoncé, who is laid out on the top of a police car, sinks into floodwaters.[1] That is the voice of Kimberly Roberts, whose footage of Hurricane Katrina was featured heavily in the documentary *Trouble the Water* (2008).[2] "Formation" becomes much more legible when we understand that it directly cites Katrina as a significant revelation of the fact that "blacks are not safe in an anti-black world."[3] Not only is it a commentary on the ways in which Black people of the bayou were abandoned by the government—on the national, state, and municipal levels—but it also responds to the anti-Blackness that characterized the coverage of the post-Katrina situation. Emphasis on "looting," crime, and questions about why people didn't evacuate (in other words, this was all their own fault) coalesced to produce a national conversation about Katrina that wasn't about the systemic unwillingness to respond humanely to this ecological crisis but predictably focused on a narrative of Black criminality. Writing about Hurricane Katrina in the context of this criminalizing narrative, Lisa Marie Cacho notes, "News media and conservative weblogs stigmatized and criminalized poor African American victims of Hurricane Katrina."[4] Human vulnerability, which should have been the focus of concern, was buried beneath the mythologized specter of Black criminality. Cacho goes on to demonstrate that looting, when done by whites, was covered as a survival strategy. The same attempts to procure resources in an emergency situation by Black people, however, were seen as crimes.[5] Hurricane Katrina, then, is a significant site where issues of anti-Blackness, precarity, and nature collide.

This chapter discusses two texts—Jesmyn Ward's *Salvage the Bones* (2011) and Benh Zeitlin's *Beasts of the Southern Wild* (2012)—that feature narratives concerned with hurricanes, Black precarity, and nature. Before turning to my analysis of these two texts, which produce radically different meanings about Black life and nature via Katrina, I want to deconstruct and look at moments where Black precarity and water meet in our culture. There is a cartography of Black suffering traceable by water: The Middle Passage, the Okeechobee Hurricane of 1928,[6] Hurricane Katrina, and Flint, Michigan. Water iterates death, especially for Black people since—as Sharon P. Holland notes above—some subjects "never achieve the status of the living."[7] That failure to achieve life is intimately tied to Blackness, and in this chapter, I want to think about how water is a kind of grave marker that exposes not only *where* the bodies are buried but also the means by which they got there. In other words, water is at once a "place" and a method, the sign of an impending end and the end itself.

To be clear, I don't mean to slander water in an absolute way. The ocean, without the Middle Passage, is something else entirely: enjoyable, beautiful, divine. A hurricane, without strategically faulty levees and structural poverty that make evacuation and rebuilding impossible, is a bad but survivable storm. In the aftermath of Katrina, the most helpless among us were abandoned to fate on rooftops, in New Orleans, at the Superdome and in the convention center. The sight of these vulnerable people threatened to break Denise Moore, who was at the convention center in New Orleans after Hurricane Katrina. Her comment about being unable to cry, for fear that doing so would kill her, reminds me of something a friend once said to me at Spelman. She said, "Black people could cry for the rest of our lives and still not be done crying."[8] Maybe, as Moore says, if we start crying, it will break us in half and kill us. I write this chapter floating in a bottomless pit of sorrow, deep and dark as the ocean itself. Katrina taught us that there is no such thing, in the eyes of the broader culture, as Black vulnerability. Even children and old folk are not considered vulnerable. Hence, it is not incidental that at the end of Beyoncé's "Formation," there is a Black boy dancing in front of a line of police officers. Behind him the words "Stop Killing Us" are spray-painted on a wall. In this way the video simultaneously references death by hurricane and death by police. By having a young, small boy dance in this scene, the video highlights that Black children are never allowed to be children, that they must always be ready to take on not only the weather but also the state. Water, Black childhood, and death coalesce in our society in a historically vicious framework produced by the political world.

In a photo often titled "The Hug Heard 'Round the World," a weeping Davonte Hart embraces a police officer.[9] The photo was taken at a Black Lives Matter protest in 2014 on behalf of Mike Brown, who had been killed in Ferguson, Missouri, by a police officer. Like Mike Brown, Davonte is also now dead, having been killed by his adoptive white mothers, Sarah and Jennifer Hart. Sarah Hart drove herself, her spouse, and their six adopted children (all Black) off a cliff and into the Pacific Ocean on March 26, 2019. There were many reports of abuse by the Harts against the children, a fact made public after the children had been murdered. Now, knowing that these children were starved and beaten by their adoptive parents, looking at Davonte's face I see not only sadness about Mike Brown's tragic death but a cry for help from an abused child. It was a cry that would go unanswered. Articles written after the deaths of these children point to the ways the state colluded to keep them in the care of the two women who would ultimately murder them, even though there were Black relatives trying to take custody of the kids.[10] Without even a direct admission of such, we discern the implication of the state's decision: that being with white caregivers is always better for Black kids than being with Black relatives. Stereotypes about unfit Black parenting are common in this culture, and these clearly structured the circumstance that kept six Black children in an abusive home. But in the context of Black life in an anti-Black society, what *are* Black children to white people? Do Black children achieve the status of aliveness for their white caregivers, or do they simply offer the same appeal of pets but, in failing to be animals (because they are not), remain subject to a literalization of their social death?

Naturalizing Black Suffering in *Beasts of the Southern Wild*

These questions frame my approach to Benh Zeitlin's film *Beasts of the Southern Wild*.[11] If Western civil society defines the Black person as always already "at one with the dead," to use Holland's phrase, then what implications does that have for Black children—both real and fictive children—who find themselves in the hands of white parents/auteurs? *Beasts of the Southern Wild* is concerned with freedom, the environment, and mythology, conveying these themes through the figure of a six-year-old Black girlchild. *Salvage the Bones* (2011), which is the subject of the second half of this chapter, is informed by a similar set of questions where wildness, in a Black context, marks the imagining of alternate modalities of existence. These texts are often read together, since both examine issues of Black precarity and the environment in the context of Hurricane Katrina. Both texts are about Hurricane Katrina, though in Zeitlin's film the hurricane remains unnamed. I discuss them here together because of the similarities in their narrative elements and because both texts speak to the cultural context of race vis-à-vis Hurricane Katrina, but in vastly different ways.

Hurricane Katrina was one of the most significant natural events to occur in the United States after 1950. An estimated 1,800 people died in Hurricane Katrina, most of them Black. Like the current water crisis in Flint, Michigan, which began in 2014 (and continues without solution as of this writing), Katrina put on display all the horrific ways that Black lives do not matter.[12] Black Lives may not matter, but *live Black matter*—stripped of all specificity and humanity, as the word "matter" implies—is ratings gold. Images of dead Black people, abandoned by rescuers, inundated the news, activating what Saidiya Hartman calls "the spectacular character of black suffering."[13] Politicians performed concern, but the president did nothing, prompting Kanye West to remark—angrily, extemporaneously, and correctly—that George W. Bush didn't care about Black people. Interrogating the query implicit in the phrase "Black Lives Matter," Calvin Warren argues, "This question re-emerges within a world of anti-black brutality, a world in which black torture, dismemberment, fatality, and fracturing are routinized and ritualized—a *global*, sadistic pleasure principle."[14] It is hard to imagine a world in which Black lives *could* matter, when the quotidian masochism that characterizes Black existence is so broadly expected and embraced that Black precarity and suffering is rendered invisible or, worse, something to be celebrated. The display of Black suffering is central to my analysis of Zeitlin's film because it raises a set of questions articulated in relation to pain and race by Hartman: "Are we witnesses who confirm the truth of what happened in the face of the world-destroying capacities of pain, the distortions of torture, the sheer unrepresentability of terror, and the repression of dominant accounts? Or are we voyeurs fascinated with and repelled by exhibitions of terror and sufferance? What does the exposure of the violated body yield?"[15] As I show in my summary below, there is no doubt that the protagonist of *Beasts of the Southern Wild* suffers in ways none of us would ever subject our children to. The questions that the display of that suffering provokes are about the consequences of occluding Black precarity in the service of a broader, Western environmental narrative, where both nature and Black people are sacrificed to an intention that does not fully know itself.

Beasts of the Southern Wild tells the story of a six-year-old girl named Hushpuppy who lives in a mythic bayou community called "the Bathtub." Her mother is absent, and her sick, alcoholic father (named Wink) is often absent for days at a time. Hushpuppy is left to fend for herself, living in an isolated wild place that is cluttered with trash. Hushpuppy becomes obsessed with a story her teacher tells her about prehistoric aurochs, creatures who are frozen in polar ice caps. But due to climate change, the teacher tells her, these beasts will be released and eat humans and anything else in their way. The hurricane hits and Hushpuppy and her father do not evacuate; they survive but Wink soon dies. Hushpuppy is briefly taken into state custody but escapes, and the film ends with her coming face-to-face with a huge aurochs, whom she miraculously tames. Critical reception to *Beasts* was overwhelmingly positive: it was heralded as "beautiful, funny, timely, and tender,"[16] while the *New York Times* also glowingly proclaimed, "the movie is a blast of sheer, improbable joy."[17] Academic response was less glowing, with bell hooks, Christina Sharpe, and Jayna Brown all bringing attention to the traumatizing vulnerability of Hushpuppy, a Black child alone in the world, in her underwear. Brown points out, "With its dystopian landscape, the film evokes the precarity, instability, and vulnerability of black life" and goes on to argue that the film "aestheticizes filth."[18] Sharpe levies similar criticism when she writes, "Hushpuppy and Wink are in and at one with the dirt. When such stark images appear in televised 'Save the Children' ads they might move some viewers to want to help Sally Struthers feed and care for little black children, but in the US, domestic blackness rarely results in something like empathy."[19] bell hooks raises many of the same issues that Brown and Sharpe do, with particular emphasis on what she sees as the sexualizing of Hushpuppy.[20] Other critics who viewed the film saw it in entirely different ways. Patricia Yaeger, whose analysis I'll discuss further below, "adored" it.[21] Nicholas Mirzoeff argues that the film is a "dramatic achievement."[22]

I think it is tempting to be seduced by the surface, ostensible claims of the film as an allegory about the substantive shortcomings of society, where consumerism has replaced community. At a moment when anyone abreast of the science of climate change cannot help but feel desperate and despairing, the seemingly simple nonconsumerist lifestyle depicted in the film offers an almost irresistible appeal. The major accomplishments claimed by Western civilization—mostly related to the ways technology has transformed our lives—have come with a devastating ecological price. *Beasts of the Southern Wild* seems to suggest that you can be whole without all the fancy stuff capitalism tells you is necessary for fulfillment. There is an unarticulated working-class ethos in *Beasts of the Southern Wild* that makes it more likely to be appealing to anyone who grew up working-class or poor (and/or perhaps anyone frustrated by the rat race). Anyone who has ever lived in a rural, working class (and/or impoverished) area knows that though mainstream society may see the folkways of people who live in such places only through a lens of depravity, that is not how the people see themselves. In a world where "bigger is better" and slogans like "whoever dies with the most toys wins," it's hard to imagine that anyone would *choose* to own less or *willfully* embrace a lifestyle that eschews the culture of the perpetual "upgrade." This is the revolutionary kernel of *Beasts of the Southern Wild*; this, I think, is what many people connect to when they see the film.

I can certainly relate to a feeling of frustration with the emphasis in American society on ownership and acquisition. When I moved out to the country, to a working-class neighborhood, almost a decade ago, I was struck by how much some middle- and upper-class folks perceived me to have hit bottom. Our house—a perfect size for two parents and two kids—was seen as pitiful. An out-of-town visitor once said to me, as if in sympathy, "I grew up around houses like these." I wasn't sure what he meant at the time, and it took me a while to understand that the location, and the absence of new-fangled amenities and decor, read as "lack" to those who managed their material lives differently than my partner and I manage ours. A film like *Beasts* speaks to the cultural silence around this kind of classism and invites us to consider that fulfillment might be found in places other than the quality (or presence) of one's kitchen backsplash. There is a rich and vibrant culture in rural areas—both white and Black—that is unavailable to the gaze of Hollywood and the media, where sociocultural indexes of wealth are the only countable measure of progress or happiness. What does it mean to reject the notion that aspiring to the attainment of middle- and upper-class accoutrements and status is the ultimate pursuit of happiness? Furthermore, how does our culture of constant material "improvement" in every area, from cell phones to our houses—involving ever-larger domiciles that are far bigger than our actual needs—destroy the environment via an endless cycle of materialist consumerism?[23] While shopping may seem like a neutral activity, consumerist culture is a leading cause of climate change. Commenting about the impact consumerism has on the environment, Gary Gardner, director of Worldwatch, notes, "Most of the environmental issues we see today can be linked to consumption."[24] So any rejection of our consumerist culture, in the face of climate crisis, seems a radical thesis. And because *Beasts* argues against the pervasive notion that the expense and fanciness of one's "owned things" is a measure of the value of one's life, I initially found it a useful critique of our relentlessly classist society.

But in the film's attempt to critique consumerism and the norms of society, what violence does it do to our most vulnerable subjects? Hushpuppy, and everyone else in the Bathtub, is framed as free and living in a mythic world of safety (Hushpuppy is never menaced or threatened). And while I do still think there are aspects of Zeitlin's film that resonate with a rebellious rejection of polite society that can be traced all the way back to Huck Finn, I am ultimately convinced by the aforementioned critiques about the ways in which Black precarity, through the figure of Hushpuppy, is romanticized. The filmmaker, and the author of the original script, did not cast Quvenzhane Wallis because she was Black, as pointed out by Tavia Nyong'o in his essay on the film. In fact, they claim to have done "blind casting" for the role, so Hushpuppy's Blackness is incidental to the way they wrote the script. Their intention does not in any way undercut the narrative effect of combining a white script with a Black actor and in fact manages to be revelatory about the ways in which the othering of the environment is inextricably linked to discourses of anti-Blackness. The film was adapted from a play by Lucy Alibar, who based the relationship between Hushpuppy and Wink on her own relationship with her father. The play, *Juicy and Delicious* (2013), initially featured a white boy as the protagonist. But when Alibar and her friend Benh Zeitlin decided to make the play into a movie, Hushpuppy became a girl and—though both Alibar and Zeitlin are white—Black. Alibar confesses that she wrote the play as a way to confront her father's death, that writing it and having it performed allowed her to move on: "After many nights of seeing Hushpuppy survive the end of the world, I started to feel like I'd be alright."[25] In talking about casting for the film, Alibar doesn't even mention Wallis's race: "After an exhaustive search, we found the transcendent Quvenzhane Wallis at a school audition just miles up the road from our production office."[26] Tellingly, Alibar finds it more remarkable that Wallis was "only a few miles up the road" than that they decided to cast a Black child to play her autobiographical role. Though we are encouraged to see such a move as racially progressive—since it is supposed to imply a kind of "postracial" logic—it quite *literally* makes Blackness not matter, since it disregards the ways in which Wallis's embodied Blackness changes and inflects the meaning of the narrative, bringing another historical reality to the enactment of Alibar's drama. If race doesn't matter, here, and Blackness always equals race, then Blackness does not, by default, matter. So, what happens when a Black child is put into white hands, narratively and otherwise?

Race has often been theorized as a projection; what the white person thinks about the other represents a shadow of that which he fears in himself. Ralph Ellison went so far as to show that "racial projection" is so powerful and thorough that white people cannot even "see" Black people; we are literally invisible.

Via Michael Omi and Howard Winant, we can argue that mainstream representations of Black people speak not to Black existence, but instead reference white epistemologies of the other.[27] Given this framework, what can we make of Hushpuppy as a white projection? Alibar is open about the fact that she struggled to write herself into her own story. There was so much pain in the story, in other words, that she could not bear to even see a person resembling herself endure it. So first she projected that experience onto a male character. Ultimately, she decided it would be okay to project it onto a Black child, counting it a victory that that child was represented as a girl. The character also went from being a teenager to a young child. So, a six-year-old Black girlchild was a fitting entity to bear the burden of her pain, a pain that she herself could not/cannot bear. Is there anything new, or "tender," to recall the language of the *New York Times* review, about Black children bearing white people's pain? Isn't racism itself just a singularly unbearable painful feeling that originates in the white mind? Blackness, through Wallis's performance, is made to bear the weight of Alibar's pain about class, about neglect, and about her father. It insults the *mattering* of Black life by suggesting that her story is the universal story, and that the Black story—which differs from the white one, as we will see in *Salvage the Bones*—has no relationship to her story without embellishment. In other words, there *is* race in Alibar's story; she simply refuses to confront it, for that, too, it seems, might be unbearable narrative weight. The ways in which hooks, Sharpe, and Brown respond to a dirty, neglected, and fearfully vulnerable Hushpuppy are precisely the reactions Alibar's deferral of identification hopes to deflect. As the white subject, admitting her own vulnerability and precarity as a child of a neglectful father is too much for her. Alibar refuses to be the vulnerable subject and in so doing, buries Black girlhood under the weight of a disowned white pathology.

Much of this goes unnoticed in mainstream reactions to the film, though, because it appears to critique environmental destruction and respectability politics. Writing about the film in her essay "Dirty Ecology," Patricia Yaeger argues that Hushpuppy "forces us to ask: What myths do we need to live in an era of global warming where every coastal community may soon look like The Bathtub?"[28] In this formulation, Hushpuppy is reduced to a device; this movie isn't about her—it's about climate change. Both the film and Yaeger's analysis reiterate Black vulnerability through the implication that Black suffering is a *requirement* for the mythological negotiation of the climate crisis. The recourse to myth suggests an almost willful and celebratory pessimism about climate change. Rather than respond to impending coastal doom with policies designed to both diminish the causes of climate change and respond well to the already inevitable consequences of it, Yaeger calls for mythology.

The Red Cross isn't coming, FEMA isn't coming, and nothing will be done to keep this from happening again—so all you Black children and elderly folk better pray, because mythology is all that is on offer for the Black person in Western society. It was not myth that caused the levees in New Orleans to break, and myth also won't stop them from breaking again. *Beasts of the Southern Wild* seems to accept this reality, offering us—as Yaeger correctly notes—a mythology, not a solution, and Western mythologies typically involve body counts.

Mythology is how a film that is about devastating climate change, and an orphaned Black child, can make us feel so good. One reason it is easy to feel good at the end of *Beasts* is because Hushpuppy's life, before the hurricane hits, is remarkably similar to the actual lives of people *after* Hurricane Katrina. Her father is only sporadically present to begin with, and it is impossible not to think of all the children who were separated from their parents and families in the aftermath of Katrina when watching the film. Additionally, the property where Wink and Hushpuppy live already looks as if it was hit by a hurricane, given the amount of debris and other detritus that clutters their living space. This similarity of her life situation, pre- and post-hurricane, suggests that despite the ostensible critique of bourgeois and consumerist values, Hushpuppy's life was always already a "disaster." Now I'd like to pause here to complicate the reading of Hushpuppy's life in these opening scenes, reading both with and against the grain of these early images. It is not my contention that because Hushpuppy is "dirty" or that because her dwelling isn't a standard home that her life is a disaster. In *Purity and Danger* (1966), Mary Douglas deconstructs the idea of "dirt" as an actual site of contagion or disease. Dirt, as part of nature, is necessary for all life (food grows in it), and disavowal of it in this society is tied to pathologies of both nature and race because dirt "offends against nature," and removal of it is understood as an attempt to "organize the environment."[29] Douglas goes on to theorize that the presence of dirt always symbolically portends disaster, and this is certainly the case with Hushpuppy. The presence of dirt in her environment and on her person symbolically marks her as worthy of disaster, hence making the consequences of climate change a natural complement to the freedom that dirt is supposed to stand in for in *Beasts*. Discourses of dirt are different in what Douglas painfully refers to as "primitive" cultures, but ultimately Douglas is making a recuperative argument for both dirt and the cultures that are not governed by dualistic notions of order/disorder, dirt/cleanliness, defilement/holiness. But in this context, the meaning of dirt in another cultural space doesn't matter because the (Western) culture that produces *Beasts of the Southern Wild* is one in which dirt always means defilement. Cleanliness is always relational, and so to make Hushpuppy dirty as a liberating practice ignores the fact that we can see her as such only relative to an implied and extradiegetic "clean" whiteness.

Embracing the precarity and vulnerability of Hushpuppy and Wink's lifestyle does not offer us a forward-looking ecological model that would protect the world; rather, their lifestyle represents a "backward" movement to a primitivism that is all too often associated with the Black other. As I demonstrated in the introduction, Western conceptions of Blackness traditionally evince notions of primitivism, dirt, and social failure. All of these characterize the lives of the people in *Beasts*, but we are supposed to see this dirtiness as an antidote to the poison of environmental degradation. In its antinature bias, Western society often associates nature with origin (and hence the past); so, whenever a recuperative move is made for nature from *within* the Cartesian dualism of Western society, it iterates nature and Blackness as "primitive" and dirty, aligned with the past. The apparatus in *Beasts* situates Hushpuppy in relation to dirt and alludes as closely as it possibly can to the idea of her as naked, by showing her frequently walking around in underpants and a T-shirt. In other words, *Beasts* wants us to think of Hushpuppy and, by extension, her father as naked primitives who are "at one" with nature, living outside of the norms of conventional society. This is a grossly racist representation of those cultures considered "primitive," because it reproduces the Western view that peoples who do not live under a technologically driven, hierarchical society are just wild and dirty, devoid of culture, intent, and intelligence. Hence, the film's recourse to primitivism is akin to the Western belief that those in non-European-style societies are unevolved. Yet we are supposed to see this as a liberal vision because it doesn't criticize primitivism, but rather seems to embrace it. In doing so, however, it cedes the ground that Black people are indeed "naturally" primitive and dirty. This move represents a profound failure of imagination, because it posits an environmentally friendly Black primitivism on one side and an ecologically irresponsible white civilization on the other. On the surface this may seem to be a pro-ecology representation, but ultimately it not only symbolically requires climate change in order to achieve mythological status but unwittingly accepts climate change itself.

One assumption that underwrites the primitivism on display in *Beasts* is that people living outside the auspices of Western society do not intentionally engage the environment. This is, of course, not true; but Wink's property is more like a junkyard than a home, and this lack of environmental shaping is the consequence of poverty—not of an ecological ethos. The collapsing of poverty with a pro-ecology politics in *Beasts* reveals a deep bias about what it means to be "pro-nature" in Western society. In other words, *Beasts* suggests that for nature to thrive, humans must live materially poor, dirty lives. In *Beasts* the elision of nature and poverty suggests that nature is a site of "lack," where survival is difficult and even unlikely. For example, when Hushpuppy finds herself alone for days, and without the meat her father is seen providing in the opening scenes, she's reduced to eating cat food out of a can. Hushpuppy, despite being a child raised almost entirely out of doors, has no knowledge of foraging or where to find wild-growing food. Compared to accounts of people who have grown up in rural and wild settings, Hushpuppy knows little about her natural environment. I can think of multiple textual and real-life examples, both historic and contemporary ones, of people knowing as children how to find food in the forest (or yard) where they lived.[30] Likewise, spending summers at my great-aunt's house, the garden was bursting with vegetables, and there was a huge pomegranate tree from which we regularly collected fruit and gorged ourselves. My partner, having grown up on seven acres in the country, often spent afternoons in the fragrant branches of a pear tree, eating his fill. It is unimaginable that as country folk without a store nearby, Wink would not have cultivated an edible garden (even a small one) and that Hushpuppy wouldn't know what to eat from such a garden. Or, if Wink didn't cultivate a garden, that no one in his neighborhood would have. Contrast Hushpuppy's food precarity, for example, to Zora Neale Hurston's description of her family's property in her autobiography *Dust Tracks on the Road* (1942): "We lived on a big piece of ground, with two Chinaberry trees shading the front gate.... There were plenty of orange, grapefruit, tangerine, guavas and other fruits in our yard. We had a five-acre garden with things to eat growing in it, and so we were never hungry. We had chicken on the table often; home-cured meat and all the eggs we wanted."[31] Hurston's description of the abundance of food, as well as of her knowing how to procure it even as a child, undermines the believability of Hushpuppy's food precarity. We know that Hushpuppy and her father raise chickens, so it is curious that she wouldn't know how to forage their eggs and cook them before she'd resort to eating pet food—after all, she does cook the cat food. The fact that Hushpuppy eats the same food as her pets (whether that is human food or cat food) animalizes her, suggesting that she too is a "beast." This cat food scene demonstrates the ways in which anti-Blackness and antinature discourses are linked and co-constitute one another. Rather than present wild and natural space as abundant and life-giving, *Beasts* presents it as one where the only food available is that which you can kill, and where in the absence of meat, nature provides nothing.

    The fact that food is not abundant, in the warm and temperate climate of the bayou, and that we never see Wink or Hushpuppy cultivating, foraging, or eating plants or fruits or eggs, speaks to a radical disconnect from nature. In fact, when Wink sees Hushpuppy eat a leaf, it's a sign that something is wrong.

He decides to teach her how to catch fish, though eventually the rancid water of the hurricane kills all the fish. In this way Hushpuppy's ability to eat is tied to the consumption (exclusively) of animal flesh. The idea of animals eating the flesh of other animals as a function of nature is at the heart of *Beasts* and seems an obvious truth about existence at first glance. The film seems to suggest that in nature it is a dog-eat-dog world, and that human precarity (as meat) is also a function of a natural unfolding, and so the film asserts that nature is a space of lack, where all animals must compete for existence and eat each other. The film projects onto nature a Darwinian social hierarchy by suggesting that you will be eaten relative to the size and brutality of the creatures you encounter, where will to power determines who eats and who doesn't. I'm not suggesting that in wild places it is impossible to be eaten, but symbolically *Beasts* aligns natural space with death rather than with life. My contention is not that life is the sole provenance of nature, but rather that *Beasts* suggests a one-sided losing proposition in relation to nature, rather than constructing it as both a life-giver and a death-bringer. And, as viewers, we are encouraged to feel okay about this because the "risks" of the natural are borne by vulnerable people, or "throwaway people," to use Yaeger's term. *Beasts* constructs nature as primarily carnivorous and in doing so implies that, for humans to survive, it must be tamed.

Hushpuppy's bildungsroman story begins with her posing a philosophical question in a voice-over about the nature of animal existence. Listening to the heartbeat of a chick, she ponders what the animal might be thinking. "Probably thinking I'm hungry or I need to poop," she speculates. This means, of course, that she already feels her separateness from the animals, even as she concerns herself with understanding their "codes." This is an important scene for understanding the moment at the end when she makes the aurochs kneel before her. The suggestion is that by learning the "secret code" of animals, she is able to tame the carnivorous beast. And if nature is itself carnivorous, then by taming it Hushpuppy enters the Western symbolic, whose goal vis-à-vis nature—going all the way back to Francis Bacon's theorization of the human fall from the Garden of Eden[32]—is to make nature less itself and more of what we want it to be. In other words, the film returns us to the same dualism that produced the Anthropocene and the ecological nightmare it seeks to address.

As Jayna Brown points out, Hushpuppy and Wink's lifestyle is not "sustainable." I think Brown's use of the word "sustainable" here is strategic and speaks to how what we see in Wink's lifestyle is not an ecological model for how we can transform our actions vis-à-vis the environment from harm to neutrality or helpfulness. Such a transformation will not occur mindlessly or by happenstance; it requires intention that must be mandated at the level of structure, not on the individual level. Upcycling and recycling may be actions that make us feel less powerless in relation to environmental destruction, but none of that will have any impact if we don't change the way global capital extracts and moves resources across the planet.[33] Brown's terminology here also makes explicit that in Wink and Hushpuppy's lifestyle there is no future; and this lack of futurity, I argue, is also why some viewers can see *Beasts* as a transcendent film. Hushpuppy, utterly parentless by the film's end, is left in a water world, orphaned at the age of six. This doesn't "read" as a horrible tragedy precisely because of the ways that anti-Blackness always inheres to vulnerability. Writing about water in another context, Ruth Meyer notes:

> All of these revisions, as different as they are, concentrate on the fantasy spaces in-between and nowhere at all, spaces that present themselves as mixed up, ambivalent, floating. The most obvious of these in-between spaces is, of course, the sea, this paradigmatic space of openness and indeterminacy which gains so radically contradictory connotations once it becomes the setting for abduction, violation, enslavement, and revolt. Placed into the context of the Middle Passage, the ocean becomes the "oceanic," as Hortense Spillers has argued, '... removed from the indigenous land and culture and not-yet American either, these captive persons, without names that their captors would recognize were in movement across the Atlantic, but they were also *nowhere* at all.'[34]

This captive status still attaches to Blackness, such that Hushpuppy's orphaned homelessness at the end of *Beasts* represents no movement at all—neither away from nor toward utopia or dystopia. As such, she's a static character—as are all Black people in the Western imagination—existing in a timeless nowhere, not actually human in the first place. Therefore, on the level of myth, the film suggests that we do not have to be worried about Hushpuppy at the end. She has tamed the aurochs, and that is all we need to know. On the level of plot, it seems clear—given that she's already once been taken into protective custody—that she likely will end up in the hands of the state, perhaps in a foster home—just like Davonte.

The Divine Unknowable in *Salvage the Bones*

> [Fred] Moten and [Steve] Harney want to gesture to another place, a wild place that is not simply the left-over space that limns real and regulated zones of polite society; rather, it is a wild place that continuously produces its own unregulated wildness.
> —Jack Halberstam

> Let our thinking lead us into the "valley of the shadow of death," and once there we can begin to imagine existence anew.
> —Calvin L. Warren

Like *Beasts*, Jesmyn Ward's *Salvage the Bones* takes up issues of race, poverty, animals, and Hurricane Katrina. Unlike *Beasts*, Ward's novel does not move toward myth, but rather "limns" the boundaries of the already magical world that its protagonist, Esch, occupies. In this section of the chapter, I want to first talk about the way that the figure of "the beast" is used in *Salvage* and then move on to a discussion of how nature and Esch's consciousness represent a mutually constitutive co-ontology that—following Fred Moten's theorization—is prior to ontology itself.[35] *Salvage* takes on the metaphor of Mother Nature both figuratively and literally through an examination of motherhood—through China and Esch—and through the force of the hurricane. In doing so Ward's novel resists both mythology and stereotype (for stereotype is a kind of mythology), insisting instead upon the actuality of the natural world, which is simultaneously miraculous and crushing. But in her insistence upon the actual over the mythological, Ward's novel reveals what Alex Weheliye calls "alternative modalities of freedom . . . [that] conjur[e] anterior futures, [and] lay claim to and make demands in the here-and-NOW."[36] *Salvage* mines the richness of a present-moment awareness that at once produces an experience of relief from what Moten calls "political death," and also suggests an "elsewhere" of existence that is remarkably divergent from the affecto-political reality of Western life. In other words, Ward's novel reveals a space of being where the notions that govern the understanding of what it means to live a Black life, from within the logic of whiteness, do not apply. It might be helpful to think of this as an entirely alternate world, where at first glance things seem to be "the same" as in the Western realm of understanding. But, upon closer examination, it becomes clear that one is in an entirely different place altogether. In my reading, this is the relationship between *Beasts* and *Salvage*; in the former, Blackness, animals, and nature all operate semiotically in recognizable and problematic ways, but in *Salvage* these signifiers at once avow and disavow their historical weight in order to divulge another realm of Black existence.

I'm not the first scholar to pair Zeitlin's film and Ward's novel. Christopher Lloyd reads the two texts in relation to their representation of "creaturely" life.[37] Animals—real and imagined—are central to the narrative of both *Beasts* and *Salvage*. To proceed, we might ask ourselves what relationship beasts (monsters) have to Black death. Perhaps there is an answer here: the last Google search that Sarah Hart performed, before driving herself and six Black children off a cliff to their watery deaths, showed that she looked up no-kill shelters for dogs.[38] Recently, there has been increasing popular attention on Black Twitter and in other closed groups on the internet about the ways in which white people value the lives of dogs over those of Black people. The fact that Sarah Hart cared about her dogs' lives but not the lives of her foster children sums up the observation that sometimes white people care more about their dogs than Black people. A person once jokingly (and frighteningly) said to me that the best way to smear a Black person would be to allege animal cruelty or mistreatment of some kind, and that this alone would instigate latent racism, which waits quietly for an excuse to crucify the Black person on the cross of a seemingly legitimate crime. On one level, love of animals evokes an Edenic fantasy where humans and animals live in harmony with each other, thus—as I discussed in the introduction—activating a long-held utopic desire present within Western epistemology to repair the damage of the fall from grace. On another level, white empathy and concern for animals, I argue, is tied to the ways that domesticated animals can live in harmonious submission to their owners. So important are pets (especially dogs) to some white people that Wink's instruction to Hushpuppy to share her food with the dog is commented on as one of Wink's winning qualities by Yaeger: "Hushpuppy's father reminds her, 'Share with the dog,' as if our main task in the Anthropocene . . . is to know ourselves as a species dependent on other species."[39] Given that Wink doesn't even show up to feed his own child sometimes, it's notable that he would be praised at all. What underlying logic must be in place to suppress the recognition of Wink's neglect of his human child in favor of emphasizing his concern for the dogs? The posthumanist notion of species interdependency skips right over the ways in which the category of the human depends upon the construction and maintenance of the Black nonhuman. Let me emphasize that I'm not at all suggesting that domesticated animals are unworthy of love; but what a text like *Beasts* reveals is how civil society can account for animals in a way that Blackness disallows because it is "unmappable in the cosmological grid of the transcendental subject."[40] Animals are appealing objects for consideration precisely because they are understood to be "mappable" in a Western cosmological sense, and that seeming access to the domesticated beast aligns animal concern and consideration with a certain fascist obsession with order and control.

We can see how attention to animal/pet life operates in contradistinction to the valuation of Black life in the Harambe incident at the Cincinnati Zoo in May 2016.[41] A Black child somehow got into Harambe's enclosure. The Cincinnati Zoo made the obviously correct call to rescue the child, which necessitated killing Harambe. Debate, in the media and in online forums, proliferated about what the zoo should have done. The people who were outraged—mostly white people—argued that Harambe probably wouldn't have hurt the little boy. An

Picture of Harambe graffiti, Goshen, Ohio. Photo by Stefanie K. Dunning.

article in the *Daily Mail* claimed that because Harambe didn't "beat his chest," his actions suggest he was protecting the child and wouldn't have harmed him.[42] Locally, white teens at the high school in the rural area where I live created T-shirts that said things like "Team Harambe" and even wrote about the gorilla in their graffiti. The "bad" Black mother who "let" her child get into the enclosure and the child himself were painted as being at fault for the death of the gorilla. Contrast the public reaction to this with the way Florida officials handled the death of a young white toddler who was eaten by an alligator at a Disney resort. Florida officials, despite knowing that the child was dead, killed dozens of alligators looking for the child's remains. The onus for this horrible tragedy was put on alligators and on the Disney resort that allows people to congregate in places where there are alligators (though there were signs posted), not on the child and not on his family. The toddler who died was even honored with a statue.[43] That Black existence emerges below that of animals in a Western hierarchy discloses the fascistic undertones of this archive of concern. This insight, about the hierarchy of Black and animal life, bears keeping in mind for my discussions in the next chapter as well.

Joseph Goebbels once famously said, "The only real friend one has in the end . . . is the dog."[44] Likewise, as Tavia Nyong'o shows, the sovereign and the beast occupy similar registers "above and below the law."[45] If white people are "above the law," and animals "below the law," then white power and animals are connected via discourses of lawlessness that enable a mutual occupation of sites of "freedom." Since Black people are always already antonymic to Western notions of freedom, they are hence symbolically powerless in relation both to white people and to domesticated beasts. Her relationship to animals is also what makes Hushpuppy so "winning" for white audiences, because a relationship to animals stands in for the relational matrix of interaction that defines agency, sovereignty, and the very category of "human" itself. Hence, Hushpuppy's taming of the prehistoric aurochs, tied as it is to eugenicist discourse as revealed by N'yongo's reading of *Beasts*, represents an iteration of this process of sovereignty, while her Blackness and the maintenance of this "speciesism" makes her available for slaughter in an economy where "everyone is meat." The aurochs in *Beasts* is framed as frightening and insensible, destined to devour everything in its path. In Jesmyn Ward's *Salvage the Bones*, the pit bull is the "beast" that, in our society, carries the weight of racial terror. Set in the few days before the onslaught of Hurricane Katrina, *Salvage the Bones* is the story of the Batiste family who live in a town called Bois Sauvage in Mississippi. The family consists of one girl, Esch, who is our narrator and protagonist, her father, and her three brothers. Her brother Skeetah owns and is breeding a pit bull named China. Esch, who is fourteen, also discovers that she is pregnant, and she attempts to grapple with what this means for her body and her life. The family does not evacuate, but they survive the storm.

The depiction of a fighting pit bull in the novel is key to Ward's examination of Black life before and after Katrina. Pit bulls may be the only dogs that mainstream society deems "killable," and they symbolically stand in for Black masculinity. Writing about the associative connection between Black men and pit bulls, Lloyd writes, "Often seen as dangerous, pit bulls and African Americans (men especially) become clearly connected; Erin Tarver suggests that this is a 'metonymic feedback loop.'"[46] Later, Lloyd notes that Michael B. Jordan, now most famous for his role as Killmonger in *Black Panther*, argued that "'Black males' are "America's pit bulls."[47] And while Black people can be seen as (dangerous) dogs, they aren't perceived as capable of properly taking care of them. Lloyd argues that one way we must contextualize the representation of animal life, through the figure of China, a pit bull, in *Salvage the Bones* is through the jailing of the NFL star Michael Vick, who was convicted of animal cruelty for dog-fighting. Ward's novel tackles difficult issues of race through a representation of dog-fighting and a pregnant, promiscuous teenager. In doing so, she activates a complicated interstice of valuation around the human and the nonhuman, revealing the ways in which the relationship between Black rural life and nature is characterized by interbeing and pervasive connectedness. For Esch, the novel's protagonist, nature is not something that exists solely for enjoyment, but rather it shapes the ways she sees and analyzes the world, functioning as the very logic that informs her consciousness. Ward alchemizes Katrina, nature, and Blackness in a way that does not reproduce Black vulnerability as the locus of consideration, or nature as a site of lack, but rather directs our gaze to an elsewhere, where Black existence is reimagined.

China presents for Esch a way to contemplate motherhood, since for most of the novel China is nursing a litter of puppies. The inclusion of China as central to the narrative also asks us to confront what is at stake in our thinking about and understanding of pit bulls, race, and the owner/pet relationship. I argue here that Ward's novel exposes the ways in which the broader society constructs relationships to animals through a model of desired relationality between master and subordinate. Consideration for animal welfare in our society is uneven at best. There is little conflict between keeping a pet and killing other animals for food (often painfully and cruelly), and there are some animals that are considered suitable for human needs and some that are considered dangerous. The pit bull, like Black people, threatens to disrupt the master/subordinate relationship desired in owner/pet situations. Pit bulls are the dogs that many people advocate be "put down" in the absence of a health problem, because they are thought of as *intrinsically* prone to attack. In other words, in the rhetoric around pit bulls, we see a return of a kind of essentialist, eugenicist logic. One article refers to pit bulls as "natural born killers."[48] All pit bulls, whether they have been trained to fight and/or attack or not, are seen as essentially hostile and hence more worthy of death than "friendlier" breeds. What this uneven approach to pets allows us to see is that when people lovingly engage their pets, the impetus is not (solely) the well-being of the animal, but that love is conditioned by the degree to which the pet can be counted on to exist within the desired relationality of the master (the human) while at the same time providing the illusion of sovereignty "below the law." Hence, pets remind us of freedom while not actually being free. This emphasis in Western society on pets, I argue, is related to the ways in which pets are the only truly reliable "good others." Humans, even if they aren't allowed into symbolic and philosophical understanding as such, are notoriously bad at being "good others." And, when pets fail to be "good others," we typically kill them.

Skeetah's relationship with China in *Salvage* asks us to consider these complicated questions, since his interactions with her do not reveal cruelty, but rather demonstrate that his care and expectations of China feature the same combination of benevolence and control that mimics the broader culture's relationship to pets. In other words, though Skeetah is "fighting" China, his treatment of her is not at all "cruel." Throughout the novel, as the Batiste family prepares for the hurricane, Skeetah's concern is for China and her puppies—not only as a source of revenue (which is an important factor), but also because he sees her as part of the family. He explains this to Esch by telling her that he and China are "equal."[49] In this way, Skeetah's way of thinking about his relation to China does not, in any way, depart from the posthumanist turn toward the idea of animals as contiguous with humans. In her discussion of this particular animal ethic, Samantha Clark notes that some eco-phenomenologists "suggest than an animal ethics based on 'sameness' or similarity with the human ... makes captives of them by 'ensnaring them in the conventions of civilized society.'"[50] Hence it is not my intention to argue that Skeetah's relationship with China, despite the dog-fighting, is somehow recuperable. Instead, I'd like to suggest that dog-fighting is not a *departure* from Western logic around animals but emblematic of it. Dog-fighting, abstracted from all the other ways in which animals are made to painfully and cruelly serve human needs in our society, reveals the uneven deployment of discourses about animal welfare, demonstrating that the actual situation is that those in power get to decide when and how animals will be treated, what is cruel and what isn't.

So what we can make of the representation of dog-fighting, and Skeetah's constant concern and care for China, is not an argument in favor of dog-fighting, but rather a call to carefully consider what is at stake in the representation of the "the other" at the locus of the racial and the animal. Black people, in their incredulity that Michael Vick was jailed for dog-fighting, felt that Vick was so harshly punished because as a "bad other" in American society, his actions harmed the "good other" that pets, and especially dogs, have come to represent in American society. Furthermore, white intervention in dog-fighting underscores a feeling of white superiority, as dog-fighting is presented as "backwards" and "unevolved." Gayatri Spivak's analysis of the colonial intervention in sati in her essay "Can the Subaltern Speak?" (1985) can model for us how to understand the interplay of animal and human at stake in thinking through dog-fighting in Ward's novel and in the larger culture. In her essay Spivak proposes a sentence (after Freud) to reveal the dynamics at play in the colonial debate around sati: "White men are saving brown women from brown men."[51] If it is true that Black people have never become human and accrue to the status of "thing" or "animal," then we can rewrite Spivak's sentence here as: "White people are saving good animals from bad animals." In doing so the white person can intervene on behalf of the "good animal's" vulnerability and put the "bad thing and/or animal" in its place—in the case of Michael Vick, in jail. The function of this salvific operation is to suppress the quotidian nature of animal cruelty and anti-Blackness and to recuperate whiteness as the site of goodness and purity.

To be clear, I am not arguing in favor of dog-fighting (or against pets). Rather, I hope to show that the logic of "the animal" in the Western imagination is perfectly consistent with dog-fighting, but that when and where intervention occurs relates to whatever mores are in fashion among those in power and does not occur because of a "pure" theory of animal treatment. Consider something like the Kentucky Derby, for instance.[52] Animal advocates have long identified the race, as well as the training it requires, as an instance of animal cruelty. Writing about the derby in *Counterpunch*, Lee Hall argues, "We humans excel at making use of other animals, extracting wealth through that use, exhausting them, disposing of them. This week, the 145th Kentucky Derby will showcase these habits. It's cruelty of the worst sort, garnished with mint and wearing a fancy hat."[53] Animals are drugged, are overworked, and frequently die from being forced to compete in ways that are decidedly unnatural. Yet the Kentucky Derby—though criticized by some—is celebrated to the extent that it is televised, bets are placed, and this form of institutionalized animal cruelty is not only allowed but encouraged and celebrated. And, if one were to do any research into the horses that are often used at tourist sites to pull carriages, one would uncover horrific living and working environments for horses (who shouldn't really be working at all) that often end in their painful deaths. Likewise, the presumably "well-treated" animals in almost all zoos are drugged because life in a cage understandably produces depression, aggression, and suicidal behavior. Hence, the emphasis on dog-fighting in Black communities buries the lede on animal cruelty in the West, where it is pervasive and accepted so long as the white supremacist culture approves the use to which the animals are being put. Likewise, white policing of dog-fighting also allows Black people to be seen as barbarous and savage, which is a conclusion white people reached about Black people long before dog-fighting ever existed in Black communities.[54] Dog-fighting simply becomes the excuse that justifies an already existent latent racism. Skeetah fights China for the same reason people race horses at the Kentucky Derby—for money. But in an anti-Black society, Skeetah's ingenuity in his care of China—under circumstances of fiscal precarity—is not seen as admirable, but rather is likely to be read as a sign of pathology.

My partner, who grew up in "the country," as Black folks say, tells a (supposedly true) story that dramatizes the gap between human desire for an obedient other and the wild. The story goes like this: a backwoods man was invited to a gathering and showed up with a raccoon on a leash. He tied the leash to a pole on the porch and went inside to the gathering. Another man, having seen him walk up with the raccoon on the leash, assumed it was a pet raccoon. This man reached out to pet the raccoon, only to have the raccoon tear him "from stem to stern." Bleeding, he went to ask the man who brought the raccoon on the leash why his pet had attacked. "Pet?" The man answered incredulously. "That's a wild raccoon that got in my house and that I was planning to let go. That raccoon's as wild as they come." This story fascinates me because it raises an interesting question: why do humans want to "pet" animals at all? What is the impulse to touch fur and to come into intimate proximity to another species? I suspect that ultimately this is about sovereignty and power, given how enamored this culture is of the possibility of "taming animals." From Cinderella to Tarzan, the ability to subdue animals is a mark of power. Yet to pet creatures is to violate their personal sovereignty and to initiate a relationship based upon subordinate/insubordinate, in which they are the inevitable subaltern. The ability to pet an animal also signals total submission, since of course a wild animal will not tolerate being petted, as they still know that humans are the enemies of their freedom. We could read petting animals, then, as an act that reinscribes human authority and power.[55] And since "petting" is read as "being nice" to an inferior creature, it also allows the human to feel benevolent and kind, while ignoring the aspects of captivity that characterize the lives of all domesticated animals.

The domestication of animals is one way that humans quite literally bring the natural world to heel. If we really believe that animals should be free, then the only "suitable wild animal ethic is an ethic based on their irreducible and implacable otherness. Wild animal Others are not polite citizens, with us, in civilized societies, enjoying all the rights and privileges pertaining thereto. We must, above all, respect their Otherness and difference and the freedom and independence that Otherness and difference imply."[56] Though the use of the term "other" in this quotation differs from how I use that word throughout this text, what the writer here alludes to is a kind of unexplainable mystery, a sovereignty of animals that is currently "disrespected" by our current use of and relationship with animals. Because we have domesticated animals to submit to the conditions of human life, they are made to mirror it in ways that reinforce a human framework that is often at odds with an animal one.

The ways animals have been trained to reflect the wishes of their human owners is evident in Ward's novel. Animals in *Salvage the Bones* are not separate from the humans they live with or come in contact with; rather, they are an extension of them. This is especially true in the case of the dogs in the text. Before talking at a bit more length about Skeetah's relationship with China, I want to point out that when Esch and Skeetah go to the white neighbor's house to steal dewormer for China, the neighbor's dog ends up chasing them all the way back to their own property. Ward's description of the man and his dog meld them as one creature throughout the encounter. The man is old and disabled, but in coloring like his dog: "And while he is too old, hair the color of his dog's, has arms that are too short and a belly, and his face is already red from trying to sprint so that he has given up running in the middle of the field, his dog is all fire, combustion and spring."[57] With hair/fur the same color, the man and the dog mirror each other, the dog's mission an extension of the man's desire. After chasing Esch and Skeetah all the way back home, the dog—whose name is Twist—encounters China and a fight ensues. After Skeetah calls China off the dog, "Twist jumps and runs, limping like his master, away to the pit and past, his panicked yelp like a siren receding in the distance, off to some other emergency."[58] Now, Twist resembles his master in both coloring and gait. This same mirroring between pet and owner is evident in Skeetah's relationship with China, and the fight scene between Twist and China—where China almost kills Twist but for being called off by Skeetah—also suggests that fighting for China is "natural." This, along with the ways in which dog-fighting is a function of not only China's captivity but Skeetah's, asks us to look closely at the human/dog interaction at the center of pit bull dog-fighting.

Skeetah's life is one characterized by constant battle—he has to fight (not necessarily physically) to feed China, to care for her (for example, by stealing the dewormer), and to keep China as safe as possible in the storm. In the one scene where we see China fight, too soon after giving birth to her puppies, we see that the fighting between the dogs bears a concentric relationship to a larger fight that is happening between Skeetah and Rico over which puppy Skeetah "owes" Rico. Before China fights, Skeetah talks to her:

> Skeetah smooths her, talks to her. Her fur looks silver in the shade. China is standing very still, staring across the clearing. Skeetah's tongue darts out of his mouth and a razor I did not know he had in his cheek flips out and over the tip of his tongue before he sucks it all back inside. He is reciting something, and he is saying it so fast it sounds like he is singing it. *China White*, he breathes, *my China. Like bleach, China, hitting and turning them red and white, China. . . . Make them runny, China, make insides outsides, China, make them think they snorted the razor, China. . . . My China*, he mumbles: *make them know, make them know, make them know.*[59]

The razor blade in Skeetah's mouth, there in case *he* has to fight, is a totem that directs his pep talk to China. He imparts his own lethal intentions to China, coaching her to be an extension of his will in the same way that Twist chased the kids to fulfill the wishes of his master. China fights because Skeetah fights; China's fights are bloody and brutal because Skeetah's life is one of blood and brutality. As beings in captivity, the conditions of their lives are not separate things, but rather of a piece. Hence, we can see the representation of China in the text as another way Ward illuminates the conditions of captivity that frame the lives of the people impacted by Hurricane Katrina. Skeetah's relationship with China is part of a larger cultural formation that inaugurates animals into a captive symbolic, where the animal's life is determined by the life of the owner. Therefore, it makes sense that China's life would require her to fight, because that is what Skeetah's life requires of him. When we bring animals into civilization, we bring them into captivity because for them to live peacefully with us, they must submit to human ways of being. As we follow Esch and her family in the days preceding Hurricane Katrina, we come to see Skeetah's love for China, which tempers whatever feelings we might have about dog-fighting. Likewise, Ward's writing asks us to consider Skeetah—subject to so much arbitrary brutality as a young Black man in America—as existing under the same conditions of precarity and vulnerability that govern China's life. What archaeology of concern can we mine for Skeetah? Where are the authorities who will come and jail those who've made a battle of his life?

It seems to me that Ward's treatment of China and Skeetah's relationship isn't meant to "excuse" dog-fighting so much as to reveal that dog-fighting is not "outside" of Western conceptions of the human/animal relationship but fully entrenched in it. At the same time, Skeetah's relationship with China is characterized not by cruelty but by love. By highlighting the complicated nexus of feeling and fighting around China, Ward disallows a dualistic reading of Skeetah and, ostensibly, any Black subject deemed "cruel" to animals because of something like dog-fighting. At other moments in *Salvage the Bones*, Ward examines alternate ways that humans and animals engage each other in life and death. Specifically, in the scene where Esch, Skeetah, and a few of their friends catch a squirrel and eat it, Ward reconfigures what it means to eat an animal. Interestingly, these country kids, whose lifestyle and upbringing seem to remind us in some ways of Hushpuppy's wild freedom, are perfectly capable of feeding themselves "in the wild." Likewise, Esch wakes up each morning and hunts for eggs, because her family keeps chickens, and they are allowed to run free on the property (free range chickens). Because they aren't kept in a coop, their eggs are everywhere, so Esch has to hunt for them. Unlike Hushpuppy, who is forced to eat cat food, Esch and her siblings know how to feed themselves without recourse to a store. In the scene where they eat the squirrel, Esch conceptualizes her consumption of the squirrel as becoming "one" with it: "I bite and I am eating acorns and leaping with fear to the small dark holes in the heart of old oak trees."[60] Eating the squirrel turns her into the squirrel, their bodies merging into one, giving Esch insight into the life of the creature. Here, Ward recontextualizes this seemingly simple encounter (hunting and eating an animal), making it larger than simply predator and prey. Instead, the act of eating the squirrel is elevated to an almost spiritual experience, as the life of the animal lives on inside of Esch. This moment in the novel reveals that nature in *Salvage the Bones* is not something the protagonist, Esch, contemplates as an object. Instead, nature informs the very way she sees the world.

Dead Wild: Generative Possibilities at the Nexus of Nature and Death

Seeing the world through the lens of the wild recurs throughout *Salvage the Bones*. When Junior, her little brother, finds their father's severed finger that still wears a wedding ring, he takes the ring off the finger and carries it around with him. His siblings are rightfully (mildly) horrified, and in attempting to explain Junior's behavior, Skeetah laughs and says, "He's dead wild."[61] "Dead" here emphasizes "wild," in that the word is used colloquially to mean something that is certain. Junior's "wildness" in this scene is about the ways in which his father's actually dead finger deters him not at all from getting the wedding ring, which stands in for his deceased mother. When asked why he takes the ring off the dead finger, Junior explains: "She gave it to him! I wanted it! Her!"[62] Junior's reclaiming of an object he considers a sacred symbol of his mother overrides any fear he "should" have of dead body parts, hence rendering him "dead wild." The double entendre here of "dead" also marks an irreducible relationship between nature (or the wilderness), Blackness, and death. In searching for his dead mother in his father's severed ring finger, Junior activates a series of unrequited familial longings that highlight the possibility of his increased vulnerability in relation to the impending storm. If their father dies in the storm, Junior—and his siblings—will find themselves as orphaned as Hushpuppy is at the end of *Beasts*. Unlike in *Beasts*, though, Junior is never alone; he has his brothers and sisters, a broader community, and family land—hurricane or not—to which he can return. And in the absence of the hurricane, the Batiste family land sustains them as a source of food, play, comfort, and family history. Like Junior, nature itself is "dead wild," but that is a reality that the Batiste children know how to negotiate since the natural world is not represented as an enemy—despite being a book about Hurricane Katrina—but rather as an extension of their lived existence. In describing her mother giving birth to her brother Junior, the last child her parents would have, Esch thinks: "Junior came out purple and blue as a hydrangea: Mama's last flower."[63] Nature is folded into the very flesh of Esch's thinking, not as a thing separate that she contemplates but as the very context through which she understands herself: "Manny threw a basketball from hand to hand. Seeing him broke the cocoon of my rib cage, and my heart unfurled to fly."[64] Esch's way of being in the world is characterized by interbeing between herself and nature, where the line between the human and the natural world doesn't just blur, it disappears: "and she moved and it looked like the woods moved, like a wind was running past the trees."[65] Throughout the novel, Esch's voice perpetually constructs both nature and people as one contiguous and unfolding process. "Manny is grinning, but he's not looking at me, and he's swimming in slow circles so he's orbiting me like the moon. Or the sun."[66] Ward's writing is poignant and evocative of the oneness of people and nature. Esch and her siblings, and their friends, are deeply imbricated in the natural unfolding that is existence on this planet. Consider this long passage:

> Away from the Pit, the pine trees reach skyward, their green-needled tops stand perfectly still. Once in a while, they shiver in the breeze that moves across their tops. They seem to nod to something that I cannot hear, and I wonder if it is the hum of José out in the Gulf, singing to himself.... Down here, the air is thick and hot. The trees are so dense that there's only a little undergrowth, and the bushes fight for their bright spots on the hard-packed, shadowy earth. There are birds, like yesterday, but these are small and brown, so small they could fit in the middle of my hand or in the maw of China's mouth. They are following us. As we walk through the wood on an unseen trail, the tiny birds fly from tree to tree, chattering sharply with each other, keeping pace with us. In the dense air, the oaks stand apart from the piney clusters: solemn, immovable. Spanish moss hangs from their arms, gray as an old king's beard.[67]

In this passage, the birds literally follow them as they walk on an "unseen trail," which reveals their deep oneness with the woods around the Pit. Esch's attention here is on the trees, the sky, the birds—there is a deep sense of embeddedness here that reveals an "elsewhere" of Black being that is "prior to ontology," as Moten argues about Blackness, understood as "ontology prior to the logistic and regulative power that is supposed to have brought it into existence."[68] Nature enables this recognition of Blackness, via Esch, as prior to ontology itself, because nature also precedes ontology. Hence, both nature and Blackness cause an "irreparable disturbance of ontology's time and space."[69] As the Zen teacher Eckhart Tolle once asked, "What time is it to a tree?"[70] Through her melding of Esch with nature via her thoughts and way of conceptualizing the world, Ward links the alternate prior-ontology of nature to Blackness to reveal the ways in which Esch's reality differs from what is typically understood to be "Black experience." So, in Esch's contiguity and embeddedness in nature, the dualism of Western ontology that divides humans from nature is undone, refiguring the relationship to "space" (land, place) and "time" (a sequence of events). That dualism relies upon a view of the natural world as a thing and as dead; Blackness in *Salvage* disallows the notion of nature as a dead thing to operate via Esch's narrative, which enlivens everything and highlights the interconnectedness of human, animal, plants, water, sky, and earth. Esch's nature consciousness perfectly illustrates the claim by Zen philosopher Alan Watts that humans didn't come "into" the world, but rather "came out of it."[71] What would this ontologically disruptive mode of being do to our conception of Black life, which so often is presumed to be devoid of value?

In reference to the Batiste family's land, Christopher Clark writes, "They live in a forest clearing called the Pit, which is both man-made and natural, adapted by Esch's family as a site of social engagement, but also a place where waste is dumped. Ward's descriptive language evokes a natural yet romanticized and almost mythologized landscape that is at the same time deprived, injured, and hurting."[72] Importantly, the Batiste family homestead is inherited from Esch's maternal grandparents, fifteen acres of land that at various times has sustained them through an edible garden and then the selling off of dirt, which creates the Pit referred to in Clark's comment. Despite Clark's assessment that the Pit is "deprived, injured, and hurting," it is also a life-giving natural space that no one in the Batiste family ever wants to leave. Existence itself is characterized by "waste" and "injury," in an absolute sense; so, saying that these define the Pit is like saying "water is wet." What Clark's comment speaks to is the way in which though Ward's novel highlights nature at every turn, it does not romanticize it. *Salvage the Bones* does not problematically romanticize nature, because it avoids making it an "other," instead emphasizing interbeing and contiguity between people and the nonhuman, and revealing how both life and death are natural. But to get to what is going on in Ward's novel, we also need to arrive at another theorization of what many would call threat and harm. Otherwise, we get stuck in a kind of dualism where nature is at once beautiful and embodies "a darker, more dangerous proposition."[73]

To do so, I'd like to highlight a vision of the natural world as articulated by Linda Hogan in *Dwellings: A Spiritual History of the Living World* (1995):

> Even wilderness is seen as having value only as it enhances and serves our human lives, our human world. While most of us agree that wilderness is necessary to our spiritual and psychological well-being, it is a container of far more, of mystery, of a life apart from ours. It is not only where we go to escape who we have

become and what we have done, but it is also part of the natural laws, the workings of a world of beauty and depth we do not yet understand. It is something beyond us, something that does not need our hand in it.[74]

Hogan's conception speaks to a way of being in relation to nature that is not one of conquest but instead highlights an acceptance of what we *cannot* know. I argue that for Esch, nature is a divine unknowable that contests the notion that everything can be comprehended through the application of intellect. At stake in both Hogan's and Esch's approach to the environment is a rejection of a Western phenomenology that conceptualizes nature as important only to the extent that it is useful to humans. Hogan's move here is important because it also unsettles Western notions of nature as the universal understanding of the phenomenological world. Thinking of nature as an external "thing" separate from human beings has several consequences, one of the most important being the erasure of alternative modalities of natural being. As Alan Watts has shown, the notion that "you" end at the boundary of your skin is a philosophical one that is "completely at odds with the rules of nature," yet it is the one that governs Western ontology.

The most intimate metaphor available to Western epistemes in relation to nature is that of Mother Nature, which is fraught with multiple categorical errors. Writing in *Undomesticated Ground: Recasting Nature as Feminist Space* (2000), Stacey Alaimo notes, "Feminism has long struggled with the historically tenuous entanglements of 'woman' and 'nature.' Mother earth, earth mothers, natural women, wild women, fertile fields, barren grounds, virgin lands, raped earths . . . these creatures portray nature as female and women as not exactly human."[75] In ways similar to Black disavowal of nature, at stake in feminist rejections of nature is an impulse to resist the ways that oppression has been naturalized, with women's exploitation being seen as a function of the natural order rather than as a consequence of structural oppression and inequality. So the representation of motherhood, both through Esch and China, risks reifying the idea that women are essentially "breeders," and that compulsory reproduction is a natural law. But Ward explicitly plays with the idea of mother/nature in *Salvage*, aligning China's birthing of a litter and Esch's pregnancy throughout with the storm itself. Hurricane Katrina is figured as a mother: "I will tie the glass and stone with string, hang the shards above my bed, so that they will flash in the dark and tell the story of Katrina, the mother that swept into the Gulf and slaughtered."[76] Mother Nature is problematized here, working against the notion that it is always generative and nurturing. Ward's depiction of motherhood as engaging both life and death unravels the simplification of women as "earth mothers" and all the implications it connotes. The contemplation of motherhood through both life and death in *Salvage* occurs via the proximity of birth and death, most especially through Esch's mother, who dies giving birth to Junior. Recourse to Mother Nature usually involves saccharine platitudes that paint nature (and by extension motherhood) as bucolic and blissful, but doing so requires that nature remain mythological in order to adumbrate the risks of both childbirth and environmental degradation. Esch's recognition of nature's bite as well as its caress situates her in the actual world rather than a mythic one. Extending the metaphor of Katrina as mother, Ward writes:

> She was the murderous mother who cut us to the bone but left us alive, left us naked and bewildered as wrinkled newborn babies, as blind puppies, as sun-starved newly hatched baby snakes. She left us a dark Gulf and salt burned land. She left us to learn to crawl. She left us to salvage. Katrina is the mother we will remember until the next mother with large, merciless hands, committed to blood, comes.[77]

By rejecting the elision of "mother" and "nurturer," Ward critiques the use to which nature has so often been put—to naturalize a woman's role as "breeder." Both scientific and symbolic representations of the "mother" have catalyzed nature as a justification for compulsory reproduction, and Ward's novel reveals that life often comes into being arbitrarily and that the title or role of mother does not inaugurate a "natural" guarantee of nurture. China gives birth to a litter of puppies but most of the time couldn't care less about them. In one scene, China kills one of her own puppies: "China snaps forward, closes her jaw around the puppy's neck as she does when she carries him, but there is no gentleness in it. She is all white eyes. She is chewing."[78] This causes Esch to ponder, "China is bloody-mouthed and bright-eyed as Medea. If she could speak, this is what I would ask her: *Is this what motherhood is?*"[79] Like Katrina, China is murderous. The storm, China's litter, and Esch's pregnancy all collide in Ward's text to render motherhood, to use Stacy Alaimo's coinage, a "natural disaster." Luce Irigaray has famously compared giving birth to going to war, and Ward's novel supports the notion that though giving birth can be miraculous in one way, it is often a physical disaster in another.[80] Esch's question here—*Is this what motherhood is?*—does not point to any murderous intent but indicates Esch's own coming to terms with bringing life into the world. Her actual mother is not there to show her, or tell her, what it is to be a mother—so Esch must look to other iterations of birth to contemplate motherhood. For Esch, the place of the mother is also symbolically a place of death, since her own mother died while giving birth to Junior. At the moment of Junior's birth, life and death were both in the room; as he came into being, Esch's mother went out of it. Esch's contemplation of motherhood, then, can be read as a blurring of the boundaries of the living and the dead, subverting the very dualism that inducts the Black person into social death. Ward's use of motherhood and (the) natural/disaster can be understood to "jam the theoretical machinery itself,"[81] in order to "expose the disruptive/creative capacity that blackness hosts/ holds"[82] in ways that refigure our notions of motherhood and of family.

We can see this creative capacity at play when Esch talks to Big Henry about the pregnancy. He asks her who the father is; Manny—who is the father—has refused to claim the child, so Esch answers, "It don't have a daddy."[83] Big Henry answers, "You wrong . . . This baby got plenty daddies."[84] Here, Big Henry turns the perceived lack of fathers on its head to argue instead for an abundance of them, suggesting that a community of men—not just one—will help raise Esch's baby. Big Henry's comment should not be read as opposition to the notion of the nuclear family that is preferred in American society and that has so often been used to define Black families as lacking, but rather as a nullification of the idea that an individualist model of family is superior to a community model. In doing so he reminds Esch of an elsewhere they can occupy on the other side of normative ideas about what constitutes a family.

At the end of the novel, the Batiste family has survived, but China is temporarily lost. Skeetah returns home to wait for her, knowing she will return. China does return, though all of her puppies have been lost to Katrina. Ward writes the last lines of the novel in a future tense, as if Esch is a seer: "She will return . . . She will look down on the circle of light we have made in the Pit, she will know that I have kept watch, that I have fought. China will bark and call me sister. In the star-suffocated sky, there is a great waiting silence. She will know that I am a mother."[85] Esch's anticipation of China's knowing of her motherhood represents her own acceptance of her pregnancy. Through this process she comes to occupy the space of the mother herself, having negotiated the divide between life and death through the storm and through her mother's absence and the presence of her unborn child.

Like Esch, I once found myself at the threshold of life and death, caught between my mother's death and becoming a mother myself. Like Esch's mom, she died young—at fifty-five; unlike Esch's mom, she was dying of lung cancer. One of the last memories I have of my mother is from a few weeks before she went into hospice. Sitting on the couch in my aunt's house together, she silently took my hand and pulled a buffer from her pocket and began to buff my nails. I knew—we both did—that it would be the last thing she ever did for me. Despite many of the hardships we faced together, there was one thing I always knew: my mother tried earnestly to take care of me throughout my life, and this was her last gesture of care, the last thing she could do for me as her own sun was setting. A few short weeks later, she was on her deathbed. My brothers and I were with her at hospice, and she told us to leave so she could rest, asking us to put on her favorite movie, *Evita* (1996). "Make sure you sing 'Don't Cry for Me Argentina' at my memorial service," she said. I went back to the hotel where we were staying so as to be near the hospice and got into the shower and cried. I knew that night was the last time I'd ever talk to her. I was five months pregnant. Standing on the cusp of being somebody's child and being somebody's mother, the mystery and complexity of our existence descended upon me, and it has yet to leave.

The end of Ward's novel returns us to a contemplation of the Black child—to Hushpuppy and to Davonte. Unlike Esch, whose sincere contemplation of motherhood helps her negotiate the death of her mother and the pending birth of her child, Davonte's adoptive mothers behaved more like the dogs of which they were so fond, murdering their children in an act of cruelty as senseless as China's eating of her puppies. I long to magically cross narratives and realms, to swim to the bottom of the ocean and find the lives stamped out by water, in the Middle Passage, in the hurricanes, and in that car as it fell from a cliff, to turn back time, to be a shelter. "Bodies tell stories," Ward writes.[86] And our bodies tell not only the story of our ancestors and our descendants, of our mothers and our children, but also the story of the earth. We evolved out of the material circumstance of this planet, and when we leave it, we must recreate an artificial copy of it. As Watts points out, we cannot live without the environment of earth, this being circumstances of soil, sky, water, and sun. We need the earth the way a fish needs water; but the earth does not need us. We are the natural stuff that is derivative and dispensable; earth is the force that will go on—even if in depleted form for a while—if we destroy ourselves. But our deaths are folded into the wild, the DNA of our bodies still circulating in the sea, the calcium of our bones nourishing the soil upon which we once walked. In this dead wild, Black lives achieve a kind of "racial eschatology"[87] through the collapse of the dualistic boundary between nature and being, through the recognition of the power of "a great waiting silence."[88]

CHAPTER THREE

Flesh of the Earth

Beyond the restoration of a lost commons through radical redistribution (everything for everyone), there is the unimaginable loss of that all too imaginable loss itself (nothing for no one). If the indigenous relation to the land precedes and exceeds any regime of property, then the slave's inhabitation of the earth precedes and exceeds any prior relation to the land—landlessness. And selflessness is the correlate. No ground for identity, no ground to stand (on). Everyone has a claim to everything until no one has a claim to anything. No claim. This is not a politics of despair brought about by a failure to lament a loss, because it is not rooted in the hope of winning. The flesh of the earth demands it: the landless inhabitation of selfless existence.
—Jared Sexton, "The Vel of Slavery"

We shine because they hate us, floss cause they degrade us
We trying to buy back our 40 acres.
And for that paper, look how low we'll stoop
Even if you in a Benz, you still a nigga in a coupe.
—Kanye West, "All Falls Down"

P(re)S(cript): Groundlessness

This chapter takes up Jared Sexton's ideas in the above epigraph as a frame for articulating a model of emancipation that differs from "the restoration of a lost commons, everything for everyone."[1] Hence, my work here is less "about" the two texts that I discuss and more about how those texts illustrate the confluence of refusal Sexton sketches in relation to "land" and "the self."

Sexton's essay "The Vel of Slavery: Tracking the Figure of the Unsovereign" is a critical intervention in discourses of land sovereignty that cause some tension between indigenous and Black scholars. It is necessary to critically explore these questions of ownership in relation to Black nature discourses precisely because the site of "land" in the Americas is a site of multiply encoded oppressions, and I do not want to write around or write over the displacement and violence experienced by Native Americans as I consider representations of nature in Black texts. After a thorough examination of the disciplinary structures around Native studies in relation to settler colonialism and land, Sexton arrives at the statement in the epigraph where he argues against the "restoration of a lost commons" (for anyone) and instead suggests the abolition of the entire structure of sovereignty, both in relation to land and "the self."[2] Sexton reveals a problem that arises between indigenous decolonizing discourses and Black antiracist discourses by noting that "settler decolonization sees in anti-racism the same pitfalls it sees in decolonization: both leave the colonizer intact and may even rely upon his continued existence for matters of recognition and redistribution."[3] Thus, it is impossible to imagine under the context of extant Western civilization a way to "restore a lost commons," for both Black and indigenous people, when the very mode of justice imagined (ownership and reparations) represents a break from the original worldview of said people before colonial/slave intervention. Ultimately, Sexton suggests that embracing land ownership (sovereignty) or self (sovereignty) will not provide the freedom (abolition) that the earth demands and requires of us. This is a far more radical suggestion than scrambling seats at the table, or on the *Titanic*, so that we preserve structures of oppression and hierarchy with a multicultural 1 percent.[4] He suggests, instead, that none of us have ground to stand upon to make a claim to any land or to any identity. Instead of this being depressing ("despair" is the word he uses), it is instead a model of what could be: selfless existence. What he is proposing here, and I will return to this fully in the last two sections of this chapter, is what in the Zen tradition is called Nibbāna, which translates from the Pali as "blowing out."[5] Another way of understanding "blowing out" is to think of it as releasing the delusion of the self, along with all the other problems that arise with it, including the notion that any "one" could own any "place." Without the presence of a "me," who is it that "owns" any place? (The end of ownership is also the end of theft.[6]) Without the construction of a "where," what is it that the illusory "me" owns?

Sexton's suggestion is radical both for indigenous and Black discourses, as it asks that two sites of loss—loss of land and loss of self—be refused as the grounds of liberation, since recovery of both depends upon notions that did not exist in many cultures prior to Western intervention. We already know that racial identity, as it exists today, was formed vis-à-vis Black people in the hold. African relations to the land, prior to slavery, differed from the Western model, even though West Africans lived in advanced civilizations. Carolyn Finney notes that "Africans believed in 'good use' of the land and the connection between the health of the land and their community."[7] Native Americans and Africans generally shared a similar view of nature, as they both "recognized that plants, animals, and humans all had a place in the world and should be treated with a respect that acknowledged the interdependence of all things. This view contrasted with the widespread belief among white men at that time who felt that nature should be dominated and exploited for profit."[8] Sexton makes note of the way these indigenous similarities between Native peoples and formerly African peoples have been galvanized for coalition building. But he argues, "If the indigenous relation to the land precedes and exceeds any regime of property, then the slave's inhabitation of the earth precedes and exceeds any prior relation to the land—landlessness. And selflessness is the correlate."[9] In the context of a Western society, justice *seems like* restoration of what was lost. But what was lost can never be restored, since history cannot be undone; the only way forward is—to use an Ellisonian phrase—to plunge outside of history,[10] which means undoing regimes of property and self. I contend that nature, as a symbol and metaphor in the texts I discuss below, helpfully reveals a need for the kind of landlessness and selflessness Sexton calls for by problematizing attempts to "restore a lost commons." It is my hope that this chapter feels as groundless and as centerless as the selfless existence Sexton proposes, so that through it we might be able to imagine another kind of being in the world, a vastly different schematic of place, one that celebrates homelessness[11] as the liberation represented by the phrase no(where) for no(body).

Land Ownership Is a Social Construction

> The first man who, having enclosed a piece of ground, to whom it occurred to say this is mine, and found people sufficiently simple to believe him, was the true founder of civil society. How many crimes, wars, murders, how many miseries and horrors Mankind would have been spared by him who, pulling up the stakes or filling in the ditch, had cried out to his kind: Beware of listening to this impostor; You are lost if you forget that the fruits are everyone's and the Earth no-one's.
> —Jean-Jacques Rousseau[12]

Rousseau's comment that the beginning of "crimes, wars, murders, . . . miseries and horrors" can be traced to the man who claimed a piece of land as his own points directly to the ethos that underlies my emphasis on landlessness in this chapter. In *Playing Indian* (1988), Paul Deloria gives us pause regarding Rousseau's critique of property by suggesting that he contributed to the notion of the noble savage. Though Rousseau never mentioned the noble savage (*bon sauvage*) in any of his work, he is often read as understanding Native peoples as simpletons who lived in an idyllic natural state. Deloria identifies two strains of noble savage ideology, arguing that Rousseau's version used the noble savage to "critique Western society."[13] Even as it can be read as invested in problematic hierarchical notions of humanity, Rousseau's critique of Western society resonates with a discourse of landlessness. The founding of civil society, which Rousseau argues begins with the claiming of land, is intimately connected in the American context to the notion that land ownership equals liberty. It is not surprising, then, that Black progress narratives would feature at their center a longing for land. Writing about what land meant to the formerly enslaved, Karen Cook Bell argues that it represented a "coda of 'full and fair compensation'" for generations of unpaid labor and abuse.[14] Forty acres and a mule, as a political promise and as a metonym for "what is owed" the descendants of the formerly enslaved, has taken on an almost-mythological status in Black American culture. As I mention in the introduction, Spike Lee's production company, Forty Acres and a Mule Filmworks, reveals through its name a deeply held memory of a Black dream deferred: the American dream of material prosperity represented as land acquisition.

Kanye West, in his perceptive critique of consumerism above, references forty acres in the song "All Falls Down."[15] Kanye reveals that Black striving for material power arises from the degradation Black people suffer under white supremacy. Furthermore, he goes on to argue that luxury items cannot mitigate the status of the Black person as "an other," when he raps, "Even in a Benz, you still a nigga in a coupe." He at once explains the urgency of Black material striving—as a reaction to oppression—and at the same time reveals that it is always already destined to fail. At the heart of this striving is land, both a literal and symbolic figure that stands in for the inscrutability and the unavailability of freedom. The connection between land and notions of freedom, between models of Western liberation in relation to chattel slavery, and the Black striving for both land and selfhood within the context of those models, informs my discussion of two texts in this chapter—the television series *Queen Sugar* (2016) and Kaitlyn Greenidge's novel *We Love You, Charlie Freeman* (2016)—where discourses of freedom are interrogated at the site of "land" and at the site of "the self." *Queen Sugar*, based on a novel of the same name by Natalie Baszile, is the story of the Bordelon family, a landed bayou family who struggle to maintain control of a sugar cane farm inherited from their father.[16] Narratively,

Queen Sugar is framed in part by an abiding concern about materiality and fiscal success in Western society, and as such it measures freedom by the ability of the Bordelon family to operate unfettered in capitalist society. *We Love You, Charlie Freeman* stages questions about liberation through the ontology of the racial self, putting pressure on the line between human and primate to reveal the ways in which racist discourses of the seventeenth and eighteenth centuries still adhere to Blackness even as the characters of Greenidge's book seek to transcend those discourses by entering white spaces and taking up white desire vis-à-vis the animal world.[17] These two texts are different from each other in many ways, but I've included them together in this chapter to demonstrate how the attainment of middle- and upper-class status brings with it inevitable conflict between power and freedom, making sites of Western liberation and self-making always already vexed for the Black person.

Both *Queen Sugar* and *We Love You, Charlie Freeman* concern middle- and upper-class Black families that find themselves at the conjunction of anti-Blackness and the natural world, and despite my perhaps counterintuitive pairing of them here, each is ultimately a thought experiment about what is possible (and impossible) within the context of Western structures for Black people. In other words, what does it mean when Black people succeed in a system that *requires* their subjugation to operate, where the very basis of historical and current societal, material, and philosophical success comes at the expense of Black humanity? And doesn't a system that works on the basis of another human being's oppression suggest its own insufficiency? These questions are at the heart of the familial and social conflict in both the texts I discuss here. Nature, in the form of land and animals in these two texts, highlights the complex problem of Western liberation for the Black subject, since Black people and nature are mutually othered, as they are co-inscribed as "wild" and in need of "taming." These two texts, I argue, use nature to illustrate *a destiny of failure* around two vectors of Western ontology: land and self.

My signaling of failure here is not the identification of a fault; rather, failure marks the site of possibility. Following Jack Halberstam's theorization of failure as "a set of oppositional tools," I argue here that the inability to fold seamlessly into systemic norms in both these texts indexes the ways in which Blackness, as the figure of the unsovereign, undoes the logic of oppression.[18] Using Sexton's notion of "landlessness" and its corollary "selflessness," I hope to show through these two texts that nature signals the ways in which Blackness always disrupts the ontology of sovereignty, returning us to what the *flesh of the earth* demands: no(where) for no(body). I explore this conjunction of failure, Blackness, and nature in four sections, alternating between *Queen Sugar* and *We Love You, Charlie Freeman*. One text (*Queen Sugar*) is concerned with land, the other with discourses of the (Black) self. In both cases, a project of Black self-making through hegemonic notions of ownership and wealth acquisition, and scientific discovery and language, results in disruptions of sovereignty when Blackness meets the natural world.

One of the aspects of slavery that Sexton discusses is that the Middle Passage represented for the African subject not only a loss of identity but also a loss of indigeneity. This loss of indigeneity meant that the newly emancipated slaves were shuttled from one end of the regime of property to another, while the overarching logic of property itself was never contested. Hence, one of the first postbellum "solutions" offered for the newly freed Black people was to give them land. This attempt to make Black people free via land ownership took place in two ways. First, the African Colonization Society was founded, and some formerly enslaved people were "given" what is now Liberia to start their own country. This was a plan Abraham Lincoln supported.[19] Of course, the results were disastrous, as the formerly enslaved disenfranchised the Mende people (who were living there when they landed) in much the same way whites had done to them in America. Even today the divisions caused by this "land acquisition" on behalf of the formerly enslaved can be seen in a relatively unending civil war in Liberia.[20]

The second attempt at bringing the formerly enslaved into the Western model of (landed) freedom, was Sherman's Field Order No. 15. The portmanteau "40 acres and a mule" can be traced to this field order, which—after the fall of the South—seized Confederate land all the way from Charleston, South Carolina, to the St. John's River in Florida, including the Sea Islands of Georgia, for distribution to the newly emancipated slaves. The order specified that over forty thousand former slaves would receive forty acres of land (the mules were added later, as leftovers from the Union army). President Lincoln signed and approved Sherman's field order—which was drafted less to give slaves reparations than to relieve the Union of providing a livelihood for the ever-growing number of Black refugees following the army—but Lincoln was assassinated before the land could be distributed.[21] The loss of slavery, to the South, was not just a shift in social relations or to a particular kind of labor system—it was quite literally the loss of revenue. The end of slavery was the beginning of the South's decline into poverty and national insignificance. To crown the South's defeat by giving valuable rice plantations and coastal land to the formerly enslaved was seen as another ideological and fiscal insult against white southerners by the North. For the freedmen, the land was quite literally a lifeline, since no infrastructure existed to manage the postbellum society of the South. Confederate sympathizer Andrew Johnson, the vice president who took office after Lincoln's death, paved the path for the rise of sharecropping, which would extend slavery's exploitation of Black labor. For many Black persons, then and now, the promise of land, and the economic stability it might have ensured, remains a symbol of a freedom that is still a dream deferred.

But at the heart of the nation's failure to right the wrongs of slavery is a deeper question about the nature of freedom itself. What would it have meant if the freedmen were each given forty acres of land? Would the racial problems that characterize our current society be absent? Would this alone have been enough to shift the tide of what would be another 150 years (and counting) of lynching, Jim Crow, the KKK, and Ferguson? While this question can never truly be answered, since it rests upon a hypothetical, I am skeptical about the "power" of land ownership to uproot the racial animus that Black people live(d) with—and that skepticism is, in part, what this chapter is about. There are two questions that form the basis of that skepticism. The first is, what does it mean to stake one's freedom in ownership of purloined land? As a continuation of this question, if you will, I wonder what it means for the Black person to participate in the mistake of European colonial domination of Native peoples' lands? And second, what does it mean to adopt and internalize the idea that land can be owned in the first place? I do not pose these questions in ignorance of the fact that, due to the way our economic system works, one is coerced into ownership of land since it is the most strategic way to proceed in a capitalist and hierarchal system where survival is difficult. Halberstam diagnoses the situation helpfully when he writes, "A market economy must have winners and losers, gamblers and risk-takers, con men and dupes; capitalism . . . requires that everyone live in a system that equates success with profit and links failure to the inability to accumulate wealth, even as profits for some means losses for others."[22] Capitalism (and the multigenerational land ownership upon which it still rests) is a kind of zero-sum game, where one must strive to be a "winner" even if it means others will lose. For the Black person, who has always been the "loser" in American history, land ownership at first glance suggests a way to win. My goal in this chapter is not to impugn the players, but rather to undermine the game itself.

When we consider the conundrum of persistent racism and white supremacy in our society, these questions of liberation (around land and self) present an almost insoluble conflict. In other words, land ownership itself (as a system) *requires* the very oppression we want to see undone. There is no way to protect the sovereignty of ownership without the police state, because land ownership, as treatment of indigenous people the world over demonstrates, can be maintained only through violence. When we realize the centrality of the police state for maintaining land rights (property rights), then it becomes clear why Native Americans are the most murdered group of citizens in the United States by the police, surpassing even the experience of Black people.[23] Consider: without a police state, how long would it be before the most disenfranchised in our society requisitioned the resources of any given place to support themselves? So, what does it mean to want property (as a sign of one's freedom) and to also simultaneously agitate against the police state? These two contradictory movements make sense only because we've confused (material) privilege with freedom. To put it another way: ownership and the police state go together, in much the same way that a body and a shadow cannot be separated. So, if one wants to maintain ownership (as a model of liberation), then the police state is necessary to protect the "freedom" of those with property.

For the Black person, this poses some categorical problems that both the texts I discuss here illuminate. And this problem is why, perhaps, Sexton argues for abolition rather than for "restoration" of a lost commons. I want to emphasize that the onus of responsibility here is not on Black people, who have achieved remarkable success in a flawed system designed to prevent such. Those achievements are not to be dismissed as unimportant or understood as responsible for our bondage; miraculously, we have made lemonade out of the lemon that is the regime of property, in which participation is compulsory. What I want to examine here is how *Queen Sugar* reveals the insufficiency of that regime for Black liberation by exposing the ways in which ownership and wealth accumulation inflect the justice of one's life choices. The idea of land as "ownable" is in direct conflict with indigenous notions of land, where the earth is perceived as a communal place, rather than as a "thing" that can be owned. The notion of land ownership, transposed to the Americas from Europe, is ultimately a monarchical one, since traditionally the sovereign owned (most) land, where the land one owns is not about communion or dwelling so much as it represents the ability to generate more revenue via rents, sharecropping, or extraction of natural resources.[24] This hegemonic model, where land possession is a bludgeon against those without it, inheres to contemporary models of land ownership and therefore always implies a cultural and economic hierarchy of value. And in that hierarchy, which still holds today, Blackness has value only as a thing itself, as an ownable asset, but is threatening at the site of self-possessed ownership because it opens the possibility of the Black monarch, a queen with the power to control whiteness and to reorder the colors, if not the system itself, of the triangular hierarchy where—for now—whiteness is at the top, and Blackness makes up the broad base. Such a rearrangement would not be freedom but would instead be another iteration of our current system. In the television series *Queen Sugar*, the tension between freedom and land ownership (which is the opposite of freedom in my formulation, following Sexton) characterizes the narrative, from the crop they grow (sugar) to the challenges they face as each character seeks agency (and success). And, through the characters of Nova and Charley Bordelon, the show undermines the materialist progress narrative that stands in for freedom in disruptive and uncomfortable ways.

This Land Is Me

> This land is me—where my spirit is happy.
> —Sounds of Blackness, *Africa to America*

Season 4 of *Queen Sugar* begins with a tight close-up of Nova Bordelon speaking into a camera. She says,

> I'm an American. And my family is an American family. And like all American families, we want the dream. Homes, Land, Space . . . Love. Being an American means we are beautiful. But it also means we have a secret, that ugliness is also within us. I believe it is our secrets that are killing us. So, in my book *Blessing and Blood*, I am offering my truth as a sacrifice; as an example of how we can all be free. And I hope all who believe that our lives depend on being better truth tellers will go on this journey with me.[25]

Nova is filming a commercial for the promotion of her book, a memoir, which is a tell-all that exposes many of the traumas and difficulties we, as viewers, have watched the Bordelons endure for the previous three seasons. In this opening statement, her words meta-narratively frame the overall logic of the series itself, highlighting the ways in which *Queen Sugar* is concerned with the pleasures and difficulties of the "American dream." Of the things she lists as part of the "dream" of her family, three out of four are about ownership and property. She articulates Black desire around Americanness through land, space, and the site of the domestic (home), and then equates all of these with love. When she says Americans are beautiful, it is clear that this rhetoric is designed to garner broad identification with the Bordelons via a kind of patriotic framing of America through its fantasy of itself. But then she disrupts her own American reverie by evoking ugliness and secrets, arguing that only by sharing those secrets with the world can she—as a "truth teller"—procure a better life for herself and for others.

What starts out as a direct address that meshes with the extradiegetic frame of the show is undone when we get an establishing shot that reveals Nova is doing an interview for her book. Her editor, who is off-screen during Nova's recitation, praises her and predicts tremendous success for the book. Nova's sincerely delivered speech is robbed of some of its impact as we realize the artificiality of her monologue, as the editor's avaricious demeanor reveals that her book is a product they are trying to sell and that Nova's rise as an author is just as much an impetus for her work as "truth-telling." Nova's construction of America in this opening monologue collapses and simplifies the complexity of the nation's history, which Hortense Spillers describes as "a dizzying concoction of writing and reportage, lying and 'signifying' jokes, 'tall tales,' and transgenerational nightmare, all conflated under the banner of Our Lord—exemplify[ing], for all intents and purposes—the oldest game of trompe de l'oeil, the perhaps-mistaken-glance-of-the-eye, that certain European powers carried out regarding indigenous Americans."[26] So though Nova sees herself as telling the unflinching truth, she does so by papering over the "dizzying concoction" of America and laying the weight of her critique on her family and not on the nation itself.

The secrets that Nova tells are not the dirty laundry of the nation. Unlike Ta-Nehisi Coates in *Between the World and Me* (2015), Nova does not use her life to illuminate the ways in which sexism, racism, and bi-phobia shape *her* lived experience. Rather, she exposes the intimate details of her family's most difficult moments (from the revelation that her brother's son is not his biological child to details of her sister's negotiation of a sex scandal while she was married to an NBA player), which places American pathology—or "ugliness"—within the context of the Black family, rather than on American structures of oppression. We can read the reaction of her family—which is negative, to say the least—not as an attempt to "hide" their secrets, but rather as a rejection of Nova's virtue signaling through her use of an anti-Black American ideology that, like the Moynihan report, constructed the Black family as the site of its own problems.[27] Though Nova's memoir is a miscalculation of how to be "free," the construction of her project in the monologue that opens season 4 is a useful frame for thinking about how the conjunction of Blackness and aspects of the "American dream" represents a kind of inevitable collision, characterized by various political and social dangers.

For the characters of *Queen Sugar*, land is at the heart of their quest for freedom. Like the broader cultural narrative evoked by forty acres and a mule, land ownership is not only a deferred dream of many Black Americans, it is the very basis upon which the United States was founded. The notion of "private property" and "land ownership," as well as the idea that land is essentially dead and exists solely for the extraction of goods, differs in important ways from the idea of "communal territory" and interdependence that characterized most other civilizations before contact with Europeans. Dianne Glave, in *Rooted in Earth: Reclaiming the African American Environmental Heritage*

(2010), notes, "For African farmers, the cycles of planning and harvesting, alpha and omega, and life and death were fundamental to nature and agriculture. Farmers consecrated and benefited from the soil, which was, in turn, a source of spirituality, nourishment, and life to humans."[28] A text like *Queen Sugar* evokes both a European and an African/indigenous notion of the farm/land, which produces various kinds of failures as well as successes in relation to natal alienation. I read *Queen Sugar* as an allegory of what happens when land, as private property, and Blackness collide, arguing that a series of problems arise that interrupt the attainment of the American dream, or the establishment of an alternative agricultural modality, because Black subjection and land ownership are historically mutually constitutive in the United States. At stake for the Bordelons is a historical progression from *owned* to *owners*, from poor to wealthy, and from powerless to powerful. The Bordelons have been brought together by their father's death and, importantly, his bequeathing of his sugar cane farm to his three children. So, their lives, and their relationship to each other, connect through the symbol of their father's land. Managing this land—and its crop—drives the narrative, staging ideas of freedom, success, wealth, and progress as a narrative experiment in Black ontology.

At the beginning of season 4, when Nova's bombshell memoir is two weeks from its release date, everything is going well for the Bordelon family. In the first episode, we see that Charley—who has been troubled in love after divorcing her husband, who turned a blind eye to the rape culture propagated by his teammates—has finally found a suitable and authentic love match, and her business, a sugar mill called Queen Sugar, is thriving despite being a subsidiary of the rival (and racist) Landry Corporation. Ralph Angel receives notification that his parole—for crimes of theft he committed in his youth—has expired and now his debt to society is paid. Aunt Vi, the family matriarch, opens a diner amidst a joyful community with the help of her supportive and loving husband, Hollywood.[29] There is nothing but good news for the Bordelons, who are doing well personally and financially: Ralph Angel's sugar cane farm is worth millions, Charley's business is thriving, and Aunt Vi's famous pies form the basis for her founding of a restaurant she has long dreamed of. At the grand opening for Vi's diner, we see Blue—Ralph Angel's son—selling candy and pies at his own little store inside Aunt Vi's store, and every time he makes a sale, he rejoices, suggesting that the habits of wealth accumulation are being passed down through the generations of the Bordelon family. The climax of the episode is when Charley attends a banquet to accept an award for an organization that recognizes women in business. As she stands up to make her speech, she's interrupted by a reporter who has read an advance copy of Nova's book, which no one else in the family has yet read. The reporter asks Charley if she's "always" supported women, and Charley replies that she has. The reporter then confronts Charley with the accusation that she suppressed the testimony of a rape victim in her husband's sex scandal to protect herself, which she read about in Nova's book. Charley is humiliated on camera, as the women at the banquet use their phones to record her shocked expression and inability to defend herself. Nova, with her truth-telling ethos, symbolically intervenes in the progress narrative represented by Charley's success. In this episode, the entanglements of "privacy" and "private property" are revealed, as Charley's "business"[30] literally intrudes upon her business.

Writing about the ways in which private property is always tied to the notion of personal privacy, Mary Choplecti notes that the 1820 *Yovatt v. Winyard* case legally "wrapped together" private property and personal privacy. She explains that in this court case, "the court extended property rights protections to cover personal secrets."[31] Following Choplecti's historicization of privacy and private property, we could argue that to be against privacy is also to be against private property. Nova's truth-telling mission not only brings what she sees as spiritually cancerous secrets to light but also implicitly attacks the logic of capitalist accumulation (private property) represented by the momentum of her family's achievements. Nova is a purist, who throughout many seasons has ended love affairs over politics. She is also the "earth mother" figure among her family and community. Charley is the sophisticate, Aunt Vi is the matriarch, and Ralph Angel represents the figure of the redeemed. But Nova is the hippie, who grows marijuana and advocates for the unfairly imprisoned. Nova represents a disruption not only of white supremacist and patriarchal politics but also the capitalist ethos represented mostly by Charley and, to a lesser degree, Ralph Angel and Aunt Vi. Nova demands a kind of Black political and interpersonal perfection, and the success of her family members is always characterized by compromise and half-gestures. But is it possible to succeed, as a Black person, in an anti-Black society without compromising with one's enemy? This is the crisis Nova faces as her book becomes a smashing success. Eventually, she is nominated for the National Book Award. Her star is rising, and she is the darling of the literary world; but by exposing her family's secrets to the world, does she collude with anti-Black ideologies that always already construct the Black family as pathological?

This is the same conundrum faced by Charley in her attempt to open the first Black- and woman-owned sugar mill in Louisiana. Though she boldly takes on the Landry family, the broader context of sugar cane and Louisiana politics forces her to make a deal with them and sell them her mill. She is coerced into doing so in a game of fiscal chess, where her only options are to sell or go under. Many of the Black farmers on the show feel alienated by this compromise and Charley's reputation takes a hit in their town of St. Jo, where she is perceived to be on the side of the whites. Likewise, though Ralph Angel wants to remain connected to many of his friends from prison and gives them jobs on his farm after their release, he must break those bonds in order to ensure the safety of his property and his child—not because his friends are engaged in criminal activity, but because the police use his attempt to help them as an excuse for unending harassment. Similarly, Aunt Vi must partner with a white businessman to distribute her pies in grocery stores. Through these narrative developments, *Queen Sugar* forces us to consider the price of the ticket in an anti-Black world, and it does so at the site of land and wealth acquisition. What does it mean when the forty acres (and then some) are achieved? In the case of the Bordelon family, material prosperity is revealed to bring with it as many problems as it solves, because the accumulation of wealth still occurs within the broader, white supremacist society. The thing that Nova really wants to tell the truth about is that money won't heal the deep brokenness caused by the oppressive structures of society, which are responsible for the tragedies in the lives of her family members. Hence, Nova's function in *Queen Sugar* is to deconstruct the dream itself, rather than emphasize its deferral.

Nova is what Sara Ahmed calls a "killjoy." In the first episode of season 4, it's clear that the ebullient, joyful hallmarks of success that everyone in her family is enjoying are "killed" by the revelations in Nova's book. But the function of the killjoy is to interrupt the problematic "pleasure" that accrues from unquestioned narratives and structures. The killjoy "exposes the bad feelings that get hidden, displaced, or negated under public signs of joy."[32] The Bordelons, at the opening of season 4, are all caught up in public (though not insincere) signs of joy due to their various kinds of material and social successes. But is material wealth the sole index of Black liberation? This is the question that I think Nova is implicitly asking. For Nova, it is not enough to rest on the notion of the "prosperity gospel" as evidence of growth and community health. Simply saving their family's farm, without talking about all the difficult secrets buried in their father's past—such as the revelation that one of his wills leaves the entire farm to Ralph Angel solely—is not enough to stand in for the "progress" that is at the heart of Black longing. But the mission of claiming the land as their own, primarily from the Landrys' greedy and destructive plans, drives the narrative of *Queen Sugar* in a way that resonates with an uneasy and compulsory desire to achieve the American dream, as a kind of antidote to the effects of slavery. The Landry family wants to steal the land from the Bordelons, and the other Black farmers of the parish of St. Jo, for the purpose of various business deals that will increase their wealth. The Black farmers of St. Jo are presented as agriculturalists who simply want to live quiet and peaceful lives growing sugar cane, and the Landry family evokes a long history of white interruption of Black attempts to live within the confines of Western society, a process perhaps best described by Saidiya Hartman as "the afterlife of slavery."[33] Parallel to Nova's literal and figurative deconstruction of ownership, *Queen Sugar* is also an exploration of the ways in which Black participation in the system is thwarted by the assumption of white entitlement to land. So while the character of Nova represents a critique of the Western progress narrative at the site of land, the show also functions as a historical treatment of the ways in which even when Black people adopt the general values of a Western-style agricultural society, racism intervenes.

Ta-Nehisi Coates, in his piece "The Case for Reparations" (2014), helpfully connects the effects of the afterlife of slavery to the material, and specifically to land, in his exposé about the ways in which land was strategically and continually stolen from Black people: "In 2001, the Associated Press published a three-part investigation into the theft of Black-owned land stretching back to the antebellum period. The series documented some 406 victims and 24,000 acres of land valued at tens of millions of dollars. The land was taken through means ranging from legal chicanery to terrorism."[34] By revealing the "legal chicanery" and "terrorism" employed by the Landrys, *Queen Sugar* highlights a history of land theft from Black Americans. The theft of Black land is a significant issue that is often unaddressed since Black people are presumed to have no land to steal, so strongly does the idea of property connect to whiteness. As of this writing, the US Congress is holding hearings on the possibility of reparations for Black people,[35] but that discussion is incomplete without a recognition of that fact that "in addition to invoking the 40 acres Black people never got, the reparations movement today should be talking about the approximately 11 million acres Black people had but lost, in many cases through fraud, deception and outright theft, much of it taken in the past 50 years."[36]

The theft of Black land in the United States presses upon an old and enduring wound of the Black person in America—that of placelessness, à la Katherine McKittrick. Though one way to understand slavery is to see it as the theft of Black persons-as-bodies, it was also simultaneously a theft of land, a literal "taking" of Africa from enslaved Africans. Hence, slavery can be understood as action against two bodies, being as it is against both the land and the people—a simultaneous theft of place and person. A Sounds of Blackness song speaks to this notion when a singer laments about Africa, "This land is me, where my spirit is happy."[37] So to take "me" is to simultaneously take "this land," as this statement collapses the boundary between person and place. The trauma of the Middle Passage was one in which the land that is "me" became no longer me, and became "elsewhere," marking a seemingly permanent displacement from an original African "self" and place. Thus, land in *Queen Sugar* signifies doubly. On the one hand, land ownership in the West always evokes the logic of conquest; on the other, for the Black person, to have land symbolically mediates against the placelessness that took hold during the Middle Passage. Because land in *Queen Sugar* represents two things—a problematic assimilative object as well as a symbol that mediates an (African) loss of place—the narrative manages to produce sympathy both for Nova's disruptive practices and for the Bordelon family members who see Nova not as a truth-teller but as a deeply damaged and disturbed troublemaker. *Queen Sugar* brilliantly illustrates the problems both with participation in an anti-Black system (land ownership) and with nonparticipation, for if the Bordelons were to give up their land as a kind of political statement—a "Blaxit,"[38] if you will—the Landry family would simply iterate Black displacement and suffering on the land ceded by the Bordelons and the other Black farmers. Furthermore, *Queen Sugar* reveals the ways in which the Bordelons—and by extension Black Americans—are emotionally invested in American society and sites of freedom in ways that are compelling and not easily dismissed, even if they are half-measures to emancipation, at best.

These complex configurations of history and progress are nowhere clearer than in the revelation that the Landry family wants to acquire the Black farmers' land because they hope to enter into a lucrative agreement with a multinational corporation to build a prison complex on the land. Narratively, sugar and prisons are historically interchangeable, as the cultivation of sugar in the seventeenth century and beyond relied upon Black bondage and fed an insatiable European appetite for the white powder, which was nicknamed "white gold," because at one time it had more value than gold did. Elizabeth Abbott's historical monograph titled *Sugar: A Bittersweet History* (2011) articulates the impact that sugar had on shaping the world as we currently know it through the "character" of an Englishwoman who was the first to put sugar into her tea: "By sipping her sugared tea, Gladys wrenched generations of men and women from Africa and transported them across the Atlantic to slavery. She ordained the sugar agriculture of the fertile colonies of the Caribbean Sea. She rewrote the map of North America, ensuring that Dutch-held New York and French-held Canada were returned to Britain."[39] It would not be an overstatement to say that sugar shaped the modern world—from its geography, to its economic system, to its labor practices. I read sugar as standing in for oppression, as we can see in Kara Walker's sculpture *A Subtlety: An Homage to the unpaid and overworked Artisans who have refined our Sweet tastes from the cane fields to the Kitchens of the New World on the Occasion of the demolition of the Domino Sugar Refining Plant.*[40] The sculpture is a huge mammy figure carved out of sugar, naked and posed as an Egyptian-style sphinx. Symbolically, sugar iterates

Black subjugation, and as a highly desired object it is also worshipped. Walker's sculpture simultaneously captures the reverence for sugar and the ways in which the production of it depend upon a history of oppression and slavery. As a consumable, the sugar sphinx can quite literally be eaten, representing the consumption of Black suffering.

The fact that the Bordelon family is growing sugar cane highlights the complicated site of their liberation, given that the nascent addiction to sugar in the West fueled slavery for hundreds of years. Like cotton, sugar is a tainted "good" that was produced in the cruelest and most brutal working conditions. According to Lizzie Collingham in *The Taste for Empire: How Britain's Quest for Food Shaped the Modern World* (2017), the conditions of West Indian sugar plantations were so lethal that slaveholders needed to bring in "20,000 new African slaves per year to maintain the labor force."[41] Upon seeing the brutality of sugar cultivation in the West Indies, a British ship purser wrote, "I never more will drink sugar in my Tea, for it is nothing but Negroes blood."[42] Hence, the sugar cane at the heart of *Queen Sugar* can be read as a mobile signifier that moves along a spectrum of freedom and bondage. Sugar, as a crop, is not neutral. Rather, it is overburdened by a history of violence; it is quite literally historically soaked in "Negroes blood." For the Bordelon family to be cultivators of sugar highlights the ambivalent and vexed nature of Western progress for the Black subject. As the historical site of the plantation, the Bordelons' sugar cane fields must undergo a transition from being the location of bondage to being a place of freedom. A simple transferal of ownership cannot accomplish this desired rupture between plantation and farm, between slave and owner, or between being a "thing" and being an owner of things. The specter of the slave plantation haunts the cane fields, even as we imagine that slavery has ended.

The symbolic complexity of the cane field is deepened by the contiguity between the plantation and the prison in contemporary society.[43] The elision between the cane fields/slave plantation and the modern-day prison industrial complex occurs when Charley learns that the Landry family wants to buy up all the Black farmers' land (at the lowest possible price) in order to build a prison complex. The prison that the Landry family plans to build is historically interchangeable with the cane fields, which traditionally were worked by—but not owned by—Black people. But the Landry family's desire to build a prison on the land is not just about profit; it is also about continuing to define Black relationship to place through imprisonment. Though cane farms at one time relied exclusively on slave labor, now that Black farmers are in a position to cultivate their own and, perhaps, different relationship to the land (of the kind Glave describes above), the white society of St. Jo moves to perpetuate the history of bondage against Black people *in that place* by putting a prison in the space of the Black farm. The prison, then, is a reiteration of the plantation, reinscribing Black propertylessness and placelessness. As Ralph Angel and the other Black farmers begin to imagine a life of independence and self-determination, and to feel the groundedness of generations of their ancestors working that land, the Landry family can see imprisonment only as the link between place (land) and Blackness. It is quite likely, in fact, that the prison will continue to grow sugar cane but that the prisoners will have to grow and harvest it basically for free—so that the prison is literally an extension, through time, of slavery.

The prison, as a modern-day plantation, ensures the continuation of Black placelessness. Writing about the plantation, Katherine McKittrick argues, "The plantation evidences an uneven colonial-racial economy that . . . legalized black servitude while simultaneously sanctioning black placelessness and constraint."[44] As a site of bondage, the slave's relationship to the land could never affectively be like home. Even though slavery persisted for hundreds of years, the hope that the plantation was a temporary site—a place one would either flee or be liberated from—persisted. Racism interrupts the Black person's ability to cathect to place, creating the placelessness McKittrick theorizes about in ways that "spacialized domination."[45] The modern-day prison industrial complex, in real life and in *Queen Sugar*, symbolically serves the same function that the slave plantation did. Hence, the Bordelon struggle for relation to the land is not only about the always already problematic pursuit of ownership; it is also about contesting the very ground of Black placelessness in American society. For the Bordelon family, the farm is not only "a place" but also a multidimensional *space of being* that holds the family together in an affective ecological field.[46]

For Charley, Ralph Angel, and Nova, the farm represents their father's actual body, an extension of him that they must retain to promote the health and well-being of the family. In season 1, when the children and Aunt Violet gather to hear the reading of their father's will, he leaves them his farm with these words:

> To my children Nova, Charlotte, and Ralph Angel Bordelon, I bequeath 800 acres . . . equally. With each Bordelon generation, we work to do a little better than the last. Nova, Charlotte, Ralph Angel, you are now in this line. Out of every place in this whole big world, this land bears your name. Farm it, nurture it, love it, pass it on to your children and for every Bordelon that will come next. Your forever loving father, Ernest.[47]

It is important that he mentions their names, first and last, twice in these few lines. In doing so, he inscribes their beingness into the land. The land, he says, "bears their name," and so he defines the land as a Bordelon, too. In this way, he ties "land" to "self," demonstrating as Sexton notes, that the two correlate to each other. If part of making a person a slave is natal alienation, as Orlando Patterson argues, then Ernest Bordelon (the father leaving this land behind) is using the land here to create a family history through both place and name.[48] His words imbue the land with the power to "do a little better" with each generation, to achieve the American dream Nova references in the opening of season 4. His words underscore the importance of that place above all others, since he suggests that they can buy other property, but none will be "theirs" as this cane farm is. In doing so he rejects the notion of Black placelessness and creates the context for place, and hence selfhood, that property ownership—over generations—implies. The Bordelon family farm can be read as representing a "paradoxical space," where ideologically the sugar cane farm/Bordelon land "would be mutually exclusive if charted on a two-dimensional map . . . but are occupied simultaneously."[49] Notions of "doing a little better" in each generation are bound up with a complicated sense of self that is implicated in place, such that *who* the Bordelons are, and *where* they are, co-constitute each other in paradoxical ways that simultaneously undermine and support the project of Black freedom.

Queen Sugar at once encourages its viewers to laud Black success and demonstrates both its limits and its failures. I want to look closely at two narrative arcs that intervene in the racial progress narrative of the Bordelon family. The first is the scandal that Charley's husband, Davis West, an NBA player, is involved with in season 1. The second is when undocumented workers on the family farm die in a hurricane because they've been urged to work past the point of safety by Charley and Ralph Angel. In the first example, Charley's husband was present when his teammates sexually assaulted a woman named Melina. Charley, a wealthy businesswoman who sees every problem as one that can be solved through a combination of manipulation, diplomacy, and lawyers, dealt with the problem by offering Melina a huge settlement, thinking that her husband was innocent of rape. But at the meeting, Melina reveals (through a secretly recorded phone conversation) that Davis was a callous philanderer who paid her for sex and saw her as available to his teammates because she was a sex worker, hence denying her rape. When Charley runs out of the mediation room, she says to Davis, "You're a monster. And now you've made me a monster too."[50] Charley's first reaction to the scandal—which was to protect Davis, herself, and Micah, their son—reveals that initially her reputation and wealth are more important than retribution for a victim of sexual assault. Though she ultimately regrets the way she protected Davis (and leaves him as a result), *Queen Sugar* suggests that Charley is corruptible because of her thirst for success and status.

This same drive for success as the site of her corruptibility is also why, despite an approaching hurricane, Charley asks the undocumented workers on the sugar cane farm to work past the point of safety. If the hurricane hits and the cane hasn't been cut, the Bordelons stand to lose a lot of money. Later, when Charley and Ralph Angel inspect the farm for flooding and hurricane damage, they come across the dead bodies of two of the workers who had been robbed and shot during the hurricane. Charley realizes she doesn't even know their names, and she must reckon painfully with the role her decisions played in their deaths. Both these incidents reveal the underbelly of material success, and in both cases ugly compromises were made that destroyed people's lives, literally and figuratively. In both instances Charley—and, to a lesser extent, Ralph Angel in the second—occupies a position of financial and social power relative to the people she's dealing with, and in both cases, she uses her privilege in precisely the same way any member of the Landry family would. *Queen Sugar* invites us to consider closely what wealth means and at what personal cost it is procured. We are all the keener to interrogate Charley's actions because we are inclined to assume that as a Black woman, she would make commitments on the side of social justice. But for Charley, who thinks far less about society and injustice than Nova does, her wealth and status define her outlook more than political or social considerations. Her story, over four seasons, seems to suggest that part of her growth as a character is to develop a more "people-centered" approach to life. Through her character and Nova's, the show asks us to consider what victory there is in winning the game of wealth and material acquisition in Western society for Black people. Fred Moten and Stefano Harney articulate this well when they write, "The settler, having settled for politics, arms himself in the name of civilization while critique initiates the self-defense of those of us who see hostility in the civil union of settlement and enclosure. We say, rightly, if our critical eyes are sharp enough, that it's evil and uncool to have a place in the sun in the dirty thinness of this atmosphere."[51] There is a double meaning of "settler" in the quote above; it speaks at once to settlers who settle down in a place and to the "settling" for wealth acquisition as freedom, which is really the failure of emancipatory Horatio Alger narratives to mitigate anti-Blackness. If the anti-Blackness of Western civil society is central to the way it works, then internalizing its norms and succeeding at its game doesn't signal freedom for the Black person, but defeat.

The Self Is a Social Construction

What white people have to do is to try and find out in their own hearts why it was necessary to have a nigger in the first place. Because I am a not a nigger; I'm a man. But if you think I'm a nigger, it means you need it.
—James Baldwin

> Illusions are experiences in the mind, but they are not out there in nature. Rather, they are events generated by the brain. Most of us have an experience of a self. I certainly have one, and I do not doubt that others do as well—an autonomous individual with a coherent identity and sense of free will. But that experience is an illusion—it does not exist independently of the person having the experience, and it is certainly not what it seems.
> —Bruce Hood

In *Notes on the State of Virginia* (1787), Thomas Jefferson advocated for the perpetual and heritable state of slavery as a way of controlling Black people, whom he saw as irredeemably inferior to whites. In his list of the many shortcomings of Black people, Jefferson claims that Black men prefer white women as "orangutans prefer black women over those of their own species,"[52] thereby in a double stroke—by metaphor and by suggesting that Black women have sex with monkeys—aligning Black people with primates. The purpose of this long meditation on supposed Black inferiority was a defense of eternal slavery; but in arguing for slavery, Jefferson does so on ontological ground. Jefferson's comparisons between orangutans and Black people persist in racist ideology today, since the most fundamental basis for racism is the notion that people of different phenotypes represent different types of "beings." This was evident when Meghan Markle, a mixed-race Black American, and Prince Harry of England gave birth to their child in spring 2019, and the BBC radio host Danny Baker tweeted a photo of a couple and a monkey with the caption "Royal Baby Leaves Hospital." One of the most ridiculous beliefs of white supremacists is that Black people are a kind of monkey or some form of simian species, and Baker's tweet revealed the dangerous asininity of this belief.

Underlying this elision between primates and Black people is a questioning of Black ontology that reveals that in the context of Western society, Black people have never gained access to the category of the human, which always already inheres to whiteness. Writing about this problem of Black ontology, Calvin Warren asks, "Is the black, in fact, a human being?" He goes on to explain that "black ~~being~~ incarnates metaphysical nothing . . . in an antiblack world."[53] Warren repurposes the term "the Negro question" to get at the ways in which Blackness and ontology collide to reveal the management of a terror around being that characterizes Western discourses of the self. The function of these comparisons of Black people to primates is to socially construct the distance of a human/nonhuman binary upon phenotypically diverse bodies that otherwise (without being constructed as such) doesn't exist. Warren goes on to argue, "The Negro is not a human, since ~~being~~ [is] not an issue for it, and instead becomes 'available equipment,' as Heidegger would call it, for the purpose of supporting the existential journey of the human being."[54] This existential journey of the human being (read: white person) is actually the foundation of the ontological crisis posed by "the Negro question," since the deepest terror of the racist person is that they may, indeed, be the same as a Black ~~being~~. And the Black ~~being~~ that they have imagined into existence, the "nigger," to use Baldwin's phrasing, is the literal containment of everything they fear about existence itself.

The impulse of Western (presumably) antiracist movements, going all the way back to the slave narrative, was to prove that Black people were *not* monkeys. It was thought that this could be proven (primarily) in two ways: first, through mastery of reading and writing, and second, through conversion to Christianity. Therefore, in almost all slave narratives, there is an emphasis on learning to read and also upon coming to knowledge of Christ. The assumption was that no animal could do these things, so if Black people could, then they must be human. But staging Black ontology as "the Negro Problem" or "the Negro Question" as a way of grappling with a difficult bundle of pathological antisocial issues assumes that the problem is Blackness, when in fact, the problem is—and has always been in the context of America—whiteness. James Baldwin gets directly to this idea in the quote above.[55] The real question is not what should be done for or about Black people; the real question is what sort of ontology produces the systems we live with, and have lived with, today? What "self" produced the modern world? What "being" is responsible for the civilization we live in now? In other words, why would anyone want to achieve the ontological status of Thomas Jefferson? Not only was he a slaveholder, he was a rapist.[56] If ideas of the "human" that we've inherited from the Enlightenment, which was when "racial essentialism and scientific notions of superiority and inferiority of the world's people first became clearly associated," produced the results of Western civilization we live with now, I'm left to wonder: who wants to be human anyway?[57] Speaking about human behavior in the twentieth century, the Zen teacher Eckhart Tolle asserts, "Humans are a dangerously insane and sick species. That's not a judgment; it's a fact."[58] The basis of his assertion is that human beings killed "in excess of one hundred million fellow humans in the twentieth century alone."[59] If whiteness is the index of the human, as humanity (as whiteness) is constitutive of genocide, chattel slavery, Jim Crow, and imperialism, is the category of "the human" as a "self" really an attainment worth striving for?

The existential journey of the white person, both in the macrohistorical sense and in the micro-individual sense, is the foundation of Western philosophy. An important (if not the most important) question this journey attempts to answer is "What or who am I?" Historically, questions of identity have been handled via essentialism, wherein your recognized race, gender, and class explained everything about who you were, what you were capable of, and what your place in society should be. Obviously, this way of thinking about categories of being was problematic, as it gave birth to all the "isms" we now find ourselves mired in. Poststructuralism managed to undo the notion of "essence," which in itself questions the fundamental Cartesian assertion that thinking is the ground of being. In trying to understand "being" or the self, poststructuralism has suggested that the category of "I" is far more playful, speculative, and performative than early philosophers supposed. Foucault interrogates the notion of the self in his lecture "The Culture of the Self," in which he deconstructs the self by asking, "What are we in actuality?"[60] Alan Watts, the Zen philosopher, asks a question about being, a question that begins to untangle the delusion of Western ontology: "I wonder what you mean when you use the word 'I'?"[61] Watts, rather than ask who am "I," asks instead, "What do you mean by 'I'?" The I (or the self) is a social construction that aligns (or tries to) with power. I = 1, I = Aye, and I = 👁. All of these, in number, word, and sense, speak to a sort of primacy, a kind of supreme agency, the affirmative center of being. The project of the self, then, is about power, and because it is about power, it is inevitably involved in the oppression of those who are not "I," the other(s). I have long maintained that the next stop on the philosophical "train" after poststructuralism is Zen, where not only is the "self" not essential but the "self" ceases to exist as a useful category of knowledge and being altogether.

In his talk "Not What Should Be but What Is," Watts goes on to deconstruct the "I" entirely: "I've come to the conclusion that what most civilized people mean by the word is a hallucination that is at complete variance with the facts of nature."[62] This hallucination, or social construction, of the "human" requires for its existential journey a mechanism whereby it can do something about "the nothing that terrorizes us, that destabilizes our metaphysical structure and ground of existence."[63] In the West, that mechanism has been the negation of Black humanity. Warren further explains that "black ~~being~~ helps the human being re-member its relation to Being through its lack of relationality.... Black ~~being~~, then, is precisely the metaphysical entity that must remain for the postmetaphysical enterprise of freedom to occur for human beingness."[64] What this means is that the entire ground of being in a Western context is a hallucination that depends, for its existential journey toward humanness, upon Blackness to occupy the space of the nonhuman, of "nothingness." But the Negro question raises another: is it possible to engage discourses of the self, of the "I," or of the "human" at all without also activating anti-Blackness? And, to wit, what structures require a "self," and why? What I'm getting at here is a parallel with what I argued about land in the first part of this chapter: can Black liberation be achieved through the attainment of humanity, if the ground of "humanity" as it has been defined in the modern world requires "an other" to come into existence?

Problems that arise at the site of the (human) self when it collides with Blackness do not reveal the insufficiency of Blackness (the people who are named such), but rather illuminate the ways in which the categories of Western being are in conflict with "the facts of nature," to use Watts's term. In her essay "The Pedagogy of Buddhism," Eve Sedgwick notes that Buddhist practice is a "mysteriously powerful solvent of individual identity."[65] Buddhist practice and philosophy complete the arc of poststructuralist interrogations of the "essential self" and provide a useful means by which we can reveal that entity of the "self" to be little more than an illusion produced out of a certain cognitive function. Bruce Hood, author of the book *The Self Illusion: How the Social Brain Creates Identity* (2012), explains to Sam Harris that the thing we think of as our "self" actually doesn't exist:

> For most of us, the sense of our self is as an integrated individual inhabiting a body. I think it is helpful to distinguish between the two ways of thinking about the self that William James talked about. There is conscious awareness of the present moment that he called the "I," but there is also a self that reflects upon who we are in terms of our history, our current activities and our future plans. James called this aspect of the self, "me" which most of us would recognize as our personal identity—who we think we are. However, I think that both the "I" and the "me" are actually ever-changing narratives generated by our brain to provide a coherent framework to organize the output of all the factors that contribute to our thoughts and behaviors.... In other words, the brain is hallucinating the experience. There are now many studies revealing that illusions generate brain activity as if they existed. They are not real but the brain treats them as if they were.[66]

Hood's insights into the illusory nature of "the (human) self" echo those of ancient Buddhist texts, which reveal that Siddhartha Gautama's discovery was that the sense of individual identity is a delusion. It is a powerfully dangerous delusion, since the notion of separation, of a fundamental split between "I" and "others," and specifically for my consideration here, from nature, is the foundation of every "ism" that plagues our lives and has for centuries. Zen and the Afro-pessimist theorizations I cite here propose the concept of oneness, even as evoking it engenders critical risk. Writing about oneness, Kevin Quashie notes, "The concept of oneness is often used to characterize human essence, the energy of the inner life that constitutes a person's being. This idea is distinct from notions of the individual, which is a modern classification based on the ideal of liberal humanism."[67] Quashie goes on to acknowledge the risk of talking about oneness. Oneness, I argue, as a state can never satisfy the egotism of empiricism, so it is always easily dismissed as a New Age fantasy, a dismissal that fails to acknowledge the insubstantiality of the category of the "individual," which also cannot be produced as anything more than a phantom. Quashie argues, "Oneness, then, constitutes a sense of being capable of and related to everything."[68] These investigations into the illusory nature of the self return us to Sexton's provocative suggestion: selfless inhabitation. No(where) for no(body). If land ownership and/or land sovereignty is a social construction that unleashes a scourge of murder into human society, and "the self" is the corollary to that social construction of ownership, how much more violence, then, results from notions of "who I am" and "who you are" as separate and distinct entities? The existential journey to selfhood always requires "an other" and so always involves violence; hence, Black journeys into the Western hinterland of self-making always involve self-violence.

(Rosalee)(12")/(Rosalee) (34") > (Nymphadora) (42")/(Nymphadora)(36")

Strange things happen when you combine epistemes of human superiority over the natural world with Blackness. How would we read Jane Goodall if she were a Black woman? Would we still see her as the brave and brilliant environmental scientist, fighting on behalf of the earth and its animals —or would we be unable to ignore the history of comparison between her Black self and the primates she was so interested in? Another question we can ask ourselves is: What happens when Black people (or characters, in this case) do a white thing? In Kaitlyn Greenidge's novel *We Love You, Charlie Freeman*, the "white thing" is a project at a scientific think tank called the Toneybee Institute, founded for the purpose of teaching chimpanzees how to talk. Set in the 1990s, the novel concerns the Freemans, a Black family fluent in sign language, though none of them are deaf. As a child, the mother of the family, Laurel Freeman, learns sign language from some children at a school for the deaf near her home. Captivated by the language, she makes it her career and eventually teaches the entire family to sign. As a result of this unique fluency, they are invited to the Toneybee Institute to take into their family a chimpanzee named Charlie, to see if they can teach him how to talk using sign language.

The family consists of two other Charlies, Charlotte, the oldest daughter, nicknamed Charlie, and the father Charlie, so that narratively the chimpanzee's name makes a triplet of the moniker in the family—a troubling parallelism that signifies on the racist history of comparing Black people to primates. The youngest child in the family, Callie, is most affected by the shifting dynamics of her family after they move into the institute. The book is told chapter by chapter from multiple character points of view, with one of the storylines being about a woman named Nymphadora,[69] who, some years before the current events are taking place, became a subject of interest to a scientist, Dr. Gardner, at the Toneybee; he sketched her—both clothed and totally naked—as part of his "studies." Nymphadora is a "secret name" of a Black woman named Ellen, who belongs to an exclusive group called the Stars of the Morning, where secret names are chosen by randomly picking a page of the Bible. An unmarried and lonely middle-aged teacher, Nymphadora falls in love with Dr. Gardner and fails to accept that his interest in her—as a Black woman—is tied to his interest in primates, an uncomfortable comparison that drives her to free one of the chimpanzees, Rosalee, when she discovers her. The narrative reaches a kind of climax when it is discovered that Laurel has been breastfeeding the chimpanzee Charlie in order to bond with him. This ruins the marriage and the family, and ultimately ends the Toneybee experiment for the Freemans. Laurel remains at the institute but is never again allowed to be alone with the chimpanzees.

Nature in this text is represented by Charlie the chimpanzee, who—like all the other primates held captive at the Toneybee—exists in an unhappy limbo between the human and the animal worlds. Charlie, alienated from a free and natural chimpanzee life by human experimentation, is perpetually depressed. It is also unclear why Laurel fails to realize the absurdity of the experiment. She seems obsessed with doing what "no one has ever done before," as if somehow proving a white premise will redeem her. Like the white people who hire her, she blurs the line between Blackness and the monkey; in her baffling ambition to get Charlie to behave like a human, she emotionally destroys her husband and her children in the process. Laurel's treatment of Charlie, as an actual member of the family, a baby that she feeds at her own breast, is simply an extension of the institute's founding premise that nonhuman animals are capable of doing human things. And though breastfeeding animals is not unheard of in some indigenous cultures, the purpose of such breastfeeding seems related to domesticating the animal rather than testing the limits between human and nonhuman.[70] But is it even possible for us to read those words without conjuring up ideas of primitive others? And, if a white person does what Laurel did (such as when Tori Amos features a picture of herself breastfeeding a pig in the liner notes for *Boys for Pele*), do we feel the same way about the collapsing of the distinction between human and animal? Thus, the posthumanist impulse at the site of Blackness always and only reinscribes the problematic ontology of Blackness as social death.

But if white self-making happens through a process of objectification, whereby a line is drawn with Black people and chimpanzees on the opposite side of human, then from the position of Blackness, there is no other representational possibility vis-à-vis Charlie and the mother except the collapse of distinction between the two. Racist narratives about Black being make the boundary between the Freeman family and Charlie extremely fragile—not from within their own experience—but from without, by the other (white) people working at the Toneybee. The mother seems interested in a project of self-making that follows a (white) Western trajectory but fails to recognize the ways in which her Blackness vis-à-vis Charlie "unmakes" her, rather than confers subjectivity. Hence, Greenidge's novel questions the very basis of subjectivity itself, of Western self-making as we know it. It does so by showing the fraught nature of Western modes of self-making at the site of Blackness. The goal of teaching chimpanzees how to talk is problematic for several reasons, all of which are tied to white conceptions of self. Indeed, the entire project arises out of Julia Toneybee-Leroy's guilt about having killed a chimpanzee on safari in Central Africa decades earlier. She believes that the chimpanzee she killed spoke to her before it died, so she dedicated her life to proving that chimpanzees can, indeed, talk. In other words, her project is tied to her own problematic white guilt. It's not clear how, though, actually getting a chimpanzee to talk will absolve her guilt. In fact, the institute's *failure* to get a chimpanzee to talk has a greater chance of assuaging her guilt, because as long as none of them speak, it means she doesn't have to consider the possibility that she killed a creature who "deserved" to live. Furthermore, her mission suggests that being able to talk would mean something about the value of the chimpanzee—a standard not unlike that imposed around literacy for those who were enslaved. For the Black person, such a project can only result in disaster, as it does both for the Freeman family and for Nymphadora. But this isn't to say that Greenidge's book invites us to be outraged because Black people are humans and chimpanzees are lowly animals. Greenidge's book instead suggests that though chimpanzees and (Black) humans are clearly not the same species, Western bondage confers a mutuality that characterizes their situations vis-à-vis white society.

This recognition of that mutuality dawns on Nymphadora when she finds Dr. Gardner's notes and drawings of herself and of the chimpanzee Rosalee. She observes, "She was posed the way I had been, our first time together: on her knees, pressed down on her elbows. Of course, he could not have gotten her to actually pose this way. This could not have been from life: no wild animal would consent to that. Only dumb, lovesick human beings would consent to that."[71] Nymphadora's comments do two things here. First, they show her finally admitting what we readers suspect all along: that Dr. Gardner's drawing sessions with her are about a comparison with the chimpanzees, despite his protestations otherwise. After all, he isn't also drawing any white ladies for the fun of it. But Nymphadora's internal dialogue also shows the difference between her and Rosalee, because she notes that Gardner never could have gotten an animal to pose the way she did, which emphasizes her humanity in distinction to Rosalee's animality—a difference Gardner failed to grasp.

The second and most baffling revelation Nymphadora has is that Gardner not only animalized her but actually admires Rosalee more than he does her:

> On a few, a name appeared. *Rosalee*. It must be hers, I thought. And this was the greatest insult. He only ever sketched my body in those drawings. Never my face. But the chimp was drawn precisely, her every mood lovingly captured, the wrinkle of a pensive brow, the scurrilous raise of an eyebrow, the pensive suck of a lower lip, the large brown eyes soft and inviting. He drew her like he loved her, like he loved her face, and I realized I had been wrong to be jealous of Julia Toneybee-Leroy.[72]

So while Nymphadora was mistaking Gardner's sketching of her as interest in her, she failed to see that for Gardner, the chimpanzee Rosalee would always be a preferable object precisely because there was no question about her status vis-à-vis humans; as a wholly captive creature, she had little power to act against her captors at the Toneybee. Nymphadora, on the other hand, becomes the subject of Gardner's sketching because she stops him from observing Black children at the playground and sketching them. He essentially refuses, at her request (and she is representing the whole community of her town Spring City when she approaches him), to stop sketching the Black children and agrees to do so only if she sits for him instead.

Their sessions start off with her fully clothed and sitting in a chair but eventually proceed to nudity and poses that expose her in blatant ways. Dr. Gardner is able to convince Nymphadora that he is not a racist and is an anthropologist who "loves" Black people and admires the work of W. E. B. Du Bois. Dr. Gardner's lack of malicious intent—for he does seem sincere in his claim that he isn't trying to harm anyone—demonstrates that even in the absence of willful racism, the Black person's status as "nothing," as noted by Warren, always returns to the "structural position" of the nonhuman. Furthermore, Nymphadora's status in Gardner's mind is summed up by an equation she finds in his notes: "(Rosalee) (12")/(Rosalee) (34") > (Nymphadora) (42")/(Nymphadora) (36")."[73] We learn only that these are "measurements"; what they are measuring is never revealed. The "greater than" sign that indicates that Gardner sees Rosalee as literally "more than" Nymphadora reveals not only that she is "like" a monkey but that the monkey has more value in Gardner's taxonomy than she does.

Realizing this structural mutuality between herself and Rosalee, Nymphadora decides to free Rosalee. She sneaks into the Toneybee Institute and finds Rosalee's cage:

> We studied each other for a good while. I had not held eye contact with any being, human or otherwise, for a long time and I found myself, again and again, following the curve of her perfectly made eyes, large and amber, and the very elegant slope of her brow. I thought, with a flash of bitterness and insane panic, Of course he prefers her. All the while, Rosalee gazed steadily back at me, probably taking in my goggled eyes and dead tooth with a curiosity that in a human would be called sympathetic. Then she leaned forward and took a long, theatrical sniff. I help my fingers up the bars so she could know me better. To my surprise, she grasped my two longest fingers in her hand, brought them close to her mouth and pressed them to her lips.[74]

In this scene, Greenidge powerfully limns the boundary between animal and human in a way that emphasizes their difference ("a curiosity in a human that would be called sympathetic") and also connects the woman and the chimpanzee through the bars of visible and invisible cages. Rosalee's cage is physical and literal, while Nymphadora's is symbolic and ideological. And though they are different species, they are mutually constrained by the existential journey of white self-making. The moment when Nymphadora frees Rosalee from the cage is one of profound intimacy, as the two run from the site of their bondage together: "I drew my hand away very slowly and then I reached up and unlatched her cage. I waited a few seconds more. So did she. Then I reached into the cage and held out my arms and she crawled right into them, she did not even hesitate, and I embraced her."[75] Rosalee does not protest when Nymphadora opens her cage and holds out her arms. Rosalee climbs willingly into Nymphadora's arms, and they silently leave the Toneybee Institute together. Rosalee and Nymphadora's actions mirror one another in a way that aligns them against the oppression represented by Gardner and the institute, and by extension the ideology that holds both Black people and animals captive. Given the violence that attaches to the depiction of Black people as monkeys, Greenidge takes a narrative risk by bringing Nymphadora closer to Rosalee, and by bringing the Freeman family to the institute. It seems counterintuitive to align Nymphadora with Rosalee, given the stakes around "proving" Black humanity, but Greenidge's novel demonstrates the need to "disinvest our axiological commitments from humanism and invest *elsewhere.*"[76] If my introductory claim—about the way that the othering of nature precedes anti-Blackness—holds up, then we can conclude that moving away from nature (in an attempt to embrace the Western self/human) will not interrupt the momentum of racism. So were Nymphadora to recoil in horror from Rosalee at the shock of Gardner's comparison, she would repeat the mistake of Western ontology—the same mistake from which her subordinate status proceeds. Instead, Greenidge manages to reveal Nymphadora's humanity (in contradistinction to Rosalee's animality) and align Nymphadora's liberatory impulses *with* Rosalee rather than *against* her. By turning away from Gardner and toward Rosalee, Nymphadora (who, after leaving Rosalee in the woods, departs Spring City for good) "disinvests from the axiological commitment" of the human and seeks, both literally and figuratively, an "elsewhere."

Callie's story echoes Nymphadora's. At the end of the novel, we learn that Callie is estranged from her family and lives in social isolation. In the final pages of the book, Callie informs Charlie (her sister) and Laurel that she is taking a job at an ape sanctuary in Kinshasa, Congo. While Charlie, who is repulsed by her mother, the Toneybee Institute, and animals in general, sees her family's time at the Toneybee through the lens of the sordid, Callie still loves Charlie (the chimpanzee) and her mother. Sister Charlie is invested in the "axiological commitments" of humanism, while Callie is not. Like Nymphadora, Callie recognizes not a contiguity between herself and primates, but rather a mutual status of degradation, confinement, abuse, and precarity. The final words of the book are about Callie, though told through Charlie's narration:

> I watch her from across the table. I know, a few months from now, she will stand at the side of some unknown heat-broken highway. She will stand at the brink of a great wide forest. It will be night. She will hear through the brush that familiar, piercing cry, but it won't be frightening. She'll recognize it as the sound of home. Callie will not hesitate. She will step off the broken road into the brush and she will walk straight into the cool of the trees and she won't ever come back. I see all this, sitting across from her in the diner, my forearms sticking to the stray maple syrup tacked across the tabletop. I lift my right hand.
> *Good-bye.*
> Callie smiles back.
> *Good-bye.*[77]

Callie leaves her human family behind and, in Charlie's telling, also human society itself. Stepping off the broken road into the woods, never to return, Callie illustrates the divestment from the human, and from Western civilization, that selflessness—no(where) for no(one)—requires. When Charlie says that "she'll recognize it as the sound of home," about the animal sounds coming from within the forest, she gestures toward Callie's transcendence of the limited (human) self that is so concerned with establishing its own superiority that it takes animals from the jungle to be studied in cold, New England climates where they lead miserable lives in scientific prisons. Instead of taking animals from their homes, Callie returns to our real home—the wilderness itself, paradoxically into homelessness—and in so doing, symbolically liberates both herself and the animals she now knows how to live with in harmony. She does this by giving up the ideas and lifestyle of the human as a situation to attain and moves away from the human toward the natural world. Choosing flora and fauna for her environment, Callie enters a space where the notion of the human (or the striving to be such) collapses in the absence of civilization due to the presence of a broader, interdependent ecological field. She becomes no(one) in an untamed wilderness, where the bondage of material acquisition and land ownership (no[where]) falls away. In short, Callie becomes free.

P(ost)S(cript): Homelessness

In Zen the phrase "a life of homelessness" is synonymous with a practitioner's decision to devote oneself to spiritual attainment by becoming a nun/monk. Homelessness in Zen, then, is also tied to "selflessness." As one lets go of the material striving that characterizes human society, so too does one give up being a human altogether. In the book *Zen Teachings of Homeless Kodo* (2014), Kosho Uchiyama Roshi explains that the Zen concept of homelessness is not about "nowhere to live" as much as it is a recognition that there is no place we can call our own. He says, "People call me Homeless Kodo, but I don't think they particularly intend to disparage me. They say 'homeless' probably because I never had a temple or owned a house. Anyway, all human beings without exception are in reality homeless. It's a mistake to think we have a solid home."[78] In a society where the ultimate "dream" (and index of success) is to own a home (the more spectacular the better), Roshi's words seem counterintuitive and perhaps dangerous. But what Roshi is saying here is that "home," "land," and "ownership" are all social constructions that obscure the actual reality of existence, which is that nothing can be owned. It can only be *imagined* as owned; there is no such thing as ownership the way there is such a thing as poop. There is no "is-ness" to ownership, and so we are all, in reality and without exception, always already homeless. And though we've been conditioned to fear homelessness as a worst-case scenario, in Zen it is the path of true liberation.

This homelessness is also tied to selflessness, as the goal of Zen is the extinguishing of the "self." As we release our attachment to things we once constructed as "mine," so too do we start to lose our grip on that construct called "me." To go into a life of homelessness and selflessness is "to sit immovably in the place where being superior or inferior to others doesn't matter."[79] The liberation of Zen is akin to the abolition Sexton talks about, an abolition that Sexton says "the flesh of the earth" demands of us. Zen also points not toward the human but away from it. "It disinvests from humanism," to reference Warren, because "to practice Zazen is to stop being an ordinary human being."[80] One is no longer an ordinary human being because it means "ceasing to be a person always gauging gain and loss."[81] A life of selfless inhabitation facilitates the shift from a gain/loss regime (what can be lost, and who is there to lose it?) into a "spiritual practice with entirely different aims."[82]

In my experience, the seemingly difficult task of losing one's land-imaginary (ownership) and self-imaginary (the category of human) is much easier to do in nature. Reading the last lines of Greenidge's novel, with the image of Callie stepping into a thick, lush forest—I know the feeling of freedom being referenced there. It's the same way I feel when I load a forty-pound pack with essentials and disappear into the wilds for a week, far beyond the reach of satellite signals, cars, police, and pop culture. After a few days with only the things you absolutely need in the wilderness, your thinking starts to shift. The mind becomes quieter. You learn to listen, smell, and see differently. Without all of our machines, humans in the wild must respect the territories and habitats of snakes and bears and coyotes. As the Dalai Lama is said to have once pointed out, nothing will reveal your ultimate powerlessness in the face of the totality of nature like a mosquito.[83] You must be mindful of where you step, where you place your hand, where you dispose of your bodily waste. When there is no store a short walk or drive away, you don't waste food. When you have to filter all your water and walk half a mile to get it from the creek, you don't squander it. Nature confers conservation and care without the need of intent, or a human self to "decide" to be wise about resources. The value of everything is apparent just by being alone in the woods, without machines. I rarely bring books to read or things to write with when I go into the wild, and when I come back to civilization, it takes a moment for me to recognize words and a few more to be able read them. Deep immersion in nature shifts our cognition, such that "'in the absence of any written analogue to speech, the sensible, natural environment remains the primary visual counterpart of the spoken utterance. . . . The land, in other words, is the sensible site or matrix where meaning occurs and proliferates.'"[84] While written language is linear—and is hence a reduction of experience to symbols—land is a matrix that moves us dimensionally from a 2-D experience of reading and writing to the 4-D experience of being. Language is the menu, while nature is the actual meal. It is difficult to be nourished in a symbolic world, especially when those symbols are imbricated with suffering and oppression. After a few hours back in civilization, slowly my mind switches back over to the highly ephemeral and symbolic nature of human society, and I feel the profound emptiness of civil society, where "success" is material acquisition and fulfillment is reduced to things you can buy online or at the mall.

John Zerzan, in "Finding Our Way Back Home" (2008), considers the problem I lay out above—between the freedom of the natural world and the constraint of civilization—when he writes,

> Where do we look for rescue? Our predicament points us toward a solution. The crisis of modernity is, in a very basic sense, a failure of vision in which our disembodied life-world has lost its "place" in existence. We no longer see ourselves within the webs and cycles of nature. The loss of a direct relationship to the world terminates a once universal human understanding of our oneness with the natural world. The principle of relatedness is at the heart of indigenous wisdom: traditional intimacy with the world as the immanent basis of spirituality. This understanding is an essential and irreparable foundation of human health and meaningfulness.[85]

We lose our "direct relationship to the world" and our "oneness" at the precise moment Rousseau describes, when we construct "me" so that any particular piece of land (or any object) can be "mine." To go into the woods, as Callie does, is to refuse the human and property grounds of civil society and to embrace freedom, which is a release of both the self and property.

In a piece for BlackLandProject.org, a website and an ongoing grassroots organization that collects stories about Black people and their relationship to land and place, a writer named Aquimin articulates a relationship to the land that rejects the regime of property, instead emphasizing an interbeing that I've argued earlier characterizes many Black nature texts. He writes,

> As a child I had a very intimate relationship with the creek and woods in the valley, one that despite my young age, I now understand was ancient in its nature. A few new people moved into the area, drawn by its beauty, and in the tradition of the suburban dream, trampled all over that beauty with gaudy uncreative architecture, hideous grass lawns, and infernal lampposts that stay lit around the clock, alienating the nocturnal creatures they claim to love and marring the night sky. Regardless of my observations of their intrusion, I was dedicated to maintaining my relationship with the creek much like I had been, visiting her, cheering her up, bringing her gifts, telling her my stories and listening to hers.[86]

An "ancient" exchange is described above, where nature ceases to be a "thing" and instead is revealed to be alive and inextricably connected to human experience.

Aquimin laments the encroachment of civilization and goes on to recount how eventually someone yelled at him to "get off my property." Outside of a regime of property, when one is existing in a selfless inhabitation, such a statement (to get off one's property) makes no sense at all: "It seemed the most preposterous thing to me, that someone could claim ownership or dominion over nature like that, that someone would WANT to, disregarding nature's role in our life as a guide and protector, an elder. Do you own your friends too? Your parent? Your dog? Do you own that rock over there? How about this cloud?"[87] I can relate to this sense of nature as a space of freedom, as an unownable totality in which I am simply enmeshed and not the master of. When I am in the wilderness, it feels like home even though when I am there I am technically homeless (without a home, without property to call my own). I experience a deep feeling of "rightness" being in a forest that is absent for me in civil society. When I am here, with my laptop and all the killing clutter (for the earth suffers horribly so we can have all these endless goods), I feel away from my true home, disconnected from life—a cell caught within a cancerous web of consumption, hoping that practices of self-care can somehow ameliorate the parasitical energy of civilization, which hates my Blackness, my womanness, and my queerness.[88]

We see all around evidence of impending doom and collapse because civilization is not sustainable, nor has it ever been. Writing about the end of the regime of property, Raoul Vaneigem notes, "The end of the reign of the economy is not the end of the world—merely the end of the economy's totalitarian hold over the world."[89] We fear the fall of civilization; we catastrophize about apocalypse and imagine that we will perish painfully. But what if the fall of civilization is the rise of equity; what if the disruption of apocalypse is actually natural justice; what if abolition is not the end of us, but the beginning of us?

CHAPTER FOUR

Plant Life (Notes on the End of the World)

I do believe that there is a way out. But I believe that the way out is a kind of violence so magnificent and comprehensive that it scares the hell out of even most radical revolutionaries. So, in other words, the trajectory of violence that Black slave revolts suggest, whether it be in the 21st or the 19th century, is a violence against the generic categories of life, agency being one of them. Marx posits an epistemological crisis, which is to say moving from one system of human arrangements and relations to another system of relations and human arrangements. What Black people embody is the potential for a catastrophe of human arrangements writ large.... And as Saidiya Hartman says, "A Black revolution makes everyone freer than they want to be." A Marxist revolution blows the lid off of economic relations; a feminist revolution blows the lid off of patriarchal relations; a Black revolution blows the lid off the unconscious and relations writ large.
—Frank B. Wilderson III

It's the end of the world as we know it and I feel fine.
—REM

I begin with a question: What does the end of the world look like?

I'm inside an MRI machine at Yale. I've been invited to participate in a test of advanced meditators. I'll meditate in the machine, and they will take pictures of my brain. They think this might tell them something about what meditation does to the brain. Earlier, they showed me fast-moving pictures to measure my response, to see how reactive I am to all sorts of scenes—from the horrific to the joyful. A few hours after my MRI is complete, the director of the study tells me that they found something on my scan and that I need to speak to the oncologist on staff. The oncologist explains that I have a brain tumor, probably benign, but that as soon as I return home to Ohio I need to have it evaluated. I take in this news calmly, oddly not entirely surprised, and the director of the study remarks that if anything can attest to the power of meditation to help us respond calmly to bad news, it is me talking to that oncologist in 2011. This is the moment that meditation has been preparing me for all these years. At the Vipassana retreat, the word "anicca" is intoned again and again as we sit in meditation. It means "impermanence." Confronted with my own impermanence, I found myself repeatedly contemplating what it would mean to be dirt: "ashes to ashes, dust to dust." My primary concern was for my daughter, who was only five years old at the time—the same age I was when my father died. No amount of concern for my daughter would make my tumor go away, so I did what I could and sat in stillness with my diagnosis, waiting to find out more. I was compelled to ponder: was this the end of the world for me? Or is the world characterized by a perpetual loop of endings and beginnings, since we will all live and all die?

My consideration of apocalypse here is bookended by my personal confrontation with death on the one end and also by a textual exploration of the "death" of Western civilization as we know it on the other. There are a few ways to answer my opening questioning, which I hope to do below in an analysis of two apocalyptic texts, Octavia Butler's *The Parable of the Sower* (1993) and the film *The Girl with All the Gifts* (2016), but first I want to think about how—presently and historically—the end of the world (the fall of civil society) has been represented and what ends such representation serves. The first feature-length film ever made, *The Birth of a Nation* (1915), was a huge hit that mediated fears about the possible dissolution of the American nation.[1] Heralded as a success by everyone in American society except the NAACP, D. W. Griffith saw it as a film based on the "realistic" history of how a previous "aggregation of jangling, discordant, antagonistic sections" finally became one country.[2] When charges of racism were laid against the film, Griffith argued that anyone who opposed the film had misunderstood "the great historical purpose of the picture, which is not an attack on any race or section of the country. It is a most powerful sermon against war, and in favor of brotherly love in all sections and nations."[3] The basic premise of Griffith's film was that in a post-slavery world, whites better unite across North-South divides if they were to protect themselves from Black people. The film represents emancipated Blacks as taking over Congress, turning it into a bacchanalian insult to order, and attempting to rape white women. The rise of the KKK at the end of the film is presented as a triumphant moment, when whiteness consolidates against the threat that is an emancipated Blackness. Griffith's film built upon earlier proslavery propaganda that argued for the continuation of slavery on the basis of Black savagery. In its representation of free Black people as rapacious brutes and buffoons, it discloses the possibility of the Black citizen and reveals how the self-making of the human relies upon an unconscious anti-Blackness to bring coherence and "unity" to the white citizen. Griffith's insistence that the film was not meant to be an affront to "any race or section" isn't an attempt to camouflage his political intentions. Rather, Griffith's unwittingly racist film uncovers the link between humanism and anti-Blackness. The effect of Griffith's film not only was mollifying for whites who desired to feel no longer at political and geographical odds but also united whites around an unconscious fear that Black people would unmake the nation. By presenting Black freedom as the white apocalypse, the film reinforced the social death of the formerly enslaved. So dead were they, in fact, that Griffith couldn't even figure out what they were objecting to; the critique of Black criminality could not land in Griffith's (or anyone else's outside of the Black community's and the interracial NAACP's) consciousness, because the Black human did not exist.

Griffith's film tapped into fear of an "uncontrollable" Black population and pandered to lurid white fantasies of rape, murder, and "takeover" that whites presumed would follow in the wake of emancipation. It collapsed the boundary between nation and race, making white unity the foundation for the advancement of American statist ideals. *The Birth of a Nation* gave voice to the relegation of Blackness to threat as a palliative response to white crisis. That crisis was the possible "end of the world," or the end of American civil society as it had existed theretofore, and Griffith's film not only inaugurated new and powerful filmic tools that bolstered its ability to persuade but also provided a kind of pedagogy of white unity that persists even today, largely for the purpose of maintaining the state. *The Birth of a Nation* was a cautionary tale about what happens when Blackness is freed from the prison of enslavement, and narratively it suggested to its white viewers the need to be wary of Blackness, which it effectively relegated to the unconscious realm of the subversive. Of course, the fears sensationalized in *The Birth of a Nation* turned out to be emotional phantoms rather than realities. The newly free people were concerned not with retribution against whites, but with education, jobs, political representation, and community building. Despite white fears, the actual Black community did not launch a full-scale guerrilla war against white people or their interests. No vigilante organization of similar kind to the KKK was founded in the Black community; instead, Black people founded colleges,[4] formed civic organizations (like the NAACP), and in some cases, founded Black towns.[5] In other words, Griffith's film mirrored not the political or social reality of 1915; instead, it mirrored the fears of white people, unleashing a series of regulatory structures designed to shape the behavior of citizens (who are always already understood to be white) in support of the state.

Fears about the dissolution of the state persist in American film and letters, and though contemporary films about apocalypse do not (always) represent the end of the world as a threat from literal Black people, we can map representations of the end of the world through the anti-Black unconscious. If popular culture is any indication of collective concerns, the end of the world ranks high as one of society's greatest fears. There is a vast catalogue of films and television shows that are about impending apocalypse or the end of the world (*Children of Men*, *2012*, *The Road*, *Final Impact*, *Independence Day*, *The Terminator*), and there are just as many movies that try to imagine human life after the end of the world as we know it (*Mad Max*, *I Am Legend*, *Waterworld*, *World War Z*). Surviving and living in a postcivilization world is a behemothic preoccupation of contemporary science fiction, and these narratives reveal an underlying sense of the precarity in our current society. Like Griffith's film, fears about the end of the world are projected almost always onto "humanish" and nonhuman others: zombies, aliens, superbugs, or nature (asteroids, tsunamis, earthquakes, etc.). So in almost all mainstream representations of the fall of the state, or the end of the world, the anti-Black unconscious returns to menace normal society. The effect of these films, like Griffith's, is disciplinary. Writing about the prevalence of apocalypse in American film, David Christopher notes, "All are concerned with horrific visions of a world in which patriarchal capitalism has either been annihilated or corrupted, and all . . . function as warnings or harbingers . . . of what must be changed and what must be protected for patriarchal capitalism to survive."[6] Thus, in order to theorize about what the end of the world might look like, we must first cut through the skein of images that have successfully inculcated in most of us such an intense fear of the fall of the state that we advocate for its continuation even in light of the bald facts of its foreordained brutalities.

But what does the end of the world really mean? Natural disasters? If this is the case, then the world is ending regularly—from the tsunami of 2004 that killed over 200,000 people in fourteen countries, to Hurricane Katrina, or flooding in Bangladesh that left over a million people homeless, to ravaging wild fires in California. The climate apocalypse is upon us. Does it mean war? If so, we've been in a perpetual apocalypse for (at least) the past two decades.[7] Does it mean disease? Because since 1980 the prevalence of infectious diseases has significantly increased on a global scale.[8] Is the end of the world a brain tumor? The only thing that forestalls recognition of the apocalyptic nature of our current situation is one's proximity to capital, which serves as a fiscal and social buffer to the effects of collapse. As Franklin Ginn, rephrasing a famous line from William Gibson, has said, "The apocalypse is already here; it's just not very evenly distributed."[9] Christopher elaborates on this idea when he writes that by presenting scenarios that are "ostensibly worse than our own," these films and texts work "to ideologically mask the fact that the horrific side-effects of capitalism . . . are representations of relations that already exist."[10] Christopher's emphasis on capitalism can be elaborated to more precisely uncover a broader unconscious that is characterized by anti-Blackness as I've shown. Failure to recognize that we are *already* living in apocalyptic conditions serves the state well, because such a presbyopic view enables the articulation of a catastrophizing about the collapse of the state that levies investment in it across every sector of society. Hence, apocalyptic narratives convince us, through horrific representations of violence in the absence of "patriarchal capitalism" and the state, that we need authoritarian structure to survive even when that same authority operates on a model that requires our social and literal death. In other words, every apocalyptic narrative is *The Birth of a Nation* redux, where the fall of society is the end of whiteness and the triumph of what the state defines as "otherness."

I do not mean to suggest that the state's continued dominance is by any means assured and that predictions about the collapse of civilization are completely misplaced. Considerations of the end of the world are of concern outside of Hollywood as well. Silicon Valley millionaires are preparing for end-times by buying million-dollar bunkers in New Zealand.[11] Even NASA funded a study that concluded that the collapse of civilization was likely, given climate change and the increasingly unequal distribution of wealth.[12] Importantly, the NASA study goes a bit further in its conclusions by offering this insight: "Noting that warnings of 'collapse' are often seen to be fringe or controversial, the study attempts to make sense of compelling historical data showing that 'the process of rise-and-collapse is actually a recurrent cycle found throughout history.' Cases of severe civilizational disruption due to 'precipitous collapse—often lasting centuries—have been quite common.'"[13] This not only clarifies the inevitability of collapse but also highlights the predictability of collapse based upon the long history of civilization itself. Hence, another unconscious implication of the apocalyptic genre is that the state is vulnerable, that it is always on the precipice of collapse, and that without our support and participation, it may well crumble. This, despite how we have been trained to fear it, is good news.

In this light, the chorus of REM's song quoted above is less menacing and more intelligible: what if the collapse of civilization is the liberation we have all been waiting for?[14] The fall of the state—or the collapse of civilization—it seems to me, is the "way out" that Frank B. Wilderson III references in the quote above. This is the dream of abolition. And though Wilderson is vague about what he means by "violence," I would like to suggest that the catastrophic violence that could bring down the state won't come from outside its framework, but from within. The perpetuation of its own violence will destroy itself, which is what the two texts I analyze in this chapter show. These protagonists do not "fight the system." The system, in both texts, destabilizes and ultimately undoes itself. The state, in both of these texts, is the source of the catastrophic violence that Wilderson speaks of, which ultimately enables the coliberation of Blackness and nature.[15] I argue in this chapter that Octavia Butler's *Parable of the Sower* and the film *The Girl with All the Gifts* detail the end of the world as a triumph over anti-Blackness and gesture toward the beginning of an alternate world in which the old oppositions of human/nonhuman, social death/social life no longer exist. In both texts a Black young woman (Lauren Olamina) and girl (Melanie) usher in a new age, where both the state and the human—as a particular metaphysical agent—are undone. I will show how an intimacy with nature, and the inevitable destruction of the state due its own unsustainability, enables these protagonists to bring about an alternate world. Both texts "blow the lid off the unconscious," because their protagonists represent the Black person's embodiment of catastrophe vis-à-vis "human arrangements," which is the end of human life[16] and the beginning, I argue, of plant life—an ontological subversion that mediates against the rupture wrought by Enlightenment thinkers between humans and nature, and which salvifically resutures the world.

In Butler's text knowledge of the natural is emphasized as one of the ways that people will survive the inevitable last vestiges of Western-style civilization, as is an ideology Lauren calls Earthseed, which theologically frames an understanding of our place and responsibility in the world; in *The Girl with All the Gifts*, a new fungal plant turns all humans into flesh-eating zombies, and women who become zombies while pregnant produce a new kind of human—people who are "intertwined" with the plant and so are immune to insensate zombification. "Becoming plants," literally in one case (Melanie) and symbolically in the other (Lauren), is how these texts suture "the person" back into the natural world. For Melanie in *The Girl with All the Gifts*, she is quite literally half plant and half human; in *Parable of the Sower*, the community that Lauren Olamina founds after her home is destroyed by looters is called Earthseed, so that symbolically humans are transformed into plants, arising out of the earth rather than existing as apex predators in opposition to flora. Furthermore, neither narrative is the articulation of a Black world, since "the work of Blackness as a category of difference fits the Hegelian movement but has no emancipatory power."[17] Thus, as Denise Ferreira da Silva shows, figuring existence under the sign of the plant and not the human, both narratives "signals ∞, another world: namely, that which exists without time and out of space, in the plenum."[18] When both time (history) and space (property) are lost, we witness the emergence of alternate orders of existence. Nature, and interbeing with it, is central to these two apocalyptic narratives, because the collapse of civilization means an end to material and epistemological structures that incentivize our rupture from nature. In both of these texts, we are ultimately invited to realize that, as Calvin Warren argues, "black freedom would constitute a form of *world destruction*,"[19] and that liberation from the oppressive arrangements of our society will happen only when the society itself falls, when there is, to recall Sexton, "nothing for no one." And while for some this may sound grim, these two texts suggest that the end of the state is the beginning of true freedom.

Learn (Survival)

Learn or die.
—Earthseed: The Books of the Living, *Parable of the Sower*

Every step toward the wild outer rim of the seminary seemed like a step toward doom, dragging me backward in time. In front of me was the infinite green mystery of the jungle, speaking a language I could not decipher; behind was the sealed door of a haven of security and protection that had suddenly been transformed into an inimical alien world.
—Malidoma Patrice Somé

At the house I share with my partner, in the countryside, I often lie in the grass for hours, looking at the sky. And though anyone I tell about my brain tumor is horrified and scared for me, I feel mostly at peace. Back when I was first diagnosed, I reminded myself of a favorite Zen koan often: "What is the cause of death?" The answer is "birth." In other words, though I might not have known how I was going to die, I knew the day would one day come. All who are born must die—and so, if the brain tumor was going to kill me, the tragedy would be only in the timing (I was thirty-six) and not in the outcome in a broad way. While waiting to see first one, then a second neurologist, I browsed urns. There are tree-pods you can deposit your ashes into, and I told my partner I wanted one of these. If this was not possible, I said, bury me at Foxfield Preserve, a local natural cemetery. In the meantime, while I was still alive, I wanted to be outside as much as possible. As a family, we spent as much time as we could camping, hiking, kayaking, gardening, and sitting in the yard. Parallel to my personal concerns about my death, politically I was never more aware of Black death than during this time. Police and "stand your ground" murders were on my mind. I participated as much as I could in community initiatives, but mostly I sought refuge in nature. The possibility of my personal death's impact on my daughter forced me to confront the world I'd be leaving her to if I died. The social world seemed charged with danger.

One day while entering a trailhead off a bike path in my neighborhood, I saw a police officer eyeing me suspiciously in the parking lot. I was tying my shoelaces and getting my water and keys situated in my pockets for my hike to the riverbank, where I would sit in quiet contemplation for an hour before picking my daughter up from school. He got out of his car to check if I had paid the $5 fee for a sticker for the parking area (I had), and I took in his outfit from the corner of my eye. His flat dress shoes were ill equipped for gravel, dirt, let alone mud, slush or high grass. His pressed pants and shirt were also bad for hiking, as they made him walk in a stiff and overly upright manner. As I entered the forest and followed a deer trail, disappearing into the thick embrace of trees, I smiled to myself—knowing that he could not find me in those woods even if he tried. For just one hour, I could at least *feel* free of the state. I decided that I wanted to teach my daughter the power of trees and the comfort of wild places, so that if I was soon to pass out of existence, she might find a trace of me in the forest.

In his memoir *Of Water and the Spirit: Ritual, Magic, and Initiation in the Life of an African Shaman* (1994), Malidoma Patrice Somé recalls his experience growing up in a French mission school in his country of Burkina Faso. The treatment he received there was predictably racist, harsh, and abusive; one day, when he could no longer stand the cruelty of the priests, he left the school, heading—without money, food, or even a map—into the jungle. He didn't know how far away his village—which he hadn't visited for at least a decade—was from the seminary. He knew only that it was east. With this scant knowledge, he walked home, sleeping every night in the jungle, watching the animals in order to find food, digging deep into his boyhood memories of how to forage, and continuing in an eastward fashion. He soon learned that he walked 100 kilometers in two days. He walked another four days, and finally found a village that was 55 kilometers from his village. He couldn't be sure how far he walked—but, at the rate of 50 kilometers a day, it is a fair estimate to guess that he walked a total 355 kilometers (approximately 220 miles). Somé, upon his seditious departure from colonial society, relied upon the cover and sustenance of plants (the forest and the jungle) to uphold his existence. The "infinite green mystery" of the jungle drags Somé "back in time," so that as he gets farther away from the French seminary, the site of his bondage, he loses his chains and also time (history). The longer he is in the jungle, the more the colonial society he once thought of as safe is transformed into an "inimical foreign world."[20] Though Somé is understandably consumed by "doom" when he begins his long journey home, he eventually begins to learn how to *be* in the jungle: "I began to feel like it was perfectly natural to be out there in the middle of nowhere trying to go somewhere. Is this the first sweet taste of freedom?"[21]

Released from the taxonomy of the seminary's time and space arrangements, Somé begins to affectively enmesh with the ethos of the wild; he is "nowhere" going to an indefinite and undisclosed "somewhere." His time in the jungle is characterized by a total immersion in plant life: "The landscape around me was beautiful because of its diversity. The succession of mountains and valleys added to the panoramic aspect of the place. There was a creek or a river in every valley I crossed. The unpolluted water was refreshing to drink. The abundance of fruit trees saved me from fear of starvation. I had gotten used to living in the bush."[22] Somé goes on to describe the psychological struggle he endures to be as free in his mind of the seminary as he is in his body. But his "first sweet taste of freedom" occurs in the jungle, where the vastness of the wilderness reveals the existence of another realm, rendering the scaffold of Western civilization an "alien world." Harriet Tubman, whose multiple journeys from South to North in the service of emancipating slaves required the same reliance upon the wild that Somé's journey did, speaks to the onto-spatial shifts that occasion flight from an oppressive society. She noted, "When I found I had crossed that line, I looked at my hands to see if I was the same person. There was such a glory over everything."[23] Crossing over into freedom produces in her a shock of misrecognition, such that her old "self" no longer exists; it falls away and gives rise to glory. In both cases, shifts in the conditions of existence catalyze the process of liberation such that time and space are radically permutated, enacting an incorporeal catastrophe that does irredeemable, and hence generative, violence to the assemblages of self and state. Wilderness facilitates these shifts, and so incursions into a being's coadunation with nature—an effect, if not an intention, of civil society—is imbricated in bondage. The diminishment of wild spaces, as well as the cultivation of ignorance about how to exist in the wild, consubstantiate captivity by atrophying both ability and desire vis-à-vis the natural world.

In *Parable of the Sower*, set in 2024, Lauren Olamina is the "Black Moses" of her people, urging them to "rewild" so that they can learn how to survive when their civilization, which is on the brink of collapse, finally fails. Lauren, unlike most of the other characters in the novel, can see that her community is living on the precipice of disaster; hence, she admonishes them to "learn or die." Lauren is the daughter of a minister and a teacher, living in a self-sufficient gated community, Robledo. Outside the gates, "pyros," drug addicts who set things on fire, and a variety of other criminal elements, prey upon vulnerable people and property. The US government is all but defunct, with the only remaining order being a loose, and corrupt, configuration of corporate power. Lauren is an empath, the result of her mother's drug use when pregnant with her, and experiences the pain and pleasure of anyone she touches. Eventually, she has to leave Robledo, takes to the road to survive, and joins a band of survivors who travel with her until they find land where they can form a small, anarchic community that they name Acorn. The decline of civilization does not transform society into a dangerous place so much as make evident the elements of brutality naturally characteristic of it; so the threat represented in *Parable of the Sower*, set just twenty miles north of Los Angeles, simply exaggerates the already-existing features of the city that has, in our contemporary moment, earned the nickname "Hell-A." Though her family, and the other people in the Robledo community, laments the loss of a civilization Lauren doesn't remember, she is constantly warning them that things will decline further—that they must learn, from the past and how to survive outside of civilization or die.

Lauren muses about the possible benefits of civilization and also contemplates its decline when she writes, "When civilization fails to serve, it must disintegrate unless it is acted upon by unifying internal or external forces." (90) The decline of civilization in the past often meant that populations dispersed—and when humanity was still close enough to its hunter-gatherer roots, it meant a return to the oldest way of human life on this planet. Lauren's imperative to herself and others to "learn," is about relearning all the skills that humanity has lost as captives of civilization. This is evident in a conversation Lauren has with Jo, a Robledo community member, who confronts Lauren about her esoteric reading habits and her strange attempts to practice living without the conveniences of civilization:

> "What are you doing?" she asked. "Trying to learn to live off the land?"
>
> "I'm trying to learn whatever I can that might help me survive out there. I think we should all study books like these . . . I think we should make emergency packs—grab and run packs—in case we have to get out of here in a hurry . . . I think we should fix places outside where we can meet in case we get separated. . . . Every time I go outside, I try to imagine what it might be to live out there without walls, and I realized I don't know anything."[24]

Trying to imagine a life "without walls" is at once frightening and challenging for Lauren—later, when her father asks idly if the world is coming to an end, Lauren thinks no, it's not, but "your world is coming to an end and you with it."[25] In this sense Butler's character anticipates Melanie from *The Girl with All the Gifts*, a human adaptation who, like Lauren, ultimately chooses herself and an alternate world over the Western one. Lauren is always thinking of another world and another way to be, while everyone around her is focused on trying to fix their lives into place, to resist the changes that become more visible each day. Lauren, on the other hand, embraces change and makes it her religion. But before Lauren can enact her religion or even teach it to others, she must first survive the downfall of her own community.

When the walls around Robledo come tumbling down, and pyros and looters enter the compound, killing everyone in sight and taking anything that isn't nailed down, Lauren grabs her survival backpack, flees, and hides. The future she predicted is now her present, and everything she has tried to learn about survival becomes of utmost importance. And despite all she has read, Lauren is keenly aware—once she has revisited a burned-down Robledo for whatever supplies and money are left—of what she doesn't know:

> Here are some of the things I learned today:
> Walking hurts. I've never done enough walking to learn that before, but I know it now. It isn't only the blisters and sore feet, but we've got those. After a while, everything hurts. I think my back and shoulders would like to desert to another body. Nothing eases the pain except rest. Even though we got a late start, we stopped twice today to rest.[26]

Walking all day, for days on end, is not something one can prepare for by reading a book, and by emphasizing the difficulty of moving from one place to another without the conveyances of civilization, Butler exposes what people have forgotten and lost under an oppressive, but technologically driven, society. Lauren also learns that when their initial food supplies run low, they will have to forage in whatever way they can. She learns that animals are just as dangerous as people, if not more so. She learns to avoid dogs and to kill them if they approach her. When animals are no longer captive to human civilization, they return to the their feral (and natural) state. Civilization suppresses these insights beneath a veneer of ease that sustains, but dissimulates, the arrangements of captivity.

Butler suggests that forgetting about the natural world is dangerous, because if we no longer remember how to survive or what survival takes, if we lose what I'd like to call our Earth-wit, then we are vulnerable to a paradigm that presupposes the necessity of the state. In order to survive when Robledo falls, Lauren—and the crew of people she slowly gathers on her way to forming a new community she calls Earthseed—must walk far away, into the most isolated and deepest wilderness they can find, which happens to be land owned by Bankole, one of their community members. Bankole, who eventually becomes Lauren's partner, has three hundred acres of uncultivated land that become the site of Lauren's new Earthseed community. Lauren says the land is as wild and empty as any she has seen. Nature, then, becomes the only available haven for these refugees from civilization. Yet living outside of civilization, rather than dying without it, is possible only if one learns how to do so. Thus, we can read Butler's book as revealing the investment of statist structures in the vitiation of natural craft and affinity.

Not only does Lauren conceptualize liberation through the ability to survive in the natural world, but she also reconceptualizes existence itself through the ontology of plant life rather than human life. Writing about her philosophy of survival, Earthseed, she pens: "We are Earthseed. We are flesh—self-aware, questing, problem-solving flesh. We are that aspect of Earthlife best able to shape God knowingly. We are Earthlife maturing, Earthlife preparing to fall away from the parent world. We are Earthlife preparing to take root in new ground, Earthlife fulfilling its purpose, its promise, its Destiny."[27] Lauren aligns being not with the metaphysical human of Western society, but rather with the Earth itself. By locating being in "seeds," rather than, say, Eartheggs, Butler implicitly references a botanical taxonomy that aligns people-being with plant-being. And while this may sound entirely like science fiction, recent studies have identified a genetic link between humans and plants, which will have more relevance as our analysis of plant life develops below.[28] Plant ontology antagonizes discourses of agency, which are invested in the constitutive status of humanism. Because we perceive plant life to be fixed and incapable of self-defense, abolishing human life in favor of plant life perhaps evokes a sense of powerlessness. But the death of power, and the cultivation of "Earthlife," is the only viable trajectory for survival. Hence, plant life is also the death of agency if we understand "agency" to refer to the behavior of metaphysical humans to act upon their environment. These alternate arrangements around plant life, agency, and the human are revealed in Rarámuri ethnobotanist Enrique Salmon's description of the difference between the cultural narratives of his people and the West. He writes, "The focus of Western cultural history is heroes. Those people who influence events usually dominate, lead, and conquer. The focus of Rarámuri cultural history is the landscape. The heroes are the trees, plants, animals, and children. The land, the plants, and people share the landscape rather than dominate it."[29] Salmon undermines agency here by situating being in a collective and broad ecological field, where "land, plants, and people" co-constitute one another. Survival is counterposed in *Parable of The Sower* against world-making through the figuration of organic growth versus the establishment of a human society. Earthseed is not a city on a hill; it is the recession of the human—and all its structures—into the earth; it is a surrender to flow rather than a commitment to reform. Plant life in *Parable of the Sower* discloses a horizon of living freedom, for all entities, "that unleashes Blackness to confront life."[30]

The emphasis on survival strategies in *Parable of the Sower* is not an iteration of agency, because Lauren's preparations are not proactive measures designed to bring about (violently or otherwise) the world she anticipates. I am not suggesting, though, that she is invested in the old world and so holds off a revolution. Rather, her observations reveal that the old society, the state, the gated community of Robledo, will implode. Hence, Lauren's preparations relate to her enactment of change and adaptability, aligned with the natural world, that forms the basis of her model of existence. The protagonist of *The Girl with All the Gifts*, Melanie, also does not plot to undermine the humans who cruelly hold her in bondage. The children in *The Girl with All the Gifts* live in dehumanizing conditions, more often referred to by a number than by their names. Interestingly, the novel version of *The Girl with All the Gifts* by M. K. Carey features a white girl protagonist and a Black teacher, but the film version reversed the races of these characters.[31] The children are not seen as human, and the concentration-camp-like setting they find themselves in is eerily reminiscent of the camps currently in operation at the US-Mexico border as of this writing. Ultimately, the facility collapses. Melanie escapes and is saved because Dr. Caroline Caldwell, a research scientist, still holds out hope of using her in an experiment, one that will kill her but (presumably) produce a vaccine for the dwindling human population. Melanie must decide if she will save humanity or embrace the fungal world, the plant within her, and build an alternate community instead. Melanie, who is incredibly intelligent and is cathected to her teacher Ms. Justineau, must decide toward the end of the film if she will save the humans by allowing Caldwell to experiment on her. Caldwell, on one of their expeditions for food after the facility is invaded and destroyed by zombies, shows Melanie the pods of the fungi that have infected earth, causing the apocalypse. She informs her that if the pods were ever to open, it would be a point of no return for humanity. In the end, Melanie sets fire to the pods, releasing their spores, choosing herself and the wild fungal-human children over humanity. The only "human" left is Ms. Justineau, whom Melanie commissions to teach her small group of fellow plant-human hybrids the same Greek myths she was teaching Melanie and her classmates at the facility.

Melanie, whose thoughts we don't have as much access to as we do Lauren's, given the epistolary style of *Parable of the Sower*, remains mostly curious about the people who imprison her. We see her, alone in her cell, looking at pictures of cats and counting—but we never see her cry or become angry or even invent clever ways to annoy or subvert the rule of the guards. Melanie's attitude suggests a sense of awareness about the unsustainability of the facility and the

Dr. Caldwell and Melanie observe a zombie tree, *The Girl with All the Gifts* (2016), directed by Colm McCarthy.

precarity of the human world. This is a logical conclusion to reach, for a world in equilibrium has no need to imprison children. Melanie's "waiting and watching" affect aligns with plant life, for she is quite literally part plant. Given the precarity of human society, Melanie need not ever act against any humans for the old world to come to an end. Like *Parable of the Sower*, this film departs in important ways from the genre of science fiction concerned with apocalypse. As Kimberly Hale and Erin Dolgoy note, *The Girl with All the Gifts* doesn't portray societal collapse as "a negative development, there is no clear sadness associated with its [humanity's] demise."[32] Melanie's decision not to preserve the human world is a rational one, based not only upon the unlikelihood of survival even if a vaccine is found, given the weakness of human infrastructure at this point in the story, but nothing about how she was treated at the facility where she grew up encourages her to see humanity as worth saving. Her decision to release the spores of the pods isn't represented as the gleeful act of an aggrieved noncitizen. It is, instead, the next logical step in an organic process whereby the distance between the human and the natural is foreclosed as the human literally recedes back into the realm of plants. The zombies eventually sprout roots and come together to begin to form a huge tree. When one of the characters asks Caldwell what would happen if the spores were ever released, she says, "The end of the world, probably."[33] As with Lauren, whose father asks

A "hungry" pushes a stroller, *The Girl with All the Gifts* (2016), directed by Colm McCarthy.

her if the world is ending, only to have Lauren think (to herself) that *his* world is ending, but not hers—this must be the sort of thought that occurs to Melanie, who sees not death in the zombie tree but life.

There is a palpable sense in the film, when Caldwell makes an impassioned plea to Melanie to help her save the world by sacrificing herself, that the argument for human continuation requires a willful elision of what "humanity" has wrought on itself and the natural world. And again, I must emphasize here that the term "human" is never neutral or universal. Thus, when we think through the genre of "the human," we are never talking about a broad, inclusive term—but instead about a very specific subject of Western ontology, the white subject. We can read post-humanity, to use Hale and Dolgoy's term, in the film as also indicating post-whiteness. Caldwell's attempt to produce a vaccine indicates an anxiety about the continuation of humanity as she knows it, and this anxiety is evident through her emphasis on babies and children. While Caldwell has "no problem vivisecting the [hybrid] children without anesthesia," she is on the other hand obsessed with the possibility of "her" type of human life continuing.[34] This is evident in a scene where Caldwell, Justineau, two military men from the facility, and Melanie are walking quietly through a mall full of "hungries" (the term in the film for zombies). In this film, zombies identify humans through smell, so

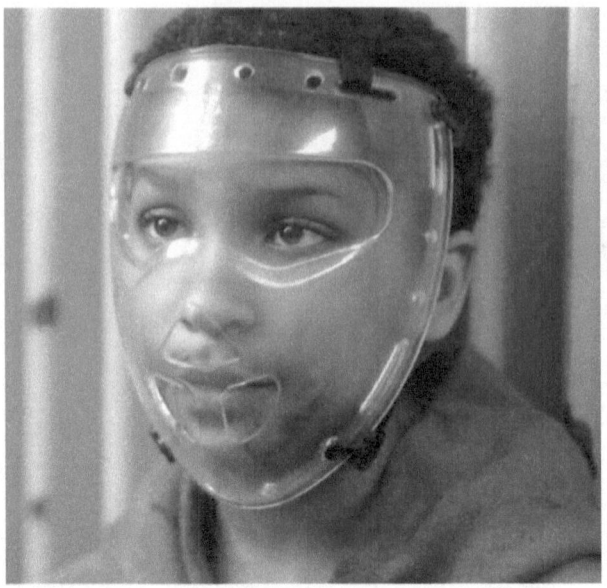

Melanie in her mask, *The Girl with All the Gifts* (2016), directed by Colm McCarthy.

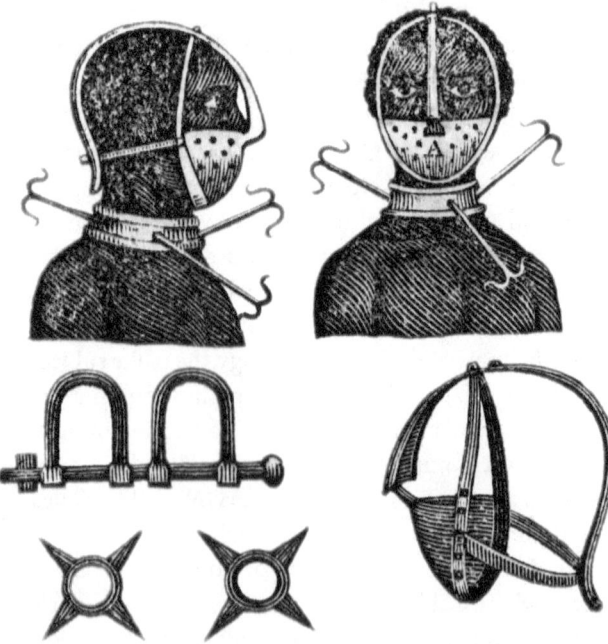

Slave masks, circa 1750. From Thomas Branagan, *The Penitential Tyrant; or, Slave Trader Reformed* (New York: Samuel Wood, 1807).

the humans have slathered themselves with a cream that suppresses their scent and are walking very quietly and successfully through a crowd of hungries. A zombie pushing a stroller, which appears to have a baby covered in a blanket, is walking through the crowd as well. Caldwell becomes fixated upon the zombie pushing the stroller and the movement of the blanket within. She puts her foot in front of the stroller to stop the zombie-woman from moving away and pulls back the blanket, revealing not a baby but a bloody rat eating the corpse of a baby. Caldwell reacts in horror, endangering the group by rousing the hungries. In this scene Caldwell's naive hope for the possibility of a human future is evident in her fixation on the stroller. The zombie mother's automatic and unthinking pushing of the stroller suggests the emptiness of human mothering, and the rat eating the child suggests the unviability of the human future Caldwell is trying to save. Checking to see if a baby is there is foolhardy, because if it were, all the hungries would smell it and instantly devour it. So Caldwell's thin faith that a human baby might be in the stroller also reveals her level of denial about the former-humans (the hungries) that she is surrounded by.

Caldwell's concern for the possibility of a human child in the stroller throws her dismissal of Melanie into sharp relief. Her willful blindness to Melanie's humanity is so absolute that she is unaware of the moral contradiction between her need to check for the presence of a (human) child in the stroller while accompanied by one in a mask. For most of the film, Melanie is forced to wear a mask to protect the humans from being eaten by her, thereby reinforcing a visual of bondage that can be traced back to slavery. The mask she is forced to wear is revealed to be more a function of cruelty than safety, since for most of the film, the humans with Melanie navigate successfully around "hungries," who are maskless and far more prone to attack than is Melanie, who unlike the zombies can think.

As a scientist Caldwell represents eugenics, and in her attempt to rescue humanity from the fungi, she also represents Western notions of the human. So when she explains to Melanie that children like herself live as "symbiotes" with the fungi, part human and part plant, she fails to realize that the cure she is looking for (a way for humans to be immune to the zombifying effects of the fungus) is standing right next to her. Living in symbiotic harmony with the plant world, Melanie represents the collapse of the Western opposition between the natural world and the human world, the literal unmaking of the Enlightenment philosophy that first made the animal and plant world "other."

In her essay "The Malaise of Civilization," Suzanne Césaire writes about the diasporic Black person through the national lens of Martinique. Her insights can be broadly applied, though, since she is tracing the development of an existential position arising out of slavery, "where the adaptation of an African population has taken place."[35] She writes, "What is the Martinican?–A plant human."[36] She goes on to explain:

> Like a plant, he abandons himself to the rhythm of universal life. There is not the slightest effort to dominate nature. Mediocre farmer. Perhaps. I am not saying that he makes the plant grow: I am saying that he grows, he lives in a plant-like manner.... And always and everywhere in the slightest manifestations, the primacy of the plant, the plant trampled underfoot but still alive, dead but reviving, the plant free, silent, and proud.[37]

In articulating a theory of freedom, Césaire produces a natural ontology that reimagines humanoid existence in precisely the same ways evident in *The Girl with All the Gifts*. Césaire rejects Western ontology via the merging of the plant world and the person world, offering an alternate theorization about the ways in which the Black person has been excluded from the category of the human. In doing so she does not lament that exclusion but celebrates it. Symbolically, this closing of philosophical distance between "the human" and the natural world is the end of whiteness as we know it, which also co-deconstructs civilization as we know it. The figure of the human in *The Girl with All the Gifts* is no longer viable, so that "they either adapt, thereby revealing humanity's true potential, or die."[38] Echoing Butler's charge to "learn or die," Hale and Dolgoy point out here that in *The Girl with All the Gifts*, those who do not adapt (learn) do indeed die. The lesson of the film seems to be that our war against the natural world (plants) is fated to failure, and that if we could only open our eyes (as Caldwell is unable to do), we might see that in adaptability there is new life. The implication of the symbiotic relationship between humans and the plant in the film is that, ultimately, nature wins. "We" could win too if only we recognize that nature is not "other than us," that nature *is*, indeed, us. As the environmentalist Andy Goldsworthy notes, "We often forget that *we are nature*. Nature is not something separate from us. So when we say that we have lost our connection to nature, we've lost our connection to ourselves."[39] This disconnection from oneself is evident in Caldwell, who cannot recognize in Melanie her like, even though with her intelligence, curiosity, and ingenuity Melanie shares some traits of brilliance with Caldwell. Her failure to recognize Melanie's humanity is her downfall; her clinging to a dying human model prevents her from seeing the possibility of an alternate world.

Die (Abolition)

> Modern industrial civilization has developed within a certain system of convenient myths. The driving force of modern industrial civilization has been individual material gain, which is accepted as legitimate, even praiseworthy, on the grounds that private vices yield public benefits in the classic formulation.

Now, it's long been understood very well that a society that is based on this principle will destroy itself in time.
—Noam Chomsky[40]

Let us cite further the decree of January 3, 1788, requiring free men of color "to take out permits to work *anywhere other than in the fields*." One will understand that from that point forward the fundamental goal of the colored man became assimilation. And with overwhelming force, a disastrous confusion takes place in his mind: liberation means assimilation.
—Suzanne Césaire[41]

I did not die, nor did death seem to be imminent. My tumor was discovered to be benign. Rather than have invasive surgery, which would require cutting into the language center of my brain, I opted for treatment by gamma knife, a direct and very precise form of radioactive treatment. Tracking progress with this form of treatment was slow, and it took two years of regular monitoring MRIs and meetings with neuro-oncologists before it was clear that my tumor was shrinking. Each year, my brain tumor grows a little smaller. Since it was benign and I was asymptomatic, the therapeutic goal was always to keep it from getting any bigger. My treatment was successful, and I began to consider that I might have a lot more life to live. Still, I craved being outside. Though I was undergoing MRIs frequently and talking over treatment options with my partner, I found myself mostly thinking about nature and trying to be in nature. I stood for hours outside with bare feet, feeling the earth and ants beneath my toes. I spent whole afternoons staring at the sky, and during both day and night, contemplating clouds and stars. I slept outside whenever I could, attuning to another world.

Though I survived the tumor, there had been a bigger shift in me, indicated by a turn away from achievement, social status, people-pleasing, and materiality, and toward wildness, trees, and freedom. I experienced a micro-apocalypse, only to discover another way of being on the other side of disruption. Is it possible that the same could be true on a macro level? Is this the liberating potential that these two texts point to? Narratively, Butler's *Parable of the Sower* closes the door on civil society and suggests the necessity of an alternate way of living. Given the catastrophizing that characterizes narratives about the end of civilization, it is easy to read the fall of Robledo *only* as a tragedy. And it is tragic—after all, when the pyros come through the wall, they kill almost everyone in the community.[42] But Butler's novel suggests that Robledo, despite its wall and managing to respond well to the increasingly unstable situation outside, is also rife with problems. The way of life in Robledo is not utopic;

in fact, it is a response to the emergency of a declining civilization. Despite the comforts provided inside the walls, Keith, Lauren's brother, is murdered because he refuses to stay inside and goes looking for riches and power in the "wild west" that is the world outside of Robledo. And though there is danger outside the community, it is clear that in *Parable of the Sower*, no place is safe—there are only different degrees of danger. While the danger outside the wall is heightened, there are dangers within as well. And the wall that separates these varying zones of danger is constantly in need of policing; the limited safety the people in Robledo experience is tenuous at best and must be defended at gunpoint. Our current society, only four years younger than the one depicted at the start of Butler's novel, is no different. We live in a society where one is subject to random, unpredictable death at school, at the movie theater, at the mall, at the grocery store, at church, during a police stop, or at the hospital. One can be killed by anyone—a fellow citizen, a police officer, or off-duty military personnel. As Butler predicted, in the United States we currently live under tyranny:

> When apparent stability disintegrates,
> As it must—
> God is Change—
> People tend to give in
> To fear and depression,
> To need and greed.
> When no influence is strong enough
> To unify people
> They divide.
> They struggle,
> One against one,
> Group against group,
> For survival, position, power.
> They remember old hates and generate new ones,
> They create chaos and nurture it.
> They kill and kill and kill,
> Until they are exhausted and destroyed,
> Until they are conquered by outside forces,
> Or until one of them becomes
> A leader
> Most will follow,
> Or a tyrant
> Most fear.[43]

Critics have noted that the dystopian world presented in Butler's novel is only a slight exaggeration of the current state of affairs in the United States. Madhu Dubey notes that *Parable of the Sower* is so close to actual reality that it produces "a shock of familiarity rather than estrangement."⁴⁴ Hence, Butler's novel strikes a pessimistic note about the possibility of the country, as it was conceived originally, ever living up to its promise of "life, liberty, and the pursuit of happiness." Though current critical race theory has taken a decidedly pessimistic turn, the historiography of Black letters is replete with optimistic appeals to the American ideal of justice and freedom. That optimism is perhaps nowhere more apparent than in Martin Luther King Jr's speech at the March on Washington. He compares the American promise of liberty to a promissory note, calling it a check yet to be cashed for the Black American. With rare, stirring power he expressed belief that it is possible, still, for the nation to make good on its promise: "But we refuse to believe that the bank of justice is bankrupt. We refuse to believe that there are insufficient funds in the great vaults of opportunity of this nation. So we have come to cash this check, a check that will give us upon demand the riches of freedom and the security of justice."⁴⁵ He ended his speech in even more optimistic terms, repeating again and again his dream of a just nation grounded in racial equality. Though King's speech might be dismissed as predictably hopeful given his broad audience, the same kind of optimistic tone can even be found in the demands of the more militant Black Panther Party. In October of 1966 (just three years after King's speech), the Black Panther Party released a document titled, "The Ten-Point Program," which laid out a series of demands designed to address the oppressive and unequal conditions of Black life in America. At the end of this document, they quote the preamble of the Declaration of Independence, insisting, as that document does, on the right to "life, liberty, and the pursuit of happiness" as "inalienable rights" that the institution of government is supposed to provide. Of interest here is the optimism of the "The Ten-Point Program," which presumes that the American experiment in this context, and perhaps the experiment of the nation in a larger context, is *capable* of delivering happiness, life, and liberty.⁴⁶ This optimism speaks to the possibility of a Black future, of freedom, *within* the state. Despite this optimism, there is nothing on hand in the historical record to suggest that what the Black Panthers demand is even possible in the context of civilization as it has existed for the past thirteen thousand years—which is its entire history so far. In other words, for as long as civilization has existed, it has been built on brutality, slavery, and oppression. Furthermore, we have yet to find any model of civilization that doesn't rely upon bondage for its survival.

Afro-pessimism, though it rarely refers to civil society as "civilization," uncovers through its analytical framework the futility of statist optimism for the emancipation of Black people. Though it does not "categorically reject every project of reform—for decreased suffering will surely make life momentarily easier—but rather take[s] to task any movement invested in the preservation of society,"[47] the critique of efforts to transform the state into a more just entity that Afro-pessimists advance, is integral to its call for the abolition of the state. While not always directly arguing for the continuation of the state, dissenting critics of Afro-pessimism point to sites of spiritual and "internal" resistance to social death as part of what Afro-pessimism doesn't account for, as a way to recuperate Blackness from a seeming nihilistic ideological prison. In his critique of Afro-pessimism, Michael Barlow argues, "Though they exist outside of the production of the human (within the category of social death), there are Black affektual [sic] politics that have been with the slave since the ship. These are the emotional and spiritual ontologies within Blackness that connected slaves of different lands, languages, and religions into one community."[48] Barlow goes on to introduce the idea of an "intra-ontology," which characterizes Black ways of being that do not engage with civil society. He notes, "This paper uses the term intra-ontology in reference to the varying ontologies within social death. This is the Black among Blacks. These are those spaces within Blackness that only the Black can ever understand or occupy."[49] Despite the seeming opposition of thinking between those who want to emphasize, celebrate, and promote "intra-ontology" as a way to think about Black life, and those who contend that Black people operate under the mantle of social death in civil society, I think that there is a fundamental misreading of Afro-pessimism that enables this apparent schism. Jared Sexton addresses the seeming opposition of Black pessimism and optimism when he writes,

> In a way it cannot be otherwise, since the language of this difference between inside and out—and what will turn out to be a series of differences including life and death, pessimism and optimism, subject and object, object and thing, thing and case, blacks and blackness, beings and being, and so on—must be used to demonstrate why this language of difference is not what it seems or claims to be. If we could sum it up in advance (which, of course, we cannot really do), we might say that captivity is always an unsettled condition, open to an outside about which it will not know anything and about which it cannot stop thinking, a system always in pursuit of the fugitive movement it cannot afford to lose and cannot live without, if it is to go on existing in and as a mode of capturing.[50]

Here, Sexton undermines the notion that pessimist treatments are categorically at odds with optimistic ones but highlights the ways in which captivity—which cannot really be denied—is always an "unsettled condition." This "outside" of which it cannot stop thinking undermines any notion that Black liberation discourses can ever be "free" of the state of captivity that necessitates their existence in the first place. In other words, we return to that double-sided proposition of being, What is the cause of death?

Furthermore, if one is grounded in the liberation politics of the 1960s and '70s, then Afro-pessimism can seem like a slap in the face to all those who fought (and died) for the rights, including access to material prosperity, that Afro-pessimists deconstruct. This seems to be the case in a review of Ta-Nehisi Coates's book *We Were Eight Years in Power: An American Tragedy* (2017) by Darryl Pinckney titled, "The Afro-Pessimist Temptation."[51] Pinckney argues, "Unfortunately, black people who dismiss the idea of progress as fantasy are incorrect in thinking they are the same as most white people who perhaps believe still that they will be fine no matter who wins our elections."[52] For Pinckney, the "progress" he speaks of seems to be, at least in part, "unprecedented prosperity."[53] Afro-pessimism critiques a model of progress that can be measured by the accumulation of property and position and so for people who have fought and died for that version of "liberation," Afro-pessimism is incredibly threatening. To compare the theoretical deconstruction of Western civilization to being a Trump voter, as Pinckney implies above, suggests that he sees Afro-pessimism as inimical to a traditional project of Black liberation. "The 1960s and the 1970s showed that mass movements can bring about systemic change. Angela Davis said so," Pinckney argues, demonstrating that he takes umbrage at the Afro-pessimist claim that despite all that sweat, blood, and activism, we have not achieved freedom.[54] It's significant that Pinckney references Cornel West and his admittance to Harvard in the 1970s as an index of progress. But in the formulation of liberation I've been developing throughout this book, that version of progress is simply the iteration of an oppressive structure from which the Black person can never be free. Césaire takes on this idea when she writes, "The race for economic fortune, diplomas, unscrupulous social climbing. A struggle shrunken to the standard of being middle class. The pursuit of monekyshines. Vanity Fair."[55] In other words, the successful assimilation of material and cultural values (pursuit of wealth, degrees from prestigious institutions) has been mistaken for freedom. Following Césaire, I contend that Afro-pessimism's turn toward abolition is a call to "plant life." "Open your eyes," Césaire commands, "a child is born. To which god should it be entrusted? To the Tree god."[56] Césaire could be speaking across time and text to Caldwell, who fails to see the plant life in front of her. But plant life is at odds with machine life, with the material life of civil society, and so arguing for the abolition of civil society—which so many people have bought into and devoted themselves to—can feel like an attack on all that has been accomplished in the struggle since the juridical abolition of slavery.

Afro-pessimism's claim is about *civil society* (the world) and the way Blackness functions within that regime, a regime that is so often taken as the natural state of being that its presence as a structure is invisible. In other words, there is a boundary to civilization, and plant life is a call to scale the wall and go outside. The stakes of Afro-pessimist theorization are clear when Wilderson writes that Afro-pessimism proposes that one "embrace its disorder, its incoherence, and allow oneself to be elaborated by it if, indeed, one's politics are to be underwritten by a desire to take down this country."[57] Afro-pessimism's appeal, for those who no longer believe that the progress narrative of civil rights and parity with whiteness equals liberation, is that it proposes the complete abolition of the world (civilization and civil society) as we know it. And, it unmasks the ways in which a "disastrous confusion," to reference Césaire's quote in the epigraph, between liberation and assimilation[58] characterizes our visions of freedom. For those who believe that the only way to freedom is the complete dismantling of the system, of civil society as we know it, then Afro-pessimist theorizations show us the tunnel at which there is a light at the end. Taking down this country is "the way out." Ultimately, Afro-pessimism is pessimistic only about one thing: the possibility of Black liberation in civilization as it currently exists, and furthermore, of total human liberation under *any* civilizational structure. Afro-pessimism is not pessimistic about Black people or their potential; it is instead critical of the structure of the state itself. It is not, as Sexton notes, a "politics of despair."[59] Instead, it is a call to "know ourselves finally by ourselves, and here before us are splendors and hopes."[60]

Lauren comes to know herself "by herself," and not by the law of the father presented by the church or the state. Her paradigmatic Earthseed philosophy begins writing a history of an as-of-yet undisclosed realm of being. But like Afro-pessimism, Butler's novel must first diagnose the blight of current society to inaugurate the possibility of "existence anew."[61] *Parable of the Sower*, though it seems to gesture toward a utopian vision for the future, actually emphasizes the fragility of our current society, which is a departure from the tradition within Black letters to imagine the possibility of redemption in America. Writing about the novel, Jerry Phillips notes,

> And thus the sense of the redemptive or salvific potential of human agency is radically diminished in scale. . . . For, in denying the possibility of revolutionary transformation, the novel perhaps succeeds in doing the opposite of what its author intended: consolidating the crushing facticity of our present world, in which the ideal of the whole human person has all but vanished. In other words, at one level, *Parable of the Sower* transcends postmodern *incredulity*; but, at another level, it bolsters the fatalism implicit in diminished utopianism.[62]

Another way to articulate Phillips's insight is to note that Butler's novel more successfully diagnoses the end of the world than it manages to imagine a new one. The solidity of the previous civilization, as it dissolves, leaves chaos in its wake. Butler's prophet and protosavior of the world, Lauren Olamina, less imagines a concrete alternative to the old world than thinks of the future through a kind of dialectic of change. Change, as a metaphor that guides the formation of Earthseed, at once reduces the possible future to nothing and expands it to anything. This, I argue below, is an abolitionist ethos, which arises out of a pessimistic backward view at human civilization heretofore.

Writing in *Against the Grain: A Deep History of the Earliest States* (2017), James C. Scott argues that all states—from their beginning—relied upon bondage to exist. He writes, "It would be almost impossible to exaggerate the centrality of bondage, in one form or another, in the development of the state until very recently."[63] His conclusions are relevant for our contemporary state as well, since the material circumstance of civilization at the current moment cannot exist without the exploitation of labor and the discursive structures that support the suppression of strategic communities within society. If it is true, as Afro-pessimist scholars maintain, that the Black subject remains in an existential and unending state of captivity and that the state requires anti-Blackness to operate as it was intended, then we can see that for the Black person, at this moment and in *this* state, freedom necessitates the fall of the state. The collapse of the state is not an anomaly in the history of civilization, but rather a predictable consequence of the oppressively hierarchal nature of civilization itself, as indicated by the previously cited NASA study and by Scott's insights. And, following Chomsky's observation in the epigraph to this section, the collapse of civilization—given the way we've maintained structural inequality—is inevitable. We have all been encouraged to see the collapse of civilization as a bad thing, the onset of which we are told would result in a murderous anarchy that would threaten the survival of humanity. But *Parable of the Sower* suggests that the violence of Los Angeles and surrounding areas is the result of people's inability to imagine a life outside of civil society, not a result of the lack of police. Motivated by the same materialist goals of an old system, they commit crimes for luxury goods, as we see when Lauren's brother Keith shows up with wads of cash and chocolate bars. This desire for the old way of life contributes significantly to the dystopic nature of Robledo, as the unwillingness to adapt when the previous methods are failing leads to decay and destruction. Scott points out, "Only for state elites might [collapse] have been experienced as a tragedy."[64] So when we lament collapse, with whom are we aligning ourselves? Viewed through the lens of historical inevitability, societal collapse can be reframed as an opportunity for much-needed change.

"Why deplore collapse," Scott asks, "when the situation it depicts is most often the disaggregation of a complex, fragile, and typically oppressive state into smaller, decentralized fragments?"[65] And if the state is "fragile," as Scott argues, Lauren's vision is anti-fragile, which perfectly describes the society she eventually creates with her family of choice.

Defining anti-fragility in his book *Anti-fragile: Things That Gain from Disorder* (2012), Naseem Nicholas Taleb writes, "The anti-fragile loves randomness and uncertainty, which also means—crucially—a love of errors.... Antifragility has a singular property of allowing us to deal with the unknown."[66] Unlike civilization and its adherents, Lauren is adaptable, intelligent, and capable of handling unforeseen crises. Change implies fluidity, which opposes the fixity of state law. These philosophies of change and anti-fragility are especially useful in the face of a real-life apocalyptic scenario, because it doesn't ask that we know exactly how civilization might fall; it only suggests that we learn to be adaptable and anti-fragile to survive whatever comes. Embracing this way of being, which is a kind of wild ethos, means rejecting authoritarian versions of "order." Lauren's abolitionist, anti-fragile character recalls the metaphor of the seed, which is central to Butler's rendering of her philosophy and her suggestions about alternative modes of being. The same arrangements are evident in *The Girl with All the Gifts*, since both Lauren Olamina and Melanie live "under the sign of plant life."[67]

Plants are, by nature, anti-fragile and abolitionist.[68] The alignment of plant life and abolition is evident in an article by Lucy Munro. She writes,

> There's a house on the edge of nowhere, sewn into the pocket of a hillside. Standing over a hundred years old, its edges are swamped by overgrown shrubs, enormous split trees and wandering climbers; an abandoned garden in open rebellion. Nobody's been here for some time now and at every turn there is dilapidation, ruin and rot. But there's also a peculiar charm in the air, the kind that only lurks in places full of history and great stories. It's been left to its own devices—part forgotten, part ignored—and alone its grown audacious, pulling silently at the seams of formality before unravelling into all-out insubordination.[69]

Munro's use of the terms "insubordination," "audacious," and "open rebellion" reveal the freedom of plant life in the absence of human intervention—a riotous subversion of authority that gives rise to planetary health and life, even as cyclical and inevitable death are implied. A house "on the edge of nowhere" is exactly the place of abolition, where borders, flags, nations, neighborhoods, and municipalities cease to exist. Everywhere is the edge of nowhere, and plant freedom connects to our own. We have been taught to fear wilderness, jungles, and the abolition that they imply; indeed, we've been taught to fear freedom itself. In that fear lies a certain complicity with bondage, for abolition—though popular culture encourages us to imagine it as producing a lawless wasteland—is actually simply the end of state domination. Abolition should be understood as "something more free and just," in the same way that abandoned gardens are "at last, unrestrained by man and his secateurs... free to grow, twist and turn with a reckless abandon only permitted in the wild."[70] Abolition, the death of the state, is the possibility of reckless abandon (freedom) in the context of the human.

Lauren and Melanie are other versions of people; Lauren is an empath, capable of literally feeling the pain or pleasure of anyone she physically touches, and Melanie is half plant and half human. Both these protagonists represent what Calvin Warren calls a "metaphysical holocaust," which is required to "imagine existence anew." Unlike an actual holocaust, the metaphysical one kills the *social construction of the human* (while leaving the body to flourish) and gives rise instead to "existence anew" and offers us a glimpse of actual freedom. In both *Parable of the Sower* and *The Girl with All the Gifts*, we are encouraged to see "plant life," Earthseed and fungal symbiote, as symbols of the way forward. Survival, both metaphorically and literally, depends upon the extent to which we can see ourselves and plants as co-ontologies, interdependent and equally important to the continuation of all forms of life on this planet.

We can take a cue from the natural world on what interdependent co-ontology looks like. The word "fungus" typically evokes in humans a kind of dread, as for us, fungus is a condition to be cured. But for trees, interdependency with fungi is central to their health. Writing about the relationship between trees and fungi in *The Hidden Life of Trees* (2016), Peter Wohlleben explains,

> Fungi are amazing. They don't really conform to the one-size-fits-all system we use to classify living organisms as either animals or plants.... To enter into a partnership with one of the many thousands of kinds of fungi, a tree must be very open—literally—because the fungal threads grow into soft root hairs. There's no research into whether this is painful or not, but as it is something the tree wants, I imagine it gives rise to positive feelings. However the tree feels, from then on, the partners work together.[71]

He goes on to explain that fungi are a kind of helpful parasite, taking nutrients from the tree in exchange for filtering out toxins (like heavy metals) and giving the tree resistance to bacteria. Addressing trees and plants as "beings," rather than as things, Wohlleben's work—along with the work of Césaire and the texts I discuss here—seems to pose a question: what would happen to our ontology if we thought of ourselves as plants? What would it mean to live as plants do, wild, ever-growing, unfixed, and anti-fragile? The abolition implied by Lauren's and Melanie's communities represents the end of Black social death, a radical break in the realm of the "human" that upends its historical and philosophical basis. As the state dies, the Black subject—represented by Lauren Olamina and Melanie—lives. *Parable of the Sower* and *The Girl with All the Gifts* reject the social death of the Black person by representing the death of the state and embracing plant life. Maybe at the end of everything, there is a seed. And perhaps that seed, unleashed, is the beginning of another way of being.

A Question to Close: What Would It Mean to Be Alive?

My brain tumor, and its diminishment, marked the end of one life, and the beginning of another. It occurred roughly on the cusp of the dissolution of my first marriage and the beginning of my second. It also occurred with a shift in my own spiritual consciousness, which was characterized by an intellectual movement away from civilization, civil society, and the logic of the state and a deeper embrace of the wild. I moved to the country, gave up city life, and disappeared (within the limits of this regime) into the green. The *bhikkhus*, the Buddhist monks of old, who often lived in isolation in nature, represented for me a kind of poignant rejection of all that we are taught to strive for. After surviving a brain tumor, much of what I'd previously cared about was revealed to be ridiculous. Existence now seemed to me to be about interbeing, harmony, cycles, and balance. I was part of the great natural unfolding, just as a tree or a flower or a bee is. I will come and I will go, just as all living things do. In the empty space left by the decomposition of my body, new life—of some kind—will arise. Our deaths are a gracious making way for new life. This is true not only of our bodies but also of our structures and our social constructions. Hence, I do not see apocalypse or the end of civilization as disaster any more than I see the end of my own life as such. When I observe the catastrophizing that characterizes contemplations of the end of civil society, I am reminded of the doomsday scenarios that slaveholders said would ensue if Black people were freed or allowed to thrive. The wild lawlessness of the formerly enslaved that was expected never occurred. Maybe it's also true that without the authoritarian structures of the state, we might all find better and less destructive ways to live our lives. I believe that if we are to preserve our lives on this planet, and the lives of the flora and fauna as well, then we must abolish the state as it currently exists. It means giving up a bunch of "stuff." It means learning new, cooperative ways of getting our fundamental needs meet. It means shifting the entire ground and frame of our ontological thinking. It means letting go of "the self" and all that this implies about existence. I do not believe it means a "descent" into violent chaos, because violence is present now. Out here, in the natural world, there is an immediacy that is healing. There is a cooperative logic prevalent all around that can serve as a model for our relations with one another. There is a nakedness of being that feels like flying. The trees call me by no name, and in that no-naming, I am free. When I talk to the trees, I apologize. When I feed animals, I lament with them our mutual captivity. When I pray to the stars, I repeat the same words again and again: May our egos die so that the world may live.

CODA

Take Me Outside

> Take me outside, sit in the green garden.
> Nobody out there, but it's okay now.
> Bathe in the sunlight, don't mind if rain falls.
> Take me outside, sit in the green garden.
> —"Green Garden," Laura Mvula

In the music video for Laura Mvula's song "Green Garden," (2012) we see Mvula with a group of women, and then men, in an urban setting dancing and playing drums. As the song continues, we watch as the group departs the city for a rural area. Their white/light colored clothing is reminiscent of the tableaux of *Daughters of the Dust* and *Lemonade*, and signals deeper symbolic work around Blackness and nature. The line "Nobody's out there, but it's okay now"[1] marks a shift around the garden as a place of danger to one of safety. Her song performs the pastoral return I've been so concerned with in this book, as it recodes nature, for the Black person, as a place of delight and joy. Once in the garden, Mvula rests in a clearing surrounded by trees with golden light shining upon her. The next lines of the song are "I'll go, wherever you go, wherever you take me I'll go." Though she could be talking to an unnamed person (offscreen in the video), I interpret these lines to be her speaking to the earth itself—that her commitment to being in the garden is indexed by her willingness to go wherever nature takes her. This love song to the earth, to the "green garden," resonates with my sense that central to Black liberation, and to abolition, is a refusal of Western constructions of nature. It has taken time, work, and support from family, friends, and colleagues to be able to admit this, because I am aware that emphasis on nature evokes, for many people, a milquetoast approach to complicated problems.

"Green Garden" music video, Laura Mvula, 2013.

"Green Garden" music video, Laura Mvula, 2013.

When I tell people I am working on a project about nature and Blackness, I am not always met with interest or encouragement. A few years ago, when I ran into a colleague I hadn't seen in some years, at the Modern Language Association conference, the inevitable sharing of our current projects came up. When I mentioned that I was working on a project about Blackness and nature, they asked in a mildly horrified tone, "You aren't going to argue that nature is the answer—are you?" I was intimidated into silence. Their question—which had occurred to me before and had been put to me by others I'd discussed the project with—was a difficult one. Of course I didn't intend to argue—and haven't, I hope—that nature is "the answer." My contention in this book is not that nature is the answer, but rather that in certain textual enactments of absence and refusal, nature is iterated and that within this evocation of nature lies a deeper critique of Western society and civilization.

At the same time, though, it is true that for me nature inflects my life in ways that connect me to the divine and mitigate my experience of the brutalities of the state. My contemplative journey has changed how I see myself, plants, animals, and the earth itself. It seems apparent to me that the earth is a living thing and that we are constituent elements of its body. This is sometimes referred to as the Gaia theory,[2] though I didn't come to this realization via that philosophy. It is so clear, just from being in nature, that the whole of existence is one thing rather than an aggregation of separate things. So it makes sense to me that being in nature improves our sense of well-being, because going outside returns us to our larger being in the same way that taking shoes off liberates our feet. What nature does for me is help me touch, and stay connected to, what feels like life. Because she writes about survival and living in such beautifully natural terms, I end where I began—with Lucille Clifton—who articulates my feeling of joy when I am in the woods, when I wake up each day having survived both the state and the unexpected vicissitudes of health, and when I stand outside in the blackness of the night, at one with everything. In her poem "*won't you celebrate with me*," she writes,

>won't you celebrate with me
>what i have shaped into
>a kind of life? i had no model.
>born in babylon
>both nonwhite and woman
>what did i see to be except myself?
>i made it up
>here on this bridge between
>starshine and clay,

my one hand holding tight
my other hand; come celebrate
with me that every day
something has tried to kill me
and has failed.[3]

Perhaps there is a time, a moment yet to come, when we—as former captives of civilization, newly at one with the natural world—will look back upon the state, which exerted itself to death in attempts to keep us from life, and marvel that it did not succeed.

ACKNOWLEDGMENTS

I am so grateful to everyone who held me in community as I thought about, conceptualized, and wrote *Black to Nature*. It took a long time and a lot of growth for me to get to a place where I could articulate the insights contained in this volume, and I would not have accomplished it without all of the people I mention here. First, I want to acknowledge my family for their love, unending support, and guidance in all the areas of my life. My daughter Omi became a teenager over the years that I was writing this book, and her presence in my life reminds me why I felt so compelled to write about nature and Blackness. I hope that she will read within these pages the most important message that nature sends to us all: that she has a right to the tree of life. I am also grateful for my life partner, Andrew Brath, who is my constant companion to all the wild places that I've been so fortunate to visit. He also gave me space and peace to write, understanding that I quite literally needed a room of my own in order to get this work done. Likewise, my closest friend and "unbiological" sister, Candice Jenkins, gave me the courage and confidence to take up this project on my own terms. As a daily sounding board for all my ideas, thoughts, and wild intellectual meanderings, she supported and nurtured me as I brought this book into being. My brothers, Chris and Simon Dunning, my aunt Beverly Frazier, and my cousins Melissa Scott and Johnna Brantley, have all been lights in my life as I completed this work.

Among the other people who were instrumental in the creation of *Black to Nature* are my "team," as I came to fondly call them through the process. Mary Jean Corbett, my friend and colleague at Miami University, has mentored me for years. Her honest readings and thoughtful engagement with this book were deeply helpful and affirming; I am infinitely grateful to Mary Jean for her confidence in me and my work. Shanna Benjamin Greene also read the whole manuscript and offered kind and instructive feedback that gave me confidence to complete the book. Special thanks to Katie Johnson for reading several chapters of the book, and to Madelyn Detloff for mentoring me through the process of procuring a contract and for talking me through my doubts at the earliest stage of this project. I am grateful to Cheryl Johnson for her friendship and for her faith in my ability to bring something both important and beautiful to the page. I must also thank Michelle Taylor, Amritjit Singh, Sandra Garner, Helane Androne, Durell Callier, and Gwen Etter-Lewis for insightful conversations about various ideas in this book and their suggestions for research. A special thanks to Venetria Patton, who invited me to give a talk at Purdue University while I was writing this book. I'm also deeply grateful to Jennifer McZier for her friendship and support, and for putting me in touch with Wangechi Mutu, whose beautiful artwork is featured on the cover of this book. In addition to the folks above who directly influenced the writing of *Black to Nature* are a bunch of kind souls whose presence in my life—and in some cases whose mutual love of nature—shaped this work. Among them are (in no particular order) Gaile Polhaus Jr., Ethan Saulnier, Racquel Dugat, Brenda Ndiaye, Chamiya Collins, Steve Rhemus, Martin Japtok, Diana Slampyak, Kwakuitl Dreher, Alyson Jones, Mary Sarazin, LaDessa Pearson, Olga Greco, Guilherme Fernández Maciel, Patti Levin, Michelle Pichon, Rebekah McKinney Reese, Ivy Simmons, Maria Kammerer, Stefan Kostka, and Muthoni Kori Kastner. And I am grateful to Mr. Jib Walker of Sapelo Island for making space for me to visit and learn about the island and its history.

It is hard to imagine *Black to Nature* coming to fruition without the work of Thich Nhat Hanh, Alan Watts, Sharon P. Holland, bell hooks, Robert Reid-Pharr, Stacey Alaimo, David Abram, LaMonda Stallings, C. Riley Snorton, Carolyn Finney, Lauret Savoy, Linda Hogan, Jared Sexton, Jack Halberstam, Calvin Warren, James Scott, Jeffrey Q. McCune, and many others. I thank them for their beautiful, insightful work. Many thanks to Wangechi Mutu for allowing her artwork to grace the cover of this book. Likewise, the opportunity to present portions of the manuscript for the past several years at the American Studies Association conference has been extremely helpful. I also want to thank Emily Bandy, my editor, for her faith in this project, as well as the anonymous readers who gave me so much excellent feedback about how to make *Black to Nature* the best it could be. Finally, I am grateful to all those who have been kind to me and with whom I have shared some wondrous moments under the trees together. *Black to Nature* would not be here without this community of love, care, and the recognition of ourselves as the very natural world we are trying to save.

NOTES

Introduction: "a black and living thing"

1. Lucille Clifton, "the earth is a living thing," *The Collected Poems of Lucille Clifton, 1965–2010*, ed. Kevin Young and Michael Glaser (New York: BOA Editions, 2012), loc. 2958, Kindle.
2. "Black Hiker," sketch on *Funny or Die*, directed by Brad Schulz, November 24, 2009, www.funnyordie.com/2009/11/24/18021000/black-hiker-with-blair-underwood.
3. Mireya Navarro, "National Parks Reach out to Blacks Who Aren't Visiting," *New York Times*, November 3, 2010, A17, www.nytimes.com/2010/11/03/science/earth/03parks.html.
4. Aura Bogada, "Why People of Color Don't Frequent National Parks," *Colorlines*, July 13, 2015, www.colorlines.com/articles/why-people-color-don%E2%80%99t-frequent-national-parks.
5. Frank B. Wilderson III, "Afro-Pessimism and the End of Redemption." Humanities Futures, Franklin Humanities Institute, humanitiesfutures.org/papers/afro-pessimism-end-redemption/.
6. Wilderson, "Afro-Pessimism and the End of Redemption."
7. Calvin L. Warren, *Ontological Terror: Blackness, Nihilism, and Emancipation* (Durham, NC: Duke University Press, 2018).
8. This is a reference to Saidiya Hartman's diagnostic of black life and its lingering relationship to slavery (*Scenes of Subjection: Terror, Slavery, and Self-Making in Nineteenth-Century America* [Oxford: Oxford University Press, 1997]).
9. Thich Nhat Hanh's notion of interbeing is important, as it includes a consideration of the importance of social justice along with an emphasis on peace, insight, and Zen practice. See Thich Nhat Hanh, *Interbeing: Fourteen Guidelines for Engaged Buddhism* (Berkeley: Parallax, 1987).
10. Paul Outka, *Race and Nature: From Transcendentalism to the Harlem Renaissance* (New York: Palgrave Macmillan, 2008), 2. Though I collapse the terms rural, pastoral, wilderness, and nature in this text, Outka's analysis is a helpful theorization of the distinctions between them.
11. Outka, *Race and Nature*, 80.
12. Uri McMillan, *Embodied Avatars: Genealogies of Black Feminist Art and Performance* (New York: New York University Press, 2015), 9.
13. In *Slavery and Social Death*, Orlando Patterson argues that the Black person—even after the emancipation of the slaves in 1865—has never emerged from "social death" in

Western society. Orlando Patterson, *Slavery and Social Death: A Comparative Study* (Cambridge: Harvard University Press, 1982).

14. Karen Barad, "Nature's Queer Performativity," *Qui Parle* 19, no. 2 (2011): 122.

15. Bo Allesøe Christensen, "Why Do We Care about Post-humanism? A Critical Note," *Geografiska Annaler: Series B, Human Geography* 96, no. 1 (2014): 23.

16. Warren, *Ontological Terror*, 1.

17. Alex Weheliye, "'Feenin': Posthuman Voices in Contemporary Black Music," *Social Text* 20, no. 2 (2002): 23.

18. Outka explains in great and excellent detail the ways in which traditional ecocriticism excluded people of color and operated on the basis of many racist, and sometimes eugenic, theories.

19. Jared Sexton, "The Vel of Slavery: Tracking the Figure of the Unsovereign," *Critical Sociology* 42, nos. 4–5 (2016): 11.

20. Blake Burleson, "Jung in Africa: The Historical Record," *Journal of Analytical Psychology* 2008, no. 53: 209–23.

21. See Alan Watt's talk "Not What Should Be But What Is."

22. Anansi is a figure from Akan mythology. He is represented as a spider and is understood as a divine figure in West Africa and throughout the African Diaspora.

23. Alan Watts, "Not What Should Be But What Is." YouTube, 53:51, posted [August 2011], https://www.youtube.com/watch?v=8vaaJP6fpJo.

24. Alexander Blum, "How the Enlightenment Separated Humanity from Nature," *Arc Digital*, arcdigital.media/how-the-enlightenment-separated-humanity-from-nature-c008881a61b0, accessed August 25, 2019.

25. Blum, "How the Enlightenment Separated Humanity from Nature."

26. Blum, "How the Enlightenment Separated Humanity from Nature."

27. Warren, *Ontological Terror*, 2.

28. Sir Francis Bacon, *Novum Organum*, ed. Joseph Devey (P. F. Collier, 1902). Online Library of Liberty, accessed March 1, 2019, oll.libertyfund.org/titles/1432.

29. E. Montuschi, "Order of Man, Order of Nature: Francis Bacon's Ideas of a 'Dominion over Nature,'" presented at the workshop The Governance of Nature, at the London School of Economics, October 2010, https://iris.unive.it/retrieve/handle/10278/24867/23441/MontuschiBacon.pdf.

30. Richard Serjeantson, "Francis Bacon and the 'Interpretation of Nature' in the Late Renaissance," *Isis* 105, no. 4 (2014): 681.

31. This is again a reference to Orlando Patterson's notion of social death, cited above.

32. I do not mean to suggest here that preslavery Africa was utopic or perfect. Rather, I am suggesting that whites may have constructed the preslavery life of Africans through the trope of the Garden of Eden and that slaves may also have imagined Africa in such terms, given the brutality of chattel slavery.

33. I expand on the term "placelessness" later in the introduction, as well as in chapter 4, where I discuss the television show *Queen Sugar*. It's a term coined by Katherine McKittrick, a geographer whose work engages critical race theory (Katherine McKittrick, *Demonic Grounds: Black Women and the Cartographies of Struggle* [Minneapolis: University of Minnesota Press, 2006]).

34. Sounds of Blackness, "Hold On, Pt. 1," Perspective/A&M Records, 1994.

35. Jean Toomer, "Harvest Song," *Poetry Foundation*, accessed December 17, 2018. https://www.poetryfoundation.org/poems/53989/harvest-song.

36. Outka, *Race and Nature*, 27.

37. Solomon Northup, *Twelve Years a Slave: Narrative of Solomon Northup* (New York: Miller, Orton, and Mulligan), 166.

38. Northup, *Twelve Years a Slave*, 166.

39. Kimberly Smith, *African American Environmental Thought* (Kansas: University Press of Kansas, 2007), 37.

40. Smith, *African American Environmental Thought*, 8.

41. Olaudah Equiano, *The Interesting Narrative of the Life of Olaudah Equiano* (New York: Penguin, 2003), 17.

42. Henry Louis Gates Jr., "The Truth behind 40 Acres and a Mule," PBS, accessed January 12, 2020, https://www.pbs.org/wnet/african-americans-many-rivers-to-cross/history/the-truth-behind-40-acres-and-a-mule/.

43. For more on sharecropping, see Jeanine King, "Memory and the Phantom South in African American Migration Film," *Mississippi Quarterly* 63, nos. 3–4 (2010): 477–91.

44. Richard Wright, "Between the World and Me," *Partisan Review*, July/August 1935.

45. Wright, "Between the World and Me."

46. Billie Holiday, vocalist, "Strange Fruit," by Abel Meeropol, Commodore Records, 1939.

47. "History of Lynching." NAACP.org. 2020. https://www.naacp.org/history-of-lynchings/.

48. Isabel Wilkerson, *The Warmth of Other Suns: The Epic Story of America's Great Migration* (New York: Vintage Books, 2011).

49. Brentin Mock, "The Great Migration Was about Racial Terror, Not Jobs," *City Lab*, June 2015, www.citylab.com/equity/2015/06/the-great-migration-was-about-racial-terror-not jobs/396722/.

50. James Weldon Johnson, "Harlem: The Culture Capital," in *The New Negro: An Interpretation*, ed. Alain Locke (New York: Touchstone, 1999), 311.

51. Jordan Peele, dir., *Get Out*, Blumhouse Productions, 2017.

52. Carolyn Finney, *Black Faces, White Spaces: Reimagining the Relationship of African Americans to the Great Outdoors* (Chapel Hill: University of North Carolina Press, 2014), 6.

53. Please visit http://outdoorafro.com/ and https://www.melaninbasecamp.com/ for more information about these groups that promote diversity and outdoorsmanship.

54. Among the many volumes not cited in this introduction (but some of whose work appears elsewhere in this volume) that explore nature and Blackness, see the works of Dianne Glave, Anissa Janine Wardi, Drew Lanham, and Betty Reid-Soskin.

55. hooks, bell. "Earthbound," *The Colors of Nature: Culture, Identity and the Natural World*, ed. Alison Hawthorne Deming and Lauret E. Savoy (Minneapolis: Milkweed Editions, 2011), 68.

56. Sexton, "Vel of Slavery," 11.

57. The phrase "lost commons," which is a quote from Sexton's essay "The Vel of Slavery" references the notion that there is a way to repair the damage of slavery or restore something that was lost with the inauguration of chattel slavery.

58. Greg Toppo and Paul Overberg, "After 100 Years, Great Migration Begins Reversal," *USA Today*, February 2, 2015, www.usatoday.com/story/news/nation/2015/02/02/census-great-migration-reversal/21818127/.

59. Reniqa Allen, "Racism Is Everywhere, So Why Not Move South?" *New York Times*, July 8, 2017, www.nytimes.com/2017/07/08/opinion/sunday/racism-is-everywhere-so-why-not-move-south.html.

60. A central contention of Afro-pessimism is that the transition from "chattel slave" (i.e., a not-quite-human-thing) to "human" has never been accomplished in Western society.

Saidiya Hartman talks about this imagined shift from "chattel" to "man" when she writes, "By examining the metamorphosis of 'chattel into man' and the strategies of individuation constitutive of the liberal individual and the rights-bearing subject, I hope to underscore the ways in which freedom and slavery presuppose one another, not only as modes of production and discipline or through contiguous forms of subjection but as founding narratives of the liberal subject revisited and revisioned in the context of Reconstruction and the sweeping changes wrought by the abolition of slavery" (*Scenes of Subjection*, 116).

61. Sharon P. Holland, "Going South," *Southern Literary Journal* 46, no. 2 (2014): 111.

62. Holland, "Going South," 111.

63. Lauret Savoy, *Trace: Memory, History, Race, and the American Landscape* (New York: Counterpoint Press, 2015), 21.

64. McKittrick. *Demonic Grounds: Black Women and the Cartographies of Struggle.* Minneapolis, MN: University of Minnesota Press, 2006.

65. hooks, "Earthbound," 188.

66. Saidiya V. Hartman, *Lose Your Mother: A Journey along the Atlantic Slave Route* (New York: Farrar, Straus and Giroux, 2008), 117.

67. See Ntozake Shange, *For Colored Girls Who Have Considered Suicide When the Rainbow Was Enuf* (New York: Scribner, 1997).

68. Susan McFarland, "Wild Women: Literary Explorations of American Landscapes," in *Women Writing Nature: A Feminist View*, ed. Barbara Cook (Washington, DC: Lexington Books, 2007), 41–56.

69. McFarland, "Wild Women," 42.

70. Karen Bell Cook, *Claiming Freedom: Race, Kinship, and Land in Nineteenth-Century Georgia* (Columbia: University of South Carolina Press, 2018), 1.

71. See Combahee River Collective, "The Combahee River Collective Statement (1978)," accessed February 5, 2020, http://circuitous.org/scraps/combahee.html.

72. Paula J. Giddings, *When and Where I Enter: The Impact of Black Women on Race and Sex in America* (New York: Morrow, 1984), 3.

Chapter One: Natural Women

Note on chapter title: I do not mean to suggest in my use of the term "natural woman" that I am talking about cisgender women exclusively with this phrase. Here, I am playing on the title of Aretha Franklin's song to mark my discussion in this chapter which explores the conjunction of nature and Black women as represented in these two texts. "Black women," in this chapter and throughout this book, *always* means transgender and cisgender Black women.

1. The song was written specifically for Franklin. Original release, Aretha Franklin, "(You Make Me Feel Like) A Natural Woman," by Gerry Goffin, Carole King, and Jerry Wexler, *Lady Soul*, Atlantic Records, 1967.

2. Sojourner Truth, "Ain't I a Woman?" Women's Rights National Historical Park, National Park Service, accessed May 3, 2019, www.nps.gov/articles/sojourner-truth.htm.

3. Marvin Meyer, ed. *The Nag Hammadi Scriptures: The Revised and Updated Translation of Sacred Gnostic Texts in One Volume* (New York: HarperOne, 2009).

4. Hortense Spillers, "Mama's Baby, Papa's Maybe: An American Grammar Book," *Diacritics* 17, no. 2 (1987): 65.

5. Spillers, "Mama's Baby, Papa's Maybe," 65.

6. Julie Dash, dir. *Daughters of the Dust*, Kino Films, 1991.

7. German Lopez, "Police Officer Who Slammed Black Girl to the Ground at Mckinney, Texas, Pool Party Resigns," *Vox*, June 9, 2015, accessed April 20, 2019, https://www.vox.com/2015/6/7/8744011/mckinney-texas-police-officer.

8. Jenny Jarvie, "Girl Thrown from Desk Didn't Obey Because the Punishment Was Unfair, Attorney Says," *Los Angeles Times*, October 29, 2015, accessed April 1, 2019, https://www.latimes.com/nation/la-na-girl-thrown-punishment-unfair-20151029-story.html.

9. "#SayHerName Campaign," #SayHerName, http://aapf.org/shn-campaign, accessed April 15, 2019.

10. W. E. B. Du Bois, *The Souls of Black Folk* (New York: Dover, 1903), 2–3.

11. Toni Morrison, *Beloved* (New York: Knopf, 1987), 27.

12. Quoted in Jennifer Machiorlatti, "Revisiting Julie Dash's *Daughters of the Dust*: Black Feminist Narrative and Diasporic Recollection," *South Atlantic Modern Language Association Journal* 70, no. 1 (2005): 98.

13. Machiorlatti, "Revisiting Julie Dash's *Daughters of the Dust*," 98.

14. Critical race theory, sometimes abbreviated as CRT, uses interdisciplinary theory to think about the political, social, and aesthetic consequences of race and racism in contemporary society.

15. Nadia Latif, "It's Lit! How Film Finally Learned to Light Black Skin," *Guardian* Sept. 21, 2017, www.theguardian.com/film/2017/sep/21/its-lit-how-film-finally-learned-how-to-light-black-skin.

16. Will Nicholls. "A Look at How HBO's 'Insecure' Lights Black Actors So Well." *PetaPixel*, Sept. 14, 2017, petapixel.com/2017/09/14/look-hbos-insecure-lights-black-actors/.

17. "The Art of Lighting Dark Skin for Film and HD," Shadow and Act, April 20, 2017, shadowandact.com/2014/02/04/the-art-of-lighting-dark-skin-for-film-and-hd/.

18. Diana Pozo. "Water Color: Radical Color Aesthetics in Julie Dash's *Daughters of the Dust*." *New Review of Film and Television Studies* (2013): 425.

19. Jeanine King, "Memory and the Phantom South in African American Migration Film," *Mississippi Quarterly* 63, nos. 3–4 (2010): 481.

20. Akiba Solomon, "The Pseudoscience of 'Black Women Are Less Attractive,'" *Colorlines*, May 17, 2011, www.colorlines.com/articles/pseudoscience-black-women-are-less-attractive.

21. See Naomi Wolf, *The Beauty Myth: How Images of Beauty Are Used against Women* (New York: HarperCollins, 2009).

22. Tressie McMillan Cottom, *Thick: And Other Essays* (New York: New Press, 2019), 53.

23. Cottom, *Thick*, 56.

24. Cottom, when she published this piece on her blog, received irate email (from women of many races) insisting that she was beautiful and that Black women too were beautiful. These people missed Cottom's larger point about the structural role beauty plays in the maintenance of white supremacy. Furthermore, a quick survey of the Black women often thought to be beautiful (Halle Berry, Beyoncé, Ciara, etc.) reveals that their proximity to white beauty norms is what causes others to perceive them as beautiful.

25. Cottom, *Thick*, 70.

26. Cottom, *Thick*, 87.

27. Cottom, *Thick*, 86.

28. See, among others, Kobena Mercer, Vanessa King, and Ayana Bird and Lori Tharps.

29. Danute Rasimaviciute, "Artist Gives Cosmic Makeovers to Help Celebrate Black Women's Natural Hair," *A Plus*, May 10, 2016, https://articles.aplus.com/a/pierre-jean-louis-black-girl-magic-hair?no_monetization=true.

30. Black people often come under attack for wearing their hair naturally. Recently a teenager in Texas was suspended from school for wearing dreadlocks. This is a common occurrence in America, where Black people's natural hair is constantly policed. See Janelle Griffith, "Second Black Texas Teen Told by School to Cut Dreadlocks, According to His Mom," NBC News, January 24, 2020, https://www.nbcnews.com/news/us-news/second-teen-suspended-over-dreadlocks-texas-school-n1122261.

31. Kristin Denise Rowe, "Nothing Else Mattered after That Wig Came Off: Black Women, Unstyled Hair, and Scenes of Interiority," *Journal of American Culture* 42, no. 1 (2019): 21.

32. Cheryl Thompson, "Black Women, Beauty, and Hair as a Matter of Being," *Women's Studies* 38 (2009): 832.

33. Margaret Hunter, "The Persistent Problem of Colorism: Skin Tone, Status, and Inequality," *Sociology Compass* 1, no. 1 (2007): 238.

34. Hortense Spillers, "Mama's Baby, Papa's Maybe: An American Grammar Book," *Diacritics* 17, no. 2 (1987): 69.

35. Dash, *Daughters of the Dust*.

36. Anissa Janine Wardi, *Water and African American Memory: An Eco-critical Perspective*. (Gainesville: University Press of Florida, 2016), 4.

37. Nana Peazant is tied to the place of Igbo Landing, her ancestors, and nature itself. Nature, then, is not a factor that is somehow "outside" of oneself; rather, nature is contiguous with both human bodies and experience. This is an important distinction, because it means not that the Peazant family "appreciates" nature, but rather that the thing we call nature is understood to be *so* connected with human being-ness that it ceases to be an object, it ceases to be an other. As the spiritual leader of the family and the community, Nana Peazant acts in a manner described by David Abram in his book *The Spell of the Sensuous: Perception and Language in a More-than-Human World* (1996): "The traditional or tribal shaman, I came to discern, acts as an intermediary between the human community and the larger ecological field, ensuring that there is an appropriate flow of nourishment, not just from the landscape to the human inhabitants, but from the human community back to the local earth" (7). Nana is an intermediary between the ancestors, those literally "in" the earth of Igbo Landing and the Atlantic Ocean, and her descendants on the island, mediating the spiritual relationship between them and what Abram calls "the larger ecological field." Eli, who spends much of his time with Nana Peazant attempting to reconcile himself to Eula's rape, can be seen as "sick," because he is out of sync with the land upon which he was born. The rape of his wife has created within him a sense of dislocation from Igbo Landing itself, which spurs his desire to migrate north. In an important scene, Eli confronts Nana, who is sitting on the ground in the Peazant family graveyard. He asks her why her spiritual protection, which he had so believed in and relied upon as a child, had failed to protect his wife. "When we were children, we believed in the coins and the roots and the flowers," he explains.

His narration of his family's traditional spiritual beliefs is tied to a Yoruba cosmology, a West African belief system that emphasizes the embeddedness of human life in nature. I am reminded of a conversation I once had with a friend from Senegal. He told me a story about a man who once cut down some trees near his house so that he could make his house bigger. Everyone in the village advised him not to cut the tree down, because a spirit lived in that tree. To cut the tree down would render the spirit homeless and hence vengeful. The man did not listen, cut down the tree, and expanded his home into a grand palace. The story goes that within three months the man was dead. What struck me about this was the respect that the trees commanded and the unwillingness to see nature as "prosaic and predictable . . . unsuited to mysteries" (Abram, *Spell of the Sensuous*, 9). Instead, my friend's story—and Nana's spiritual lessons to Eli—demonstrate the difference between African and European constructions of nature via a discourse of spirituality. "The deeply mysterious powers and entities with whom the shaman enters into a rapport are ultimately the same forces—the same plants, animals, forests, and winds—that to literate, 'civilized' Europeans are just so much scenery, the pleasant backdrop of our more pressing human concerns" (Abram, *Spell of the Sensuous*, 9). The cautionary tale about the tree from my friend's village reveals that nature is seen not as a "thing," but rather as a being, with which we interact on a not-entirely-equal footing (i.e., nature has more power than do people). Eli's loss of faith in the "flowers and the roots" of his ancestors is a critical situation, because when nature becomes a dead "thing," then people do also. In other words, people and the natural world are one body in this cosmology, separate only via a powerful and dangerous delusion. Hence, when Nana attempts to teach Eli in this graveyard scene, her goal is to help him see the continuity of the womb and the ancestors, of people and nature, of the past and the present.

38. The elision between conversion to Christianity and racial progress goes all the way back to the slave narrative, where evidence of Christian faith was a necessary aspect of proving that one "deserved" freedom.

39. Ishmael Reed, "Foreword," in *Tell My Horse: Voodoo and Life in Haiti and Jamaica*, by Zora Neale Hurston (New York: HarperCollins, 2009), xiii.

40. Theologically speaking, Voodoo is not at all at odds with Christianity, though some evangelical people define Voodoo as the enemy of Christianity. And though our society curates the two as opposites, I want to reject this move outright. While there are certainly divergent cultural foundations for Christianity and Voodoo, for many Diasporic Black people, there is considerable and harmonious overlap between the two. From the ring shout to the veneration of saints, African beliefs inflect the practice of Christianity by many Black people all over the Diaspora.

41. Zora Neale Hurston, *Tell My Horse: Voodoo and Life in Haiti and Jamaica* (New York: HarperCollins, 2009), 9.

42. Nana says as much to Eli in the graveyard when she tells him, "I'm trying to learn you something to take North with you besides all those hopes and dreams." For Nana, the absence of an African-grounded spiritual worldview is a lethal situation for the Black person: she is tortured by the fact that her children and grandchildren believe that the mainland, and Western society, can offer them anything more valuable than their own perfect selves. For Nana, the argument that Black people were somehow in need of "progress" cuts against her deeper spiritual knowledge of her family and of her history.

43. Eve Kosofsky Sedgwick, *Between Men: English Literature and Male Homosocial Desire* (New York: Columbia University Press, 1985).

44. Thich Nhat Hanh, *Interbeing: Fourteen Guidelines for Engaged Buddhism* (Berkeley, CA: Parallax, 1987), 35.

45. Mali Collins-White, "Rethinking the Human: Anti-Respectability and Blackhood," *American Quarterly* 71, no. 1 (2019): 142.

46. "Ratchet," *Urban Dictionary*, April 27, 2014, https://www.urbandictionary.com/define.php?term=ratchet.

47. Collins-White, "Rethinking the Human 141.

48. Yohana Desta, "How Beyoncé's *Lemonade* Helped Bring a Groundbreaking Film Back to Theaters," *Vanity Fair*, August 22, 2016, www.vanityfair.com/hollywood/2016/08/daughters-of-the-dust-exclusive.

49. Collins-White, "Rethinking the Human," 142.

50. Lindsey Stewart, "Work the Root: Black Feminism, Hoodoo Love Rituals, and Practices of Freedom," *Hypatia* 21, no. 1 (2017): 104.

51. Spillers, "Mama's Baby, Papa's Maybe," 68.

52. I learned about the significance of white clothing from a friend who practices Yoruba as her religion. She always wears white on Friday, and doing so, she informed me, represents repelling negative energy. One can read about it in relation to Santeria here: http://www.aboutsanteria.com/iyaboacute.html.

53. Spillers, "Mama's Baby, Papa's Maybe," 68.

54. Jason Pham, "Serena Williams Shut Down Body Critics: 'I Am Strong and Muscular—and Beautiful,'" *Business Insider*, May 31, 2018, www.businessinsider.com/serena-williams-shut-down-body-critics-who-said-she-was-born-a-guy-2018-5.

55. Ruth Nicole Brown, "Pleasure Verses: A Five Element Set," *American Quarterly* 71, no. 1, (2019): 187.

56. Collins-White, "Rethinking the Human," 146.

57. Stewart, "Work the Root," 104.

58. Annie Earnshaw, "Our Goddess Beyoncé: Yoruba Goddesses in *Lemonade*," Medium, Accessed May 3, 2019, http://www.medium.com/beyoncé-lit-and-lemonade/our-goddess-beyoncé-yoruba-goddesses-in-lemonade-921ab922bc89.

59. Joyce Chen, "Beyonce [*sic*] and the Illuminati: Music's Most WTF Conspiracy Theories, Explained," *Rolling Stone*, Oct. 9, 2017, www.rollingstone.com/music/music-news/beyonce-and-the-illuminati-musics-most-wtf-conspiracy-theories-explained-119376/.

60. bell hooks, "The Oppositional Gaze: Black Female Spectators," *Black Looks: Race and Representation* (New York: Routledge, 2015), 115–33.

61. Wardi, *Water and African American Memory*, 1.

Chapter Two: Dead Wild

1. Beyoncé [Knowles], "Formation," Track #12, *Lemonade*, Parkwood/Columbia, 2016.

2. *Trouble the Water*, dir. Tia Lessin and Carl Deal, Zeitgeist Films, 2008.

3. Calvin L. Warren, *Ontological Terror: Blackness, Nihilism, and Emancipation* (Durham, NC: Duke University Press, 2018), 3.

4. Lisa Marie Cacho, *Social Death: Racialized Rightlessness and the Criminalization of the Unprotected* (New York: New York University Press, 2012), 1.

5. Cacho, *Social Death*, 2.

6. The hurricane of 1928 was just as deadly as Katrina. Some 4,500 people died, and it is the hurricane that is referenced in Zora Neale Hurston's book *Their Eyes Were Watching God*. See Nicole Sterghos Brochu, "Florida's Forgotten Storm."

7. Sharon Holland, *Raising the Dead: Readings of Death and (Black) Subjectivity* (Durham, NC: Duke University Press, 2000), 15.

8. "After the Flood," *This American Life*, podcast audio, Ira Glass (host), episode 296, September 9, 2005. https://www.thisamericanlife.org/296/after-the-flood.

9. The photo was taken by the photographer Johnny Nguyen. Read more about the photographer and the photograph: Joseph Rose, "Portland Photographer behind Viral Ferguson Rally 'Hug Photo' Knew 'This Kid Was Special.'" *Oregon Live: The Oregonian*. Last updated January 20, 2019. https://www.oregonlive.com/portland/2014/11/ferguson_photographer_hug_port.html

10. Stacey Patton, "Why Jennifer and Sarah Hart Killed Their Adopted Children," *Dame*, May 2, 2019, www.damemagazine.com/2018/05/02/why-jennifer-and-sarah-hart-killed-their-adopted-children/.

11. Benh Zeitlin, director, *Beasts of the Southern Wild*, Fox Searchlight Pictures, 2012.

12. Curt Guyette, "The Flint Water Crisis Isn't Over," *ACLU Blog*, April 25, 2018, www.aclu.org/blog/racial-justice/race-and-economic-justice/flint-water-crisis-isnt-over.

13. Saidiya Hartman, *Scenes of Subjection: Terror, Slavery, and Self-Making in Nineteenth-Century America*. (Oxford: Oxford University Press, 1997), 3.

14. Warren, *Ontological Terror*, 3.

15. Hartman, *Scenes of Subjection*, 3.

16. Damon Wise, "*Beasts of the Southern Wild*: 'I Didn't Expect People to Like It,'" *Guardian*, October 11, 2012, www.theguardian.com/film/2012/oct/11/beasts-of-the-southern-wild-behn-zeitlin.

17. A. O. Scott, "She's the Man of This Swamp," review of *Beasts of the Southern Wild*, directed by Benh Zeitlin, *New York Times*, June 27, 2012, www.nytimes.com/2012/06/27/movies/beasts-of-the-southern-wild-directed-by-benh-zeitlin.html.

18. Jayna Brown, "*Beasts of the Southern Wild*—The Romance of Precarity II," *Social Text Online*, September 27, 2013, socialtextjournal.org/beasts-of-the-southern-wild-the-romance-of-precarity-ii/.

19. Christina Sharpe, "*Beasts of the Southern Wild*—The Romance of Precarity I," *Social Text Online*, September 27, 2013, socialtextjournal.org/beasts-of-the-southern-wild-the-romance-of-precarity-i/.

20. bell hooks, "No Love in the Wild," New Black Man in Exile: The Digital Home of Mark Anthony Neal, September 5, 2012, www.newblackmaninexile.net/2012/09/bell-hooks-no-love-in-wild.html.

21. Patricia Yaeger, "*Beasts of the Southern Wild* and Dirty Ecology," *Southern Spaces*, February 13 2013, https://southernspaces.org/2013/beasts-southern-wild-and-dirty-ecology.

22. Nicholas Mirzoeff, "Becoming Wild," Occupy 2012, 30 Sept. 2012, www.nicholasmirzoeff.com/O2012/2012/09/30/becoming-wild/.

23. Drew DeSilver, "As American Homes Get Bigger, Energy Efficiency Gains Are Wiped Out," Pew Research Center, November 9, 2015, www.pewresearch.org/fact-tank/2015/11/09/as american-homes-get-bigger-energy-efficiency-gains-are-wiped-out/

24. Hillary Mayell, "As Consumerism Spreads, Earth Suffers, Study Says," *National Geographic*, January 12, 2004, https://www.nationalgeographic.com/environment/2004/01/consumerism-earth-suffers/.

25. Lucy Alibar, "Once There Was a Hushpuppy: On the Origins of *Beasts of the Southern Wild*," *Zoetrope: All-Story* 16, no. 1 (2012): n.p.

26. Alibar, "Once There Was a Hushpuppy."

27. Michael Omi and Howard Winant, *Racial Formation in the United States* (New York: Routledge, 1986).

28. Yaeger, "*Beasts of the Southern Wild* and Dirty Ecology."

29. Mary Douglas, *Purity and Danger: An Analysis of the Concepts of Pollution and Taboo* (New York: Routledge, 1966), loc. 276, Kindle.

30. As I will demonstrate in this chapter, Zora Neale Hurston in *Dust Tracks on the Road* emphasizes the food availability of her homestead as a child. Likewise, even in *Salvage the Bones*, the children know how to find eggs laid by their free range chickens.

31. Zora Neale Hurston, *Dust Tracks on the Road* (New York: Lippincott, 1942), loc. 152, Kindle.

32. See my discussion of this idea in the introduction.

33. Recent media attention has focused on the fact that China will no longer accept US recyclables, and neither will African countries—which had previously received the cast-off trash caused by "fast fashion"—take our recyclable clothing. So, recycling, while certainly admirable in intention, rarely has a profound ecological impact. See Alana Semuels, "Is This the End of Recycling?" *Atlantic*, March 5, 2019, https://www.theatlantic.com/technology/archive/2019/03/china-has-stopped-accepting-our-trash/584131/; and Eleanor Goldberg, "These African Countries Don't Want Your Used Clothing Anymore," *Huffpost*, September 19, 2019, https://www.huffpost.com/entry/these-african-countries-dont-want-your-used-clothing-anymore_n_57cf19bce4b06a74c9f10dd6.

34. Ruth Meyer, "Africa as an Alien Future: The Middle Passage, Afro-Futurism, and Postcolonial Waterworlds," *American Studies* 45, no. 4 (2000): 555–66.

35. Fred Moten, "Blackness and Nothingness: Mysticism in the Flesh," *South Atlantic Quarterly*, 112, no. 4 (2013): 737–80.

36. Alex Weheliye, *Habeas Viscus: Racializing Assemblages, Biopolitics, and Black Feminist Theories of the Human* (Durham, NC: Duke University Press, 2014), 15.

37. Christopher Lloyd, "Creaturely, Throwaway Life after Katrina: *Salvage the Bones* and *Beasts of the Southern Wild*," *South: A Scholarly Journal* 48, no. 2 (Spring 2016): 246–64.

38. Molly Young. "Sarah Hart's Horrific Google Searches Suggest She Prioritized Saving the Lives of Her Dogs, Not Her Children," *Oregon Live*, April 4, 2019, www.oregonlive.com/crime/2019/04/sarah-harts-horrific-google-searches-suggest-she-prioritized-saving-the-lives-of-her-dogs-not-her-children.html.

39. Yaeger, "*Beasts of the Southern Wild* and Dirty Ecology."

40. Moten, "Blackness and Nothingness: Mysticism in the Flesh," 740.

41. Living in the Cincinnati area at the time of this incident, I was privy to many conservations about Harambe and had to endure many white defenses of the gorilla over that of the Black child's life. For more information on this incident, please see Elisha Fieldstadt and Tim Stelloh, "Outrage Grows after Gorilla Harambe Shot Dead at Cincinnati Zoo to Save Tot," NBC News, May 30, 2016, https://www.nbcnews.com/news/us-news/outrage-grows-after-gorilla-harambe-shot-dead-cincinnati-zoo-save-n582706.

42. Leith Huffadine and Freya Noble, "He Didn't Beat His Chest," *Daily Mail*, May 30, 2016, www.dailymail.co.uk/news/article-3617102/Australian-animal-behaviour-expert-doesn-t-believe-gorilla-Harambe-gorilla-hurt-boy.html.

43. Allison May, "Toddler Killed by Alligator at Disney Resort Honored with Statue," *USA Today*, August 9, 2017, www.usatoday.com/story/news/nation-now/2017/08/09/toddler-killed-alligator-near-disney-resort-honored-statue/553497001/.

44. Alexander Cockburn, "Why German Nazis Were Big Fans of Animal Rights," *Seattle Times*, February 1, 1996, community.seattletimes.nwsource.com/archive/?date=19960201&slug=2311809.

45. Tavia Nyong'o, "Little Monsters: Race, Sovereignty, and Queer Inhumanism in *Beasts of the Southern Wild*," *GLQ: A Journal of Gay and Lesbian Studies* 21, nos. 2–3 (May 2015): 249–72.

46. Lloyd, "Creaturely, Throwaway Life after Katrina," 254.

47. Lloyd, "Creaturely, Throwaway Life after Katrina," 254.

48. Charles Leerhsen, "Get Rid of Pit Bulls," *Daily Beast*, March 12, 2010, www.thedailybeast.com/get-rid-of-pit-bulls.

49. Jesmyn Ward, *Salvage the Bones* (New York: Bloomsbury, 2011), 29.

50. Samantha Clark, "Nothing Really Matters: Jean-Paul Sartre, Negation, and Nature." *Environmental Ethics* 38, no. 3 (Fall 2016): 329.

51. Gayatri Chakravorty Spivak, "Can the Subaltern Speak?" In *The Post-colonial Studies Reader*, ed. Bill Ashcroft, Gareth Griffiths, and Helen Tiffin (New York: Routledge, 2006), 33.

52. Though I specifically mention the Kentucky Derby here, this critique can be applied to all horse racing.

53. Lee Hall, "The Last Kentucky Derby," *Counterpunch*, May 3, 2019, www.counterpunch.org/2019/05/03/the-last-kentucky-derby/.

54. Dog-fighting has a long history in Western civilization. See Monica Villavicencio, "A History of Dogfighting," National Public Radio, July 19, 2007, https://www.npr.org/templates/story/story.php?storyId=12108421.

55. This is why the request to touch Black people's hair is so problematic: because it positions the Black person as an animal, and the person asking to touch the hair as the sovereign.

56. Clark, "Nothing Really Matters," 329.

57. Ward, *Salvage*, 79.

58. Ward, *Salvage*, 82.

59. Ward, *Salvage*, 171.

60. Ward, *Salvage*, 49.

61. Ward, *Salvage*, 186.

62. Ward, *Salvage*, 186.

63. Ward, *Salvage*, 2.

64. Ward, *Salvage*, 5.

65. Ward, *Salvage*, 22.

66. Ward, *Salvage*, 54.

67. Ward, *Salvage*, 66.

68. Moten, "Blackness and Nothingness," 739.

69. Moten, "Blackness and Nothingness," 739.

70. Eckhart Tolle, *The Power of Now* (Novato, CA: New World Library, 2010), Kindle.

71. Alan Watts, "Not What Should Be but What Is," YouTube, www.youtube.com/watch?v=8vaaJP6fpJo, accessed July 22, 2019.

72. Christopher Clark, "What Comes to the Surface: Storms, Bodies, and Community in Jesmyn Ward's *Salvage the Bones*," *Mississippi Quarterly* (2017): 344.

73. Clark, "What Comes to the Surface," 344.

74. Linda Hogan, *Dwellings: A Spiritual History of the Living World* (New York: Norton, 2007), 45.

75. Stacey Alaimo, *Undomesticated Ground: Recasting Nature as Feminist Space* (Ithaca: Cornell University Press, 2000), 2.

76. Ward, *Salvage*, 255.

77. Ward, *Salvage*, 255.

78. Ward, *Salvage*, 129.

79. Ward, *Salvage*, 130.

80. See Alaimo, *Undomesticated Ground*, 108.

81. Alaimo, *Undomesticated Ground*, 128.

82. Denise Ferreira da Silva, "1 (life) ÷ 0 (blackness) = $\infty - \infty$ or ∞ / ∞: On Matter beyond the Equation of Value," *E-Flux* 79 (Feb. 2017): n.p. www.e-flux.com/journal/79/94686/1-life-0-blackness-or-on-matter-beyond-the-equation-of-value/.

83. Ward, *Salvage*, 254.
84. Ward, *Salvage*, 255.
85. Ward, *Salvage*, 258.
86. Ward, *Salvage*, 83.
87. Ferreira da Silva, 10.
88. Ward, *Salvage*, 258.

Chapter Three: Flesh of the Earth

1. Jared Sexton, "The Vel of Slavery: Tracking the Figure of the Unsovereign," *Critical Sociology* 42, nos. 4–5 (July 2016): 11.
2. The term "lost commons" should be understood to reference a view of progress where the notion that the restoration of lost things, especially as it relates to land and identity in this case, is what freedom looks like. If one way we understand Blackness is as a term that indicates the beginning of a loss—loss of African indigeneity, as I argue in this chapter—then it is a common loss, one that characterizes the experience of everyone who is Black.
3. Sexton, "Vel of Slavery," 5.
4. I am referring here to the notion that access to seats of power will somehow ameliorate the experience of oppression.
5. For a full explanation of the Pali translation of the word "Nibbāna," see Wikipedia, The Free Encyclopedia, *s.v.* "Nirvana (Buddhism)," accessed May 10, 2019, https://en.wikipedia.org/wiki/Nirvana_(Buddhism)
6. If no one owns anything, nothing can be stolen. Hence, private property actually creates theft.
7. Carolyn Finney, *Black Faces, White Spaces: Reimagining the Relationship of African Americans to the Great Outdoors* (Chapel Hill: University of North Carolina Press, 2014), 58.
8. Finney, *Black Faces, White Spaces*, 58.
9. Sexton, "Vel of Slavery," 11.
10. Ralph Ellison, *Invisible Man* (New York: Vintage, 1952), 377.
11. When I use the word "homelessness" throughout this chapter, I am not talking about homelessness that results from poverty. I am using the word here as it is understood in Buddhist rhetoric to refer to a movement away from ownership and acquisition as a governing logic for one's life. In other words, "homelessness" here refers to renunciation of material worldliness. See Stuart Smithers, "Homelessness into Home: On the Origins of Buddhist Monasticism," *Tricycle*, Winter 1995. https://tricycle.org/magazine/homelessness-home/.
12. Rousseau traces the origin of inequality to private property in useful ways. Jean-Jacques Rousseau, "On the Origin of Inequality of Mankind," https://www.marxists.org/reference/subject/economics/rousseau/inequality/ch02.htm.
13. Paul Deloria, *Playing Indian* (New Haven: Yale University Press, 1988), 4.
14. Karen Bell Cook, *Claiming Freedom: Race, Kinship, and Land in Nineteenth-Century Georgia* (Columbia: University of South Carolina Press, 2018), 53.
15. Kanye West, "All Falls Down," *The College Dropout*, Rock-A-Fella/Def Jam, 2004.
16. *Queen Sugar*, Ava DuVernay, dir., OWN (Oprah Winfrey Network), 2016.
17. Kaitlyn Greenidge, *We Love You, Charlie Freeman* (New York: Algonquin Books, 2016).
18. Jack Halberstam, *The Queer Art of Failure* (Durham, NC: Duke University Press, 2011), 88.

19. Marie Tyler-McGraw, *An African Republic: Black and White Virginians in the Making of Liberia* (Chapel Hill: University of North Carolina Press, 2007).

20. See Tyler-McGraw, *African Republic*.

21. Howard C. Westwood. "Sherman Marched: And Proclaimed 'Land for the Landless.'" *South Carolina Historical Magazine* 85, no. 1 (1984), 33–50.

22. Halberstam, *Queer Art*, 88. Here Halberstam is referencing the work of Scott Sandage.

23. Elise Hansen, "The Forgotten Minority in Police Shootings," CNN, November 13, 2017, www.cnn.com/2017/11/10/us/native-lives-matter/index.html.

24. See David Seipp, "The Concept of Property in the Early Common Law," *Law and History Review* 12, no. 1 (Spring 1994), 29–91.

25. *Queen Sugar*, "Pleasure Is Black," directed by Cheryl Dunye, season 4, episode 1, OWN, June 12, 2019.

26. Hortense Spillers, "Who Cuts the Border? Some Readings on America," in *Black, White, and in Color: Essays on American Literature and Culture* (Chicago: University of Chicago Press, 2003), 323.

27. Daniel Geary. "The Moynihan Report: An Annotated Edition." *Atlantic*, September 14, 2015, www.theatlantic.com/politics/archive/2015/09/the-moynihan-report-an-annotated-edition/404632/.

28. Dianne Glave, *Rooted in Earth: Reclaiming the African American Environmental Heritage* (Chicago: Lawrence Hill Books, 2010), 44.

29. Interestingly, Aunt Vi's diner and pie-making business relates to the family business of making sugar—so that the success of all the family members, except Nova, is symbolically and literally linked to sugar.

30. I am using the word "business" here to refer to the Black vernacular use of it as that which is private, as in "that's my business" or "mind your own business."

31. Mary Choplecti, "The Property Rights Origins of Privacy Rights," *Foundation for Economic Education*, August 1, 1992, fee.org/articles/the-property-rights-origins-of-privacy-rights/.

32. Sara Ahmed, *Living a Feminist Life* (Durham, NC: Duke University Press, 2016), 22.

33. See Saidiya Hartman, *Lose Your Mother: A Journey along the Atlantic Slave Route* (New York: Farrar, Straus and Giroux, 2008), 6.

34. Ta-Nehisi Coates, "The Case for Reparations," *Atlantic*, June 2016, https://www.theatlantic.com/magazine/archive/2014/06/the-case-for-reparations/361631/.

35. Sharon Gay Stolberg, "At Historic Hearing, House Panel Explores Reparations," *New York Times*, June 19, 2019, https://www.nytimes.com/2019/06/19/us/politics/slavery-reparations-hearing.html.

36. Andrew W. Kahrl, "Black People's Land Was Stolen." *New York Times*, June 20, 2019, www.nytimes.com/2019/06/20/opinion/sunday/reparations-hearing.html.

37. Sounds of Blackness, "African Medley: Royal Kingdoms," *Africa to America: The Journey of the Drum*, Perspective Records, 1994.

38. "Blaxit" is a term that combines "Black" and "exit" that was coined to describe Black exhaustion with American racism and to reference the notion of a profound (and perhaps literal) departure of Black people from American society.

39. Elizabeth Abbott, *Sugar: A Bittersweet History* (New York: Abrams, 2011), i.

40. Kara Walker, *A Subtlety*, debuted at the Domino Sugar Factory, New York, 2014.

41. Lizzie Collingham, *The Taste for Empire: How Britain's Quest for Food Shaped the Modern World* (New York: Basic Books, 2017), 50.

42. Collingham, *Taste for Empire*, 48.

43. The Netflix documentary *The 13th* explores the history of the way in which provisions around convict labor in the Thirteenth Amendment have been used to disproportionately imprison Black people. Some historians, such as Daryl Scott, however, have pushed back against this perception of the Thirteenth Amendment as being a loophole that extended slavery in a de facto fashion. For the purposes of my argument here, though, the popular understanding—due to texts like the documentary *The 13th* and the fact that both that documentary and *Queen Sugar* are directed and produced by Ava DuVernay—that contemporary prisons extend (or even expand) bondage for Black people is at play in *Queen Sugar*'s textual layering of the site of the plantation and the prison. For a rebuttal of the claims made in the documentary *The 13th*, see Patrick Rael, "Demystifying the 13th Amendment and Its Impact on Mass Incarceration," *Black Perspectives*, December 9, 2016, https://www.aaihs.org/demystifying-the-13th-amendment-and-its-impact-on-mass-incarceration/?fbclid=IwAR3T7a1sL8tE6dWqz7pVFop5c706LezaYqX0W487sMmEBTehrjD4ZQYv8Kk.

44. Katherine McKittrick, *Demonic Grounds: Black Women and the Cartographies of Struggle*. (Minneapolis: University of Minnesota Press, 2006), loc. 823, Kindle.

45. McKittrick, *Demonic Grounds*, loc. 840.

46. See David Abram, *The Spell of the Sensuous: Perception and Language in a More-than-Human World* (New York: Vintage Books, 2017), 7.

47. *Queen Sugar*, "Thy Will Be Done," season 1, episode 3, directed by Neema Barnette, OWN, September 14, 2016.

48. Orlando Patterson, *Slavery and Social Death: A Comparative Study* (Cambridge: Harvard University Press, 1982).

49. McKittrick, *Demonic Grounds*, loc. 803.

50. *Queen Sugar*, "As Promised," season 1, episode 6, directed by Victoria Mahoney, OWN, September 28, 2016.

51. Stefano Harney, and Fred Moten, *The Undercommons: Fugitive Planning and Black Study*. (Wivenhoe, UK: Minor Compositions, 2013), 18.

52. Thomas Jefferson, *Notes on the State of Virginia* (London: Prichard and Hall, 1787), https://docsouth.unc.edu/southlit/jefferson/jefferson.html.

53. Calvin Warren, *Ontological Terror: Blackness, Nihilism, and Emancipation* (Durham, NC: Duke University Press, 2018), 2, 5.

54. Warren, *Ontological Terror*, 27.

55. James Baldwin, *I Am Not Your Negro*, directed by Raoul Peck, Magnolia Pictures, 2017.

56. It is well known that Jefferson conducted a decades-long sexual assault upon Sally Hemmings, who was a slave and, as a fourteen-year-old when his advances began, could not give consent or protect herself from his advances.

57. Hamilton Cravens, "What's New in Science and Race since the 1930s: Anthropologists and Racial Essentialism." *Historian* 72, no. 2 (2010): 300.

58. Eckhart Tolle, *Power of Now*, 81.

59. Eckhart Tolle, *Power of Now*, 80.

60. Michel Foucault, "The Culture of the Self," *YouTube*, accessed April 25, 2019, www.youtube.com/watch?list=PL9C78808A41B0AC89&v=umi43H0-I24.

61. Alan Watts, "Not What Should Be but What Is," *YouTube*, accessed July 22, 2019, www.youtube.com/watch?v=8vaaJP6fpJ0.

62. Alan Watts, "Not What Should Be but What Is."

63. Warren, *Ontological Terror*, 27.

64. Warren, *Ontological Terror*, 33.

65. Eve K. Sedgwick, "The Pedagogy of Buddhism," *Touching Feeling: Affect, Pedagogy, and Performativity* (Durham, NC: Duke University Press, 2003), 160.

66. Sam Harris, "The Illusion of the Self: An Interview with Bruce Hood," Sam Harris, May 22, 2012, https://samharris.org/the-illusion-of-the-self2/.

67. Kevin Quashie, *The Sovereignty of the Quiet: Beyond Resistance in Black Culture* (New Brunswick, NJ: Rutgers University Press, 2012), 119.

68. Quashie, *Sovereignty of the Quiet*, 120.

69. Nymphadora's name, despite sounding sexual, is accidental; later, when she runs off (temporarily) into the woods, we might think of her name as pointing to the idea of woodland nymphs.

70. Frederick J. Simoons and James A. Baldwin, "Breast-Feeding of Animals by Women: Its Socio-Culture Context and Geographic Occurrence," *Anthropos* 77, nos. 3–4 (1982): 421–48.

71. Greenidge, *We Love You, Charlie Freeman*, 267.

72. Greenidge, *We Love You, Charlie Freeman*, 268.

73. Greenidge, *We Love You, Charlie Freeman*, 268.

74. Greenidge, *We Love You, Charlie Freeman*, 272.

75. Greenidge, *We Love You, Charlie Freeman*, 272.

76. Warren, *Ontological Terror*, 172.

77. Greenidge, *We Love You, Charlie Freeman*, 324.

78. Kosho Uchiyama Roshi and Shohaku Okamura, *The Zen Teaching of Homeless Kodo*, ed. Jokei Molly Delight Whitehead (Somerville, MA: Wisdom, 1981), loc. 332.

79. Roshi, *Zen Teaching of Homeless Kodo*, loc. 541.

80. This is important because it represents a spiritual way of tracking an "axiological disinvestment" from the "categories of the human," to follow Calvin Warren's philosophical model of transcendence. Roshi, *Zen Teaching of Homeless Kodo*, loc. 1080.

81. Roshi, *Zen Teaching of Homeless Kodo*, loc. 1080.

82. Warren, *Ontological Terror*, 72.

83. Though this quote is widely attributed to the Dalai Lama, I cannot find the origin or source material from which it is drawn.

84. Abram, *Spell of the Sensuous*, 140.

85. John Zerzan, "Finding Our Way Back Home," in *Twilight of the Machines* (Port Townsend, WA: Feral House, 2008), 124.

86. Aquimin, "Get off My Property," *Black Land Project*, March 30, 2019, http://www.blacklandproject.org/stories/get-off-my-property.

87. Aquimin, "Get off My Property."

88. I am bisexual and identify as queer, which I write about briefly in my book *Queer in Black and White: Interraciality, Same Sex Desire, and Contemporary African American Culture*. (Bloomington: Indiana University Press, 2009).

89. Raoul Vaneigem, *The Movement of the Free Spirit* (New York: Zone Books, 1994), 20.

Chapter Four: Plant Life (Notes on the End of the World)

1. The film was based on the Thomas Dixon novel *The Clansman*.

2. Quoted in Arthur Lennig, "Myth and Fact: The Reception of 'Birth of a Nation,'" *Film History* 16, no. 2 (2004): 120.

3. Lennig, "Myth and Fact," 120.

4. http://www.americanradioworks.org/segments/hbcu-history/.

5. https://en.wikipedia.org/wiki/List_of_Freedmen%27s_towns.

6. David Christopher, "The Capitalist and Cultural Work of Apocalypse and Dystopia Films," *Cineaction* 95 (April 2015): 56.

7. James Joyner, "How Perpetual War Became U.S. Ideology." *Atlantic*. May 11, 2011. https://www.theatlantic.com/international/archive/2011/05/how-perpetual-war-became-us-ideology/238600/.

8. Katherine Smith et al. "Global Rise in Human Infection Disease Outbreaks," Royal Society, 2014, https://www.ncbi.nlm.nih.gov/pmc/articles/PMC4223919/.

9. David Wood, Twitter post, May 20, 2017, https://twitter.com/dw2/status/869630490109767680?lang=en.

10. Christopher, "Capitalist and Cultural Work," 56.

11. See Elizabeth Stamp, "Billionaire Bunkers: How the 1% Are Preparing for the Apocalypse," CNN, August 7, 2019, https://www.cnn.com/style/article/doomsday-luxury-bunkers/index.html.

12. Nafeez Ahmed, "NASA Funded Study: Industrial Civilization Headed for Irreversible Collapse," *Guardian*, March 14, 2014, https://www.theguardian.com/environment/earth-insight/2014/mar/14/nasa-civilisation-irreversible-collapse-study-scientists.

13. Ahmed, "NASA Funded Study."

14. REM, "It's the End of the World as We Know It (And I Feel Fine)," *Document*, I.R.S. Records, 1987.

15. Frank Wilderson III, "Blacks and the Master/Slave Relation," in *Afro-Pessimism: An Introduction* (Minneapolis: Racked and Dispatched, September 2017), 30, https://rackedanddispatched.noblogs.org/files/2017/01/Afro-pessimism2_imposed.pdf.

16. I am always talking about whiteness when I evoke the human, following Calvin Warren's construction in *Ontological Terror*.

17. Denise Ferreira da Silva, "1 (life) ÷ 0 (blackness) = $\infty - \infty$ or ∞ / ∞: On Matter beyond the Equation of Value," *E-Flux*, 79, February 2017, www.e-flux.com/journal/79/94686/1-life-0-blackness-or-on-matter-beyond-the-equation-of value/.

18. Ferreira da Silva, 10.

19. Calvin L. Warren, *Ontological Terror: Blackness, Nihilism, and Emancipation.* (Durham, NC: Duke University Press, 2018), 6.

20. Malidoma Patrice Somé, *Of Water and the Spirit: Ritual, Magic and Initiation in the Life of an African Shaman* (London: Penguin Books, 1995), 141.

21. Somé, *Of Water and Spirit*, 145.

22. Somé, *Of Water and Spirit*, 150.

23. "Harriet Tubman and the Underground Railroad," National Park Service, March 11, 2017, https://www.nps.gov/articles/harriet-tubman-and-the-underground-railroad.htm.

24. Octavia Butler, *Parable of the Sower* (New York: Warner Books, 1993), 51.

25. Butler, *Parable of the Sower*, 55.

26. Butler, *Parable of the Sower*, 160.

27. Butler, *Parable of the Sower*, 137.

28. Victoria Ward, "Humans May Have Evolved Genes from Plants," *Telegraph*, March 13, 2015, https://www.telegraph.co.uk/news/science/11467685/Humans-may-have-evolved-with-genes-from-plants-study-finds.html.

29. Enrique Salmon, "Sharing Breath: Some Links between Land, Plants, and People," in *The Colors of Nature*, ed. Alison H. Deming and Lauret E. Savoy (Minneapolis:: Milkweed Editions, 2011), 74–75.

30. Ferreira da Silva, "1 (life)."

31. M. R. Carey, *The Girl with All the Gifts* (London: Orbit Books, 2015).

32. Kimberly Hurd Hale and Erin A. Dolgoy, "Humanity in a Posthuman World: M. R. Carey's *The Girl with All the Gifts*," *Utopia Studies* 29, no. 3 (2018): 344.

33. Colm McCarthy, dir. *The Girl with All The Gifts*. Warner Brothers Pictures, 2016.

34. Hale and Dolgoy, "Humanity in a Posthuman World," 343.

35. Suzanne Césaire, "The Malaise of Civilization," *The Great Camouflage: Writings of Dissent (1941–1945)* (Middletown, CT: Wesleyan University Press, 2012), 28.

36. Césaire, "Malaise of Civilization," 30.

37. Césaire, "Malaise of Civilization," 30.

38. Hale and Dolgoy, "Humanity in a Posthuman World," 344.

39. Andy Goldsworthy, *Sacred Ecology*, https://sacredecology.com/andygoldsworthy/?fbcl id=IwAR2YJZ1oxfcq6IlPot151It50aa-4IH8JFx79APVzQUJvHtoI9HQdW-z0A.

40. Quoted in Roberto De Vogli, *Progress or Collapse: The Price of Market Greed* (New York: Routledge, 2013), 204.

41. Césaire, "Malaise of Civilization," 31.

42. I'd like to point out that though we've been told that the fall of civilization is dangerous, this obscures the reality that life in civilization is *already* dangerous. The scenario Butler writes in *Parable* where Pyros destroy the community, must be what the people of MOVE in Philadelphia felt when the government firebombed their homes—killing women, men, and children in the process. The notion that without civilization we would all be in danger falsely implies that *within* civilization we are safe—which for the Black person has never been true. Furthermore, with the ever-present shootings, in schools and public places, the expansion of the carceral state, living with poisoned water and air, and a capitalist ruthlessness so pernicious that some voters once said they'd rather let someone die in the street than have universal health care, life in civilization is already, by definition, dangerous. On health care, see Jeneed Interlandi. "Why Doesn't the United States Have Universal Health Care? The Answer Has Everything to Do with Race," *New York Times Magazine*, August 14, 2019, https://www.nytimes.com/interactive/2019/08/14/magazine/universal-health-care-racism .html

43. Butler, *Parable of the Sower*, 91.

44. Madhu Dubey, "Folk and Urban Communities in African American Women's Fiction: Octavia Butler's *Parable of the Sower*," *Studies in American Fiction* 27 (1999): 106.

45. Martin Luther King Jr., "I Have a Dream," *I Have a Dream: Writings and Speeches That Changed the World* (San Francisco: Harper Books, 1986), 101.

46. Black Panther Party, "The Ten-Point Program" (1966), https://www.marxists.org/ history/usa/workers/black-panthers/1966/10/15.htm.

47. "Introduction," in *Afro-Pessimism: An Introduction* (Minneapolis: Racked and Dispatched, 2017), 11.

48. Michael Barlow, "Addressing Shortcomings in Afro-Pessimism," *Inquiries Journal: Social Sciences, Arts and Humanities* 8, no 9. (2016), http://www.inquiriesjournal.com/ articles/1435/2/addressing-shortcomings-in-afro-pessimism.

49. Barlow, "Addressing Shortcomings."

50. Jared Sexton, "The Social Life of Social Death: On Afro-Pessimism and Black Optimism," *InTensions* 5 (Fall/Winter 2011), 9.

51. Darryl Pinckney, "The Afro-Pessimist Temptation," *New York Review of Books*, June 7, 2018, https://www.nybooks.com/articles/2018/06/07/ta-nehisi-coates-afro-pessimist -temptation/.

52. Pinckney, "Afro-Pessimist Temptation."
53. Pinckney, "Afro-Pessimist Temptation."
54. Pinckney, "Afro-Pessimist Temptation."
55. Césaire, "Malaise of Civilization," 32.
56. Césaire, "Malaise of Civilization," 30.
57. Frank Wilderson III, "Blacks and the Master/Slave Relation," in *Afro-Pessimism: An Introduction* (Minneapolis: Racked and Dispatched, 2017), 78, https://rackedanddispatched.noblogs.org/files/2017/01/Afro-pessimism2_imposed.pdf.
58. By using the word "assimilation," I'm not referencing the way that word has often been used to police folks around Black authenticity. What I mean here is the degree to which one believes that this American/Western society, which is based upon anti-Blackness, bondage, and oppression, can be saved. If one believes that, this means one has already assimilated the idea that civilization itself (as it more or less currently exists) is desirable. I contend here that civilization, in every iteration, is always the opposite of freedom.
59. Jared Sexton, "The Vel of Slavery: Tracking the Figure of the Unsovereign," in *Afro-Pessimism: An Introduction* (Minneapolis: Racked and Dispatched, 2017), 169, https://rackedanddispatched.noblogs.org/files/2017/01/Afro-pessimism2_imposed.pdf
60. Césaire, "Malaise of Civilization," 33.
61. Warren, *Ontological Terror*, 172.
62. Jerry Phillips, "The Intuition of the Future: Utopia and Catastrophe in Octavia Butler's *Parable of the Sower*," NOVEL: A Forum on Fiction 35, nos. 2–3 (2002), 301.
63. James C. Scott, *Against the Grain: A Deep History of the Earliest States* (New Haven: Yale University Press, 2018), 155.
64. Scott, *Against the Grain*, 202.
65. Scott, *Against the Grain*, 209.
66. Nassim Nicholas Taleb, *Anti-fragile: Things That Gain from Disorder* (New York: Random House, 2012), 4.
67. Césaire, "Malaise of Civilization," 33.
68. It may seem odd to refer to plants as "abolitionist," but consider the fact that without constant weeding, microgardens set up by humans are soon overrun by "unwanted" plants. Plants are notoriously good at ignoring human attempts to prune them back or "keep them in their place."
69. Lucy Munro, "Abandoned Garden Anarchy," TPH: The Plant Hunter, May 25, 2018, https://theplanthunter.com.au/botanica/abandoned-garden-anarchy/.
70. Munro, "Abandoned Garden Anarchy."
71. Peter Wohlleben, *The Hidden Life of Trees: What They Feel, How They Communicate, Discoveries from a Secret World* (Vancouver, Canada: Greystone Books, 2015), 51.

Coda: Take Me Outside

1. Laura Mvula, "Green Garden," *Sing to the Moon*, RCA Records/Sony Music, 2012.
2. Wikipedia, *s.v.* "Gaia Hypothesis," last modified January 24, 2020. https://en.wikipedia.org/wiki/Gaia_hypothesis.
3. Lucille Clifton, "won't you celebrate with me," in *The Collected Poems of Lucille Clifton, 1965–2010*, ed. Kevin Young and Michael Glaser (New York: BOA Editions, 2012), loc. 2915, Kindle.

BIBLIOGRAPHY

Abbott, Elizabeth. *Sugar: A Bittersweet History.* New York: Abrams Press, 2011.
Abram, David. *The Spell of the Sensuous: Perception and Language in a More-than-Human World.* New York: Vintage Books, 2017.
"After the Flood." *This American Life.* American Public Radio. Ira Glass (host). Podcast audio, episode 296. September 9, 2005. https://www.thisamericanlife.org/296/after-the-flood.
Ahmed, Nafeez. "NASA Funded Study: Industrial Civilization Headed for Irreversible Collapse." *Guardian.* March 14, 2014. https://www.theguardian.com/environment/earth-insight/2014/mar/14/nasa-civilisation-irreversible-collapse-study-scientists.
Ahmed, Sara. *Living a Feminist Life.* Durham, NC: Duke University Press, 2016.
Alaimo, Stacey. *Undomesticated Ground: Recasting Nature as Feminist Space.* Ithaca: Cornell University Press, 2000.
Alibar, Lucy. "Once There Was a Hushpuppy: On the Origins of *Beasts of the Southern Wild.*" *Allstory* 16, no. 3. https://www.all-story.com/issues/62/stories/496. Accessed March 5, 2019.
Allen, Reniqa. "Racism Is Everywhere, So Why Not Move South?" *New York Times*, July 8, 2017. www.nytimes.com/2017/07/08/opinion/sunday/racism-is-everywhere-so-why-not-move-south.html.
Aquimin. "Get off My Property." Black Land Project. Accessed March 30, 2019. www.blacklandproject.org/stories/get-off-my-property.
"The Art of Lighting Dark Skin for Film and HD." Shadow and Act, April 20, 2017. shadowandact.com/2014/02/04/the-art-of-lighting-dark-skin-for-film-and-hd/.
Bacon, Sir Francis Bacon. *Novum Organum.* Edited by Joseph Devey. P. F. Collier, 1902. *Online Library of Liberty.* Accessed March 1, 2019. oll.libertyfund.org/titles/1432.
Barad, Karen. "Nature's Queer Performativity." *Qui Parle* 19, no. 2 (2011): 121–58.
Barlow, Michael. "Addressing Shortcomings in Afro-Pessimism." *Inquiries Journal: Social Sciences, Arts and Humanities* 8, no. 9. Accessed April 8, 2019. http://www.inquiriesjournal.com/articles/1435/2/addressing-shortcomings-in-afro-pessimism.
Bennett, Kanya. "Say Her Name: Recognizing Police Brutality against Black Women." ACLU, June 14, 2018. www.aclu.org/blog/criminal-law-reform/reforming-police-practices/say-her-name-recognizing-police-brutality.
Beyoncé [Knowles]. *Lemonade.* Parkwood Entertainment, Columbia Records, 2016.
Beyoncé [Knowles.] "Flawless." On *Beyoncé.* Parkwood Entertainment, Columbia Records, 2013.

Bird, Ayana, and Lori Tharp. *Hair Story: Untangling the Roots of Black Hair in America*. New York: St. Martin's Griffin, 2002.

"Black Hiker." Sketch in *Funny or Die*, Directed by Brad Schulz. November 24, 2009, www.funnyordie.com/2009/11/24/18021000/black-hiker-with-blair-underwood.

Black Panther Party. "The Ten Point Program, 1966." Accessed March 15, 2019. https://www.marxists.org/history/usa/workers/black-panthers/1966/10/15.htm.

Blum, Alexander. "How the Enlightenment Separated Humanity from Nature." Arc Digital. Accessed March 21, 2019. arcdigital.media/how-the-enlightenment-separated-humanity-from-nature-c008881a61b0.

Bogado, Aura. "Why People of Color Don't Frequent National Parks." *Colorlines*, July 13, 2015. www.colorlines.com/articles/why-people-color-don%E2%80%99t-frequent-national-parks.

Brochu, Nicole Sterghos. "Florida's Forgotten Storm: The Hurricane of 1928." *South Florida Sun-Sentinel*, September 14, 2014. www.sun-sentinel.com/sfl-ahurricane14sep14-story.html.

Brown, Jayna. "*Beasts of the Southern Wild*—The Romance of Precarity II." *Social Text Online*, September 27, 2013. socialtextjournal.org/beasts-of-the-southern-wild-the-romance-of-precarity-ii/.

Brown, Ruth Nicole. "Pleasure Verses: A Five Element Set." *American Quarterly* 71, no. 1 (March 2019): 179–89.

Burleson, Blake. "Jung in Africa: The Historical Record." *Journal of Analytical Psychology* 53 (2008): 209–23.

Butler, Octavia. *Parable of the Sower*. New York: Warner Books, 1993.

Cacho, Lisa Marie. *Social Death: Racialized Rightlessness and the Criminalization of the Unprotected*. New York: NYU Press, 2012.

Carey, Mike. *The Girl With All the Gifts*. London: Orbit Books, 2014.

Césaire, Suzanne. *The Great Camouflage: Writings of Dissent (1941–1945)*. Middletown, CT: Wesleyan University Press, 2012.

Chen, Joyce. "Beyonce [sic] and the Illuminati: Music's Most WTF Conspiracy Theories, Explained." *Rolling Stone*, October 9, 2017. www.rollingstone.com/music/music-news/beyonce-and-the-illuminati-musics-most-wtf-conspiracy-theories-explained-119376/.

Choplecti, Mary. "The Property Rights Origins of Privacy Rights." Foundation for Economic Education, August 1, 1992. fee.org/articles/the-property-rights-origins-of-privacy-rights/.

Christensen, Bo Allesøe. "Why Do We Care about Post-humanism? A Critical Note." *Geografiska Annaler: Series B, Human Geography* 96, no. 1 (2014): 23–35.

Christopher, David. "The Capitalist and Cultural Work of Apocalypse and Dystopia Films." *Cineaction* 95 (April 2015): 56+.

Clark, Christopher. "What Comes to the Surface: Storms, Bodies, and Community in Jesmyn Ward's *Salvage the Bones*." *Mississippi Quarterly* 68, nos. 3–4 (2017): 341–58.

Clark, Samantha. "Nothing Really Matters: Jean-Paul Sartre, Negation, and Nature." *Environmental Ethics* 38, no. 3 (Fall 2016): 327–46.

Clifton, Lucille. "the earth is a living thing." In *Black Nature: Four Centuries of African American Nature Poetry*, edited by Camille Dungy. Athens: University of Georgia Press, 2009.

Clifton, Lucille. "*won't you come celebrate with me*." In *The Collected Poems of Lucille Clifton, 1965–2010*. Edited by Kevin Young and Michael S. Glaser. New York: BOA Editions, 2012.

Coates, Ta-Nehisi. *Between the World and Me*. Spiegel and Grau, 2015.

Coates, Ta-Nehisi. "The Case for Reparations." *Atlantic*, June 2014. www.theatlantic.com/magazine/archive/2014/06/the-case-for-reparations/361631/.

Cockburn, Alexander. "Why German Nazis Were Big Fans of Animal Rights." *Seattle Times*, February 1, 1996. community.seattletimes.nwsource.com/archive/?date=19960201&s lug=2311809.
Collingham, Lizzie. *The Taste for Empire: How Britain's Quest for Food Shaped the Modern World*. New York: Basic Books, 2017.
Collins-White, Mali. "Rethinking the Human: Anti-Respectability and Blackhood." *American Quarterly* 71, no. 1 (March 2019): 141–49.
Cook, Karen Bell. *Claiming Freedom: Race, Kinship, and Land in Nineteenth-Century Georgia*. Columbia: University of South Carolina Press, 2018.
Cottom, Tressie McMillan. *Thick: And Other Essays*. New York: New Press, 2019.
Cravens, Hamilton. "What's New in Science and Race since the 1930s: Anthropologists and Racial Essentialism." *Historian* 72, no. 2 (2010): 299–320.
Dash, Julie, dir. *Daughters of the Dust*. Kino on Video, 1991.
Davis, Angela Y. *Blues Legacies and Black Feminism: Gertrude Ma Rainey, Bessie Smith, and Billie Holiday*. New York: Vintage, 2011.
Deloria, Paul. *Playing Indian*. New Haven: Yale University Press, 1988.
DeSilver, Drew. "As American Homes Get Bigger, Energy Efficiency Gains Are Wiped Out." Pew Research Center, November 9, 2015. www.pewresearch.org/fact-tank/2015/11/09/as-american-homes-get-bigger-energy-efficiency-gains-are-wiped-out/.
Desta, Yohana. "How Beyoncé's *Lemonade* Helped Bring a Groundbreaking Film Back to Theaters." *Vanity Fair*, August 22, 2016. www.vanityfair.com/hollywood/2016/08/daughters-of-the-dust-exclusive.
D.K. "Why Many British Homeowners Don't Actually Own Their Homes at All." *Economist*, June 11, 2014. www.economist.com/the-economist-explains/2014/06/10/why-many-british-homeowners-dont-actually-own-their-homes-at-all.
Douglas, Mary. *Purity and Danger: An Analysis of the Concepts of Pollution and Taboo*. New York: Routledge, 1966, Kindle edition.
Dubey, Madhu. "Folk and Urban Communities in African American Women's Fiction: Octavia Butler's *Parable of the Sower*." *Studies in American Fiction* 27 (1999): 103–28.
Du Bois, W. E. B. *The Souls of Black Folk*. New York: Dover, 1905.
Dunning, Stefanie K. *Queer in Black and White: Interraciality, Same Sex Desire, and Contemporary African American Culture*. Bloomington: Indiana University Press, 2009.
DuVernay, Ava, dir. *Queen Sugar*. OWN (Oprah Winfrey Network), 2016.
Earnshaw, Annie. "Our Goddess Beyoncé: Yoruba Goddesses in *Lemonade*." Medium. Accessed May 3, 2019. medium.com/beyoncé-lit-and-lemonade/our-goddess-beyoncé-yoruba-goddesses-in-lemonade-921ab922bc89.
Ellison, Ralph. *Invisible Man*. New York: Vintage Books, 1952.
Equiano, Olaudah. *The Interesting Narrative of the Life of Olaudah Equiano*. London: Penguin, 2003.
Ferreira da Silva, Denise. "1 (life) ÷ 0 (blackness) = $\infty - \infty$ or ∞ / ∞: On Matter beyond the Equation of Value." *E-Flux*, no. 79 (February 2017), www.e-flux.com/journal/79/94686/1-life-o-blackness-or-on-matter-beyond-the-equation-of-value/.
Finney, Carolyn. *Black Faces, White Spaces: Reimagining the Relationship of African Americans to the Great Outdoors*. Chapel Hill: University of North Carolina Press, 2014.
Foucault, Michel. "The Culture of the Self." *YouTube*. Accessed September 10, 2018. www.youtube.com/watch?list=PL9C78808A41B0AC89&v=umi43H0-I24.
Franklin, Aretha. "(You Make Me Feel Like) A Natural Woman." By Gerry Goffin, Carole King, and Jerry Wexler. *Lady Soul*, Atlantic Records, 1967.

Gates, Henry Louis Jr. "The Truth behind 40 Acres and a Mule." Public Broadcasting Service, Accessed April 14, 2018. www.pbs.org/wnet/african-americans-many-rivers-to-cross/history/the-truth-behind-40-acres-and-a-mule/.

Geary, Daniel. "The Moynihan Report: An Annotated Edition." *Atlantic*, September 14, 2015. www.theatlantic.com/politics/archive/2015/09/the-moynihan-report-an-annotated-edition/404632/.

Georgia Writers Program. *Drums and Shadows: Survival Studies among Georgia Coastal Negroes*. Athens: University of Georgia Press, 1940.

Giardina, Carol. "MOW to NOW: Black Feminism Resets the Chronology of the Founding of Modern Feminism." *Feminist Studies* 44, no. 3 (2018): 736–65.

Glave, Dianne. *Rooted in Earth: Reclaiming the African American Environmental Heritage*. Chicago: Lawrence Hill Books, 2010.

Goldsworthy, Andy. *Sacred Ecology*. https://sacredecology.com/andygoldsworthy/?fbclid=IwAR2YJZ10x-fcq6IlP0t151It50aa-4IH8JFx79APVzQUJvHt0I9HQdW-z0A. Accessed October 5, 2019.

Greenidge, Kaitlyn. *We Love You, Charlie Freeman*. New York: Algonquin Books, 2016.

Griffith, D. W., dir. *The Birth of a Nation*. Produced by D. W. Griffith. 1915.

Guyette, Curt. "The Flint Water Crisis Isn't Over." *ACLU Blog*, April 25, 2018, www.aclu.org/blog/racial-justice/race-and-economic-justice/flint-water-crisis-isnt-over.

Halberstam, Jack. "Introduction." In *The Undercommons: Fugitive Planning and Black Study*, by Stefano Harney and Fred Moten, 2–12. Wivenhoe, UK: Minor Compositions, 2013.

Halberstam, Jack. *The Queer Art of Failure*. Durham, NC: Duke University Press, 2011.

Hale, Kimberly Hurd, and Erin A. Dolgoy. "Humanity in a Posthuman World: M. R. Carey's *The Girl with All the Gifts*." *Utopia Studies* 29, no. 3 (2018): 343–61.

Hall, Lee. "The Last Kentucky Derby." *Counterpunch*, May 3, 2019. www.counterpunch.org/2019/05/03/the-last-kentucky-derby/.

Hanh, Thich Nhat. *Interbeing: Fourteen Guidelines for Engaged Buddhism*. Berkeley, CA: Parallax, 1987.

Hansen, Elise. "The Forgotten Minority in Police Shootings." CNN, November 13, 2017. www.cnn.com/2017/11/10/us/native-lives-matter/index.html.

Harney, Stefano, and Fred Moten. *The Undercommons: Fugitive Planning and Black Study*. Wivenhoe, UK: Minor Compositions, 2013.

Harris, Sam. "The Illusion of the Self: An Interview with Bruce Hood." Sam Harris, May 22, 2012. https://samharris.org/the-illusion-of-the-self2/.

Hartman, Saidiya V. *Lose Your Mother: A Journey along the Atlantic Slave Route*. New York: Farrar, Straus and Giroux, 2008.

Hartman, Saidiya V. *Scenes of Subjection: Terror, Slavery, and Self-Making in Nineteenth Century America*. Oxford: Oxford University Press, 1997.

Hogan, Linda. *Dwellings: A Spiritual History of the Living World*. New York: Norton, 2007.

Holiday, Billie, vocalist. "Strange Fruit." By Abel Meeropol. Commodore Records, 1939.

Holland, Sharon P. "Going South." *Southern Literary Journal* 46, no. 2 (Spring 2014): iii–v.

Holland, Sharon P. *Raising the Dead: Readings of Death and (Black) Subjectivity*. Durham: Duke University Press, 2000.

hooks, bell. "Earthbound." *The Colors of Nature: Culture, Identity and the Natural World*, edited by Alison Hawthorne Deming and Lauret E. Savoy, 184–88. Minneapolis: Milkweed Editions, 2011.

hooks, bell. "No Love in the Wild." New Black Man in Exile: The Digital Home of Mark Anthony Neal, September 5, 2012. www.newblackmaninexile.net/2012/09/bell-hooks-no-love-in-wild.html.

Huffadine, Leith, and Freya Noble. "He Didn't Beat His Chest." *Daily Mail*, May 30, 2016. www.dailymail.co.uk/news/article-3617102/Australian-animal-behaviour-expert-doesn-t-believe-gorilla-Harambe-gorilla-hurt-boy.html.

Hunter, Margaret. "The Persistent Problem of Colorism: Skin Tone, Status, and Inequality." *Sociology Compass* 1, no. 1 (September 2007): 237–54.

Hurston, Zora Neale. *Dust Tracks on the Road.* New York: Lippincott, 1942.

Hurston, Zora Neale. *Tell My Horse: Voodoo and Life in Haiti and Jamaica.* New York: Harper's, 1938.

Jamieson, Amber. "A School Police Officer Attacked a Black High School Student." *BuzzfeedNews*, February 6, 2019. www.buzzfeednews.com/article/amberjamieson/school-police-attack-black-student.

Jefferson, Thomas. *Notes on the State of Virginia.* London: Prichard and Hall, 1787.

Johnson, James Weldon. "Harlem: The Culture Capital." *The New Negro: An Interpretation*, edited by Alain Locke, 301–12. New York: Touchstone, 1999.

Kahrl, Andrew W. "Black People's Land Was Stolen." *New York Times*, June 20, 2019. www.nytimes.com/2019/06/20/opinion/sunday/reparations-hearing.html.

King, Jeanine. "Memory and the Phantom South in African American Migration Film." *Mississippi Quarterly* 63, nos. 3–4 (Summer/Fall 2010): 477–91.

King, Quisimbing, et al. "Black Agrarianism: The Significance of African American Land Ownership in the Rural South." *Rural Sociology* 83, no. 3 (2018): 677–99.

King, Vanessa. "The Politics of Black Women's Hair." *Cornerstone: Journal of Undergraduate Research at Minnesota State University, Mankato* 13, article 4 (2013): 1–19.

Lanham, J. Drew. *The Home Place: Memoirs of a Colored Man's Love Affair with Nature.* Minneapolis: Milkweed Editions, 2016.

Latif, Nadia. "It's Lit! How Film Finally Learned to Light Black Skin." *Guardian*, September 21, 2017. www.theguardian.com/film/2017/sep/21/its-lit-how-film-finally-learned-how-to-light-black-skin.

Leerhsen, Charles. "Get Rid of Pit Bulls." *Daily Beast*, March 12, 2010. www.thedailybeast.com/get-rid-of-pit-bulls. Accessed July 5, 2019.

Lennig, Arthur. "Myth and Fact: The Reception of 'Birth of a Nation.'" *Film History* 16, no. 2 (2004): 117–41.

Lessin, Tia, and Carl Deal, dirs. *Trouble the Water.* Zeitgeist Films, 2008.

Lloyd, Christopher. "Creaturely, Throwaway Life after Katrina: *Salvage the Bones* and *Beasts of the Southern Wild.*" *South: A Scholarly Journal* 48, no. 2 (Spring 2016): 246–64.

Machiorlatti, Jennifer. "Revisiting Julie Dash's 'Daughters of the Dust': Black Feminist Narrative and Diasporic Recollection." *South Atlantic Modern Language Association Journal* 70, no. 1 (Winter 2005): 97–116.

May, Allison. "Toddler Killed by Alligator at Disney Resort Honored with Statue." *USA Today*, August 9, 2017. www.usatoday.com/story/news/nation-now/2017/08/09/toddler-killed-alligator-near-disney-resort-honored-statue/553497001/.

Mayell, Hillary. "As Consumerism Spreads, Earth Suffers, Study Says." *National Geographic*, January 12, 2004. www.nationalgeographic.com/environment/2004/01/consumerism-earth-suffers/.

McKittrick, Katherine. *Demonic Grounds: Black Women and the Cartographies of Struggle.* Minneapolis: University of Minnesota Press, 2006.

McMillan, Uri. *Embodied Avatars: Genealogies of Black Feminist Art and Performance.* New York: NYU Press, 2015.

Mercer, Kobena. "Black Hair/Styles Politics." In *Welcome to the Jungle.* New York: Routledge, 1994.

Meyer, Ruth. "Africa as an Alien Future: The Middle Passage, Afro-Futurism, and Postcolonial Waterworlds." *American Studies* 45, no. 4 (2000): 555–66.

Mirzoeff, Nicholas. "Becoming Wild." Occupy 2012, September 30, 2012, www.nicholas mirzoeff.com/02012/2012/09/30/becoming-wild/.

Mock, Brentin. "The Great Migration Was about Racial Terror, Not Jobs." *City Lab*, June 24, 2015. www.citylab.com/equity/2015/06/the-great-migration-was-about-racial-terror-not-jobs/396722/.

Montuschi, E. "Order of Man, Order of Nature: Francis Bacon's Idea of a 'Dominion' over Nature." iris.unive.it/retrieve/handle/10278/24867/23441/MontuschiBacon.pdf. Accessed April 14, 2019.

Morrison, Toni. *Beloved.* New York: Knopf, 1987.

Morrison, Toni. *Song of Solomon.* New York: Knopf, 1977.

Moten, Fred. "Blackness and Nothingness: Mysticism in the Flesh." *South Atlantic Quarterly* 112, no. 4 (2013): 737–80.

Munro, Lucy. "Abandoned Garden Anarchy." TPH: The Plant Hunter, May 25, 2018. https://theplanthunter.com.au/botanica/abandoned-garden-anarchy/.

Mvula, Lauren. "Green Garden." *Sing to the Moon.* RCA Records, 2013.

Navarro, Mireya. "National Parks Reach Out to Blacks Who Aren't Visiting." *New York Times*, November 3, 2010. www.nytimes.com/2010/11/03/science/earth/03parks.html.

Nicholls, Will. "A Look at How HBO's 'Insecure' Lights Black Actors So Well." PetaPixel, September 14, 2017. petapixel.com/2017/09/14/look-hbos-insecure-lights-black-actors/.

Northup, Solomon. *Twelve Years a Slave.* Wikisource, November 10, 2017. en.wikisource.org/wiki/Twelve_Years_a_Slave/.

Nyong'o, Tavia. "Little Monsters: Race, Sovereignty, and Queer Inhumanism in *Beasts of the Southern Wild.*" *GLQ: A Journal of Gay and Lesbian Studies* 21, nos. 2–3 (May 2015): 249–72.

Omi, Michael, and Howard Winant. *Racial Formation in the United States.* New York: Routledge, 1986.

Outka, Paul. *Race and Nature: From Transcendentalism to the Harlem Renaissance.* London: Palgrave Macmillan, 2008.

Patterson, Orlando. *Slavery and Social Death: A Comparative Study.* Cambridge: Harvard University Press, 1982.

Patton, Stacey. "Why Jennifer and Sarah Hart Killed Their Adopted Children." *Dame*, May 2, 2019. www.damemagazine.com/2018/05/02/why-jennifer-and-sarah-hart-killed-their-adopted-children/.

Peele, Jordan, dir. *Get Out.* Blumhouse Films, 2017.

Peck, Raoul, dir. *I Am Not Your Negro.* Independent Lens, 2017.

Pham, Jason. "Serena Williams Shut Down Body Critics: 'I Am Strong and Muscular—and Beautiful.'" *Business Insider*, May 31, 2018. www.businessinsider.com/serena-williams-shut-down-body-critics-who-said-she-was-born-a-guy-2018-5.

Phillips, Kristine. "Black Teen Who Was Slammed to the Ground by a White Cop at Texas Pool Party Sues for $5 Million." *Washington Post*, January 5, 2017. www.washingtonpost.com/news/post-nation/wp/2017/01/05/black-teenager-who-was-slammed-to-the

-ground-at-texas-pool-party-sues-ex-cop-city-for-5m/?noredirect=on&utm_term
=.575ec3a90aeb.
Phillips, Jerry. "The Intuition of the Future: Utopia and Catastrophe in Octavia Butler's *Parable of the Sower*." *NOVEL: A Forum on Fiction* 35, nos. 2/3 (2002): 299–31.
Pinckney, Darryl. "The Afro-Pessimist Temptation." *New York Review of Books*, June 7, 2018. https://www.nybooks.com/articles/2018/06/07/ta-nehisi-coates-afro-pessimist-temptation/.
Quashie, Kevin. *The Sovereignty of the Quiet: Beyond Resistance in Black Culture*. New Brunswick, NJ: Rutgers University Press, 2012.
"Ratchet." Urban Dictionary. www.urbandictionary.com/define.php?term=ratchet. Accessed May 3, 2019.
Reed, Ishmael. "Foreword." *Tell My Horse: Voodoo and Life in Haiti and Jamaica*. By Zora Neale Hurston. New York: HarperCollins, 2009.
Reid-Soskin, Betty. *Sign My Name to Freedom: A Memoir of a Pioneering Life*. New York: Hay House, 2018.
REM. "It's the End of the World as We Know It (And I Feel Fine)." *Document*. I.R.S. Records, 1987.
Rousseau, Jean-Jacques. "On the Origins of Inequality of Mankind, 1754." Accessed July 22, 2019. www.marxists.org/reference/subject/economics/rousseau/inequality/.
Rowe, Kristin Denise. "Nothing Else Mattered after That Wig Came Off: Black Women, Unstyled Hair, and Scenes of Interiority." *Journal of American Culture* 42, no. 1 (March 2019): 21–36.
Salmon, Enrique. "Sharing Breath: Some Links between Land, Plants, and People." In *The Colors of Nature*, edited by Alison H. Deming and Lauret E. Savoy, 72–89. Minneapolis: Milkweed Editions, 2002.
Savoy, Lauret. *Trace: Memory, History, Race, and the American Landscape*. New York: Counterpoint Press, 2015.
Scott, A. O. "She's the Man of This Swamp." Review of *Beasts of the Southern Wild*, directed by Benh Zeitlin. *New York Times*, June 2012. www.nytimes.com/2012/06/27/movies/beasts-of-the-southern-wild-directed-by-benh-zeitlin.html.
Scott, James C. *Against the Grain: A Deep History of the Earliest States*. New Haven: Yale University Press, 2017.
Sedgwick, Eve Kosofsky. *Between Men: English Literature and Male Homosocial Desire*. New York: Columbia University Press, 1985.
Sedgwick, Eve Kosofsky. "The Pedagogy of Buddhism." In *Touching Feeling: Affect, Pedagogy, and Performativity*. Durham, NC: Duke University Press, 2003, 153–83.
Serjeantson, Richard. "Francis Bacon and the 'Interpretation of Nature' in the Late Renaissance." *Isis* 105, no. 4 (December 2014): 681–705.
Sexton, Jared. "The Social Life of Social Death: On Afro-Pessimism and Black Optimism." *InTensions*, no. 5 (Fall/Winter 2011).
Sexton, Jared. "The Vel of Slavery: Tracking the Figure of the Unsovereign." *Critical Sociology* 42, nos. 4–5 (July 2016): 1–15.
Sharpe, Christina. "*Beasts of the Southern Wild*—The Romance of Precarity I." *Social Text Online*, September 27, 2013, socialtextjournal.org/beasts-of-the-southern-wild-the-romance-of-precarity-i/.
Simoons, Frederick J., and James A. Baldwin. "Breast-Feeding of Animals by Women: Its Socio-Culture Context and Geographic Occurrence." *Anthropos* 77, nos. 3–4 (1982): 421–48.

Smith, Kimberly. *African American Environmental Thought*. Lawrence: University Press of Kansas, 2007.

Solomon, Akiba. "The Pseudoscience of 'Black Women Are Less Attractive.'" *Colorlines*, 17 May 2011, www.colorlines.com/articles/pseudoscience-black-women-are-less-attractive.

Somé, Malidoma Patrice. *Of Water and the Spirit: Ritual, Magic, and the Initiation of an African Shaman*. New York: Putnam, 1994.

Sounds of Blackness. "African Medley: Royal Kingdoms/Rise/My Native Land." *Africa to America*. Revolution Media, 1994.

Spillers, Hortense. "Mama's Baby, Papa's Maybe: An American Grammar Book." *Diacritics* 17, no. 2 (1987): 64–81.

Spillers, Hortense. "Who Cuts the Border? Some Readings on America." In *Black, White, and in Color: Essays on American Literature and Culture*. Chicago: University of Chicago Press, 2003, 319–36.

Spivak, Gayatri Chakravorty. "Can the Subaltern Speak?" In *The Post-colonial Studies Reader*, edited by Bill Ashcroft, Gareth Griffiths, and Helen Tiffin, 28–37. New York: Routledge, 2006.

Stamp, Elizabeth. "Billionaire Bunkers: How the 1% Are Preparing for the Apocalypse." CNN, October 17, 2017. https://www.cnn.com/style/article/doomsday-luxury-bunkers/index.html.

Stewart, Lindsey. "Work the Root: Black Feminism, Hoodoo Love Rituals, and Practices of Freedom." *Hypatia* 21, no. 1 (2017): 103–18.

Taleb, Nassim Nicholas. *Anti-fragile: Things That Gain from Disorder*. New York: Random House, 2012.

Terry, Josh. "10 Years Ago Today, Kanye West Said, 'George Bush Doesn't Care about Black People.'" *Chicago Tribune*, September 2, 2015. www.chicagotribune.com/redeye/redeye-kanye-west-katrina-telethon-george-bush-black-people-20150902-htmlstory.html.

Thompson, Cheryl. "Black Women, Beauty, and Hair as a Matter of Being." *Women's Studies* 38 (2009): 831–56.

Tolle, Eckhart. *The Power of Now*. Novato, CA: New World Library, 2010. Kindle.

Toomer, Jean. *Cane*. New York: Liveright Press, 2011.

Toppo, Greg, and Paul Overberg. "After 100 Years, Great Migration Begins Reversal." *USA Today*, February 2, 2015. www.usatoday.com/story/news/nation/2015/02/02/census-great-migration-reversal/21818127/.

Truth, Sojourner. "Ain't I a Woman?" Women's Rights National Historical Park, National Park Service. Accessed May 3, 2019. www.nps.gov/articles/sojourner-truth.htm.

Tyler-McGraw, Marie. *An African Republic: Black and White Virginians in the Making of Liberia*. Chapel Hill: University of North Carolina Press, 2007.

Uchiyama, Kosho, and Shohaku Okamura. *The Zen Teaching of Homeless Kodo*. Edited by Jokei Molly Delight Whitehead. Somerville, MA: Wisdom, 1981.

Vaneigem, Raoul. *The Movement of the Free Spirit*. Cambridge, MA: Zone Books, 1994.

Walker, Kara. *A Subtlety*. Debuted at the Domino Sugar Factory, New York, 2014.

Ward, Jesmyn. *Salvage the Bones*. New York: Bloomsbury, 2011.

Wardi, Anissa Janine. *Water and African American Memory: An Eco-critical Perspective*. Gainesville: University Press of Florida, 2016.

Warren, Calvin L. *Ontological Terror: Blackness, Nihilism, and Emancipation*. Durham, NC: Duke University Press, 2018.

Watts, Alan. "Not What Should Be but What Is." YouTube. www.youtube.com/watch?v=8vaaJP6fpJo. Accessed July 22, 2019.

Weheliye, Alex. "'Feenin': Posthuman Voices in Contemporary Black Music." *Social Text* 20, no. 2 (Summer 2002): 21–47.

Weheliye, Alex. *Habeas Viscus: Racializing Assemblages, Biopolitics, and Black Feminist Theories of ,the Human*. Durham, NJ: Duke University Press, 2014.

West, Kanye. "All Falls Down." *The College Dropout*. Roc-a-fella Records, 2004.

Wilderson, Frank B. III. "Afro-Pessimism and the End of Redemption." Humanities Futures, Franklin Humanities Institute. http://www.humanitiesfutures.org/papers/afro-pessimism-end-redemption/. Accessed February 15, 2020.

Wilderson, Frank B., III. "Blacks and the Master/Slave Relation." In *Afro-Pessimism: An Introduction*. Minneapolis: Racked and Dispatched, 2017. https://rackedanddispatched.noblogs.org/files/2017/01/Afro-pessimism2_imposed.pdf.

Wilkerson, Isabel. *The Warmth of Other Suns: The Epic Story of America's Great Migration*. New York: Vintage Books, 2011.

Wise, Damon. "*Beasts of the Southern Wild*: 'I Didn't Expect People to Like It.'" *Guardian*, October 11, 2012. www.theguardian.com/film/2012/oct/11/beasts-of-the-southern-wild-behn-zeitlin.

Wohlleben, Peter. *The Hidden Life of Trees: What They Feel, How They Communicate, Discoveries from a Secret World*. Vancouver, CA: Greystone Books, 2015.

Wolf, Naomi. *The Beauty Myth: How Images of Beauty Are Used against Women*. New York: HarperCollins, 2009.

Wright, Richard. "Between the World and Me." *Partisan Review*, July/August 1935.

Yaeger, Patricia. "*Beasts of the Southern Wild* and Dirty Ecology." *Southern Spaces*, February 13, 2013. https://southernspaces.org/2013/beasts-southern-wild-and-dirty-ecology.

Young, Molly. "Sarah Hart's Horrific Google Searches Suggest She Prioritized Saving the Lives of Her Dogs, Not Her Children." *Oregon Live*, April 4, 2019. www.oregonlive.com/crime/2019/04/sarah-harts-horrific-google-searches-suggest-she-prioritized-saving-the-lives-of-her-dogs-not-her-children.html.

Zeitlin, Benh, dir. *Beasts of the Southern Wild*. Fox Searchlight Pictures, 2012.

Zerzan, John. "Finding Our Way Back Home." In *Twilight of the Machines*. Port Townsend, WA: Feral House, 2008, 123–25.

INDEX

Abbott, Elizabeth, 105
abolition, 5–6, 8, 20–21, 23–27, 92, 96, 98, 121, 129, 142, 146–52, 155, 164n60, 178n68
Abram, David, 166n37
African Colonization Society, 96
African-inflected spirituality, 33, 42
Afro-pessimism, 24, 145–48, 163n60
agrarianism, 5–6, 18, 21–22, 27, 52
Ahmed, Sara, 103
Alaimo, Stacey, 87–88
Alibar, Lucy, 67–69
Allen, Reniqua, 21
Amos, Tori, 115
Anansi, 8, 43
anarchy, 26, 149
ancestors, 40, 43–44, 52, 59, 61, 90, 107, 166n37
anti-Blackness, 7, 9–10, 21, 25, 27, 55, 57, 61–62, 71, 73, 109, 127, 129–30
anti-fragility, 150
apocalypse, 123, 126, 128–29, 137–38, 152; climate and, 128; perpetual, 128
Aquimin, 122–23
assimilation, 143, 147–48, 178n58
aurochs, prehistoric, 65, 77

backwoods, 23–24, 80
Bacon, Francis, 9, 10–11, 13, 72
Baker, Danny, 110
Baldwin, James, 109, 111
Bambara, Toni Cade, 33
Barlow, Michael, 146
Baszile, Natalie, 94

Beasts of the Southern Wild (Zeitlin), 25, 63–66, 69
beauty, 14, 17, 21, 25, 27, 36–37, 39, 51, 122, 165n21
Bell, Karen Cook, 94
Beloved (Morrison), 32
Berry, Halle, 165n24
Beyoncé, 25, 30–32, 45–53, 55, 57, 59, 61–62
Bird, Ayana, 165n28
Black farmers, 16, 102–3, 105–7
Blackhood, 45–46, 51–53
Black Land Project, 122
Black Lives Matter, 7, 63–64
Black Panther, 77
Black Power Movement, 36
Bland, Sandra, 31
Blum, Alexander, 9
Boyd, Rekia, 31
Branagan, Thomas, 140
Brown, Jayna, 65, 72–73
Brown, Mike, 63
Brown, Ruth Nicole, 50
Burks, Ruth Elizabeth, 33
Burleson, Blake, 162
Bush, George W., 64
Butler, Octavia, 26, 135–36, 143–45, 148–50

Cacho, Lisa Marie, 62
capitalism, 97, 129; patriarchal, 128–29
captive bodies, 40, 47, 49
captivity, 40, 47, 81, 83, 135, 146–47, 149
Carey, M. K., 137
Cartesian dualism, 9, 34, 70

Césaire, Suzanne, 142–43, 147, 151
chattel slavery, 6, 10–11, 94, 111, 162n32, 163n57, 163n60
Chen, Joyce, 168
chimpanzees, 26, 114–16, 118–19
Chomsky, Noam, 143, 149
Choplecti, Mary, 102
Christensen, Bo Allesøe, 7
Christopher, David, 128
cisgender women, 24–25, 30, 164n (chap. 1)
Clark, Christopher, 86
Clifton, Lucille, 3, 4, 9, 157
Coates, Ta-Nehisi, 100, 104, 147
colorism, 39, 50
Combahee River Collective, 25
Continental Divide, 23
Collingham, Lizzie, 106
Collins-White, Mali, 45, 51–52
Cooper, Anna Julia, 25
Cooper, Brittany, 31
Cottom, Tressie McMillan, 35, 36, 40, 165n24

Dalai Lama, 121
Dash, Julie, 25, 31–32, 34–35, 40, 46, 56, 59, 164n6, 166n35
Daughters of the Dust (Dash), 25, 29, 30–37, 41–50, 52–55, 57, 155
Davis, Angela, 46; mentioned by Pinckney, 147
Deloria, Paul, 94
Descartes, Rene, 9
dirt, 9, 65, 69–70, 86, 126, 132
Dixon, Thomas, 175n1
dog-fighting, 78–80; pitbulls and, 82–83, 171n54
Dolgoy, Erin, 138
domesticated animals, 75, 81
Douglas, Mary, 69
Dubey, Madhu, 145
Du Bois, W. E. B., 32, 117
DuVernay, Ava, 172n16, 174n43

Earnshaw, Annie, 52
earth, 3–5, 8–9, 21, 24, 27, 37, 42, 86, 91–123, 136, 155, 157

earth mothers, 87
eco-criticism, 7, 162n18
eco-feminism, 25
ecological field: affective, 107; interdependent, 120, 136, 165n37
Eden, 10–11, 13, 162n32
Ellison, Ralph, 67, 93
Enlightenment: ideals, 9–11; philosophy, 141; thinkers, 10, 130
environmentalism, 8; Eurocentric, 20, 23
Equal Justice Initiative, 18
Equiano, Olaudah, 15–16
Eve (Garden of Eden), Black Eve, 11, 30, 43
Evita (Parker), 90

failure, 62, 70, 91, 95, 101, 108–9, 122, 129, 142
feminism, 24, 34, 87
Ferreira da Silva, Denise, 130
fields, 14, 46–48, 60, 82
Finney, Carolyn, 20, 93
food, 69, 71, 75, 78, 84, 132, 137
Foucault, Michel, 112
Franklin, Aretha, 29, 30, 32
Funny or Die, 4

Gaia theory, 157
Garden of Eden, 11, 13; and the Black Eden, 13, 72, 155, 162n32
gardens, abandoned, 150–51
Gardner, Gary, 66
gender, 24, 30, 36, 46, 111
Georgia, 13, 16, 19, 32, 59, 96
Gibson, William, 129
Gin, Franklin, 127
Girl with All the Gifts, The (McCarthy), 26, 126, 130, 134, 137–39, 140, 142, 150–52
Glass, Ira, 168
Glave, Dianne, 100, 163, 178
Goebbels, Joseph, 77
Goffin, Gerry, 29
Goldsworthy, Andrew, 142
Goodall, Jane, 114
Great Migration, 21, 163
Greenidge, Kaitlyn, 26, 94, 114, 116, 118, 121
Griffith, D. W., 127–28

Index

hair, 6, 32, 36–37, 42–43, 46, 49–50, 53, 55, 82, 166n30
Halberstam, Jack, 73, 95, 97
Hale, Kimberly, 138
Hall, Lee, 80
Hanh, Thich Nhat, 5, 44, 161n9
Harambe, 75–76
Harney, Steve, 73
Hart, Davonte, 63, 73, 90
Hart, Jennifer, 63
Hart, Sarah, 62–63, 74–75
Hartman, Saidiya, 5, 22, 24, 25, 64
Hayles, N. Katherine, 7
Hegelian terms, 11
Hemmings, Sally, 174n56
hiking, 4, 131–32
Hogan, Linda, 86
Holiday, Billie, 17
Holland, Sharon P., 22, 25, 61, 62, 63
homelessness (life of), 26, 93, 120
hooks, bell, 21, 23, 25, 53, 65
humanism, 7, 118–19, 136
Hunter, Margaret, 39
Hurricane Katrina, 25, 61–62, 64, 69, 74, 77, 83–84, 86, 128
Hurston, Zora Neale, 43, 71, 169n30

Illuminati, 52–53
interbeing, 5, 26, 44–45, 78, 85–86, 122, 131, 152
Invisible Man, 57
Irigaray, Luce, 88

Jafa, Arthur, 34
Jay-Z, 47
Jean-Louis, Pierre, 37
Jefferson, Thomas, 110–11
Jim Crow, 15, 23, 40
Johnson, James Weldon, 18
Jordan, Michael B., 77
Joseph, Kahlil, 48–51, 54–56, 58
Jung, Carl, 8–9

King, Vanessa, 165n28

Lee, Spike, 94

Lemonade (Beyoncé), 25, 30–33, 43, 45, 46–58, 98, 155
Lloyd, Christopher, 74, 77
loas, 43
Locke, Alain, 18
lynching, 6, 18, 21–22; relative to gender, 24

Martin, Trayvon, 47
McCarthy, Colm, 26
McFarland, Susan, 14
McKittrick, Katherine, 23, 104, 107, 162n33
McMillan, Uri, 7
Meeropol, Abel, 17
Melanin Base Camp, 20
Mercer, Kobena, 165n28
Meyer, Ruth, 73
Middle Passage, 41, 55, 57, 62, 73, 90, 96, 104–5
Mirzoeff, Nicholas, 65
misogynoir, 30, 32, 35, 40, 49
Monstuchi, E., 11
Moore, Denise Kristin, 61–62
Moten, Fred, 73–74, 85
Mother Nature, 24–25, 74, 87
Mvula, Lauren, 156

NAACP, 18, 126–27
Nag Hammadi, The, 30, 52
Nibbāna, 92
Northup, Solomon, 14
Nyong'o, Tavia, 67, 77–79

Okeechobee Hurricane, 62
Omi, Michael, 68
Outdoor Afro, 20
Outka, Paul, 6, 13, 161n10, 162n18

Parable of the Sower (Butler), 26, 126, 130–31, 133–34, 136–38, 143–45, 148–52
pastoral, 4; black death and, 19; lynching and, 18; pastoral spaces, 15; return, 5
Patterson, Orlando, 5
Peele, Jordan, 19
Phillips, Jerry, 149
Pinckney, Darryl, 147
pit bulls, 77–78

police: beatings and, 31, 55, 63; brutality and, 21; police state, 97–98, 144
posthumanism, 7, 8, 75
Pozo, Diana, 34
precarity, 62, 64–65, 67–68, 70–71, 80, 83, 119, 128, 138
primitivism, 10–11, 15; discourses and, 18, 42, 69–70

Quashie, Kevin, 113–14
Queen Sugar (DuVernay), 26, 94–95, 98–106, 108–9, 162n33

ratchet, 45
Reed, Ishmael, 42
REM (the band), 125, 129
respectability politics, 22, 45, 46, 51, 68–69
Riou, Edward, 12
Roberts, Kimberly, 61
Roshi, Kosho Uchiyama, 120
Rousseau, Henry, 11–13
Rousseau, Jean-Jacques, 93–94
Rowe, Kristen Denise, 37

Said, Shukri Ali, 31
Salmon, Enrique, 136
Salvage the Bones (Ward), 25, 62, 64, 68, 73, 77–78, 81, 83–86, 169n30
Sapelo Island, 59–60
Savoy, Lauret, 20, 23
Say Her Name, 30–32, 35, 39, 49
Scott, James C., 149–50
Sedgwick, Eve, 44, 113
Serjeantson, Richard, 11
Sexton, Jared, 5, 8, 21, 22, 24, 26, 93, 95–96, 98, 107, 114, 121, 146, 148
Sharpe, Christina, 22, 25, 65, 68
Sherman's Field Order No. 15, 16, 96
Shire, Warsan, 52
Snake Charmer, The, 11, 12
social death, 5, 11, 17, 63, 89, 115, 127, 130, 146, 152, 161n13
Somé, Malidoma Patrice, 26, 131–33
Sounds of Blackness, 13
Smith, Kimberly, 15
Spelman College, 31–32, 59, 62
Spillers, Hortense, 25, 31, 40, 47, 49, 73

Spivak, Gayatri Chakravorty, 79
Stevenson, Bryan, 18
Stewart, Lindsey, 46, 52

tableau vivant, 34
Taleb, Naseem Nicholas, 150
Taylor, Breonna, 31
This American Life, 61
Thompson, Cheryl, 37
Tolle, Eckhart, 85
Toomer, Jean, 13, 14
Tree of Snakes, The, 12, 13
Transcendentalism, 6, 8
transgender women, 24–25, 30, 164
transphobia, 6
Truth, Sojourner, 29, 43–44
Tubman, Harriet, 26, 133

Underwood, Blair, 4

Vaneigem, Raoul, 123
Vick, Michael, 77–79
Voodoo, 42; as neo-African spirituality, 42–44, 53, 59

Wallis, Quvenzhane, 67–68
Ward, Jesmyn, 25–26, 62, 74, 78–79, 81–90
Wardi, Anissa J., 41, 163n54
Warren, Calvin, 5, 7, 10, 22, 64, 74, 110, 112, 121, 131, 151, 175n82
Watts, Alan, 9, 86, 95, 98, 112
Weheliye, Alex, 7, 74
We Love You, Charlie Freeman (Greenidge), 26, 94–96, 114
West, Cornel, 147
West, Kanye, 64, 94
Wilderson, Frank, III, 5, 22, 125, 129, 130, 148
Wilkerson, Isabel, 18
Williams, Serena, 49–51
Winant, Howard, 68
Wohlleben, Peter, 151
Women's Rights Convention, 29
Wright, Richard, 17

Yaeger, Patricia, 65, 68–69, 72, 75
Yoruba, 49
YouTube, 52

Zeitlin, Benh, 25–26, 62–64, 67, 74
Zen, 5; *bhikkus* and, 152; Buddhism and, 113–15, 120; Buddhist rhetoric and, 172n11; frameworks and, 26; life of homelessness and, 115; oneness and, 44, 112
Zerzan, John, 122

ABOUT THE AUTHOR

Stefanie K. Dunning is associate professor of English at Miami University of Ohio. She is a graduate of Spelman College and the University of California, Riverside, and a Ford Fellow. She is author of *Queer in Black and White: Interraciality, Same Sex Desire, and Contemporary African American Culture*. Her work has been published in *African American Review*, *MELUS*, *Signs*, and several other journals and anthologies. She sometimes publishes under the pen name Zeffie Gaines.

www.ingramcontent.com/pod-product-compliance
Lightning Source LLC
Chambersburg PA
CBHW022021220426
43663CB00007B/1159